THE BROKEN RING

JEAN BORELLA

The Broken Ring

<----------->

A HISTORY AND THEORY OF THE SYMBOL

Translated by Alexander Burdge

Angelico Press

First published in French as *Histoire et théorie du symbole* by Editions L'Harmattan in 2015.
Copyright © L'Harmattan, 2015
Copyright © Angelico Press 2025

All rights reserved:
No part of this book may be reproduced or transmitted,
in any form or by any means, without permission

For information, address:
Angelico Press, Ltd.
169 Monitor St.
Brooklyn, NY 11222
www.angelicopress.com

ppr 979-8-89280-159-1
cloth 979-8-89280-160-7

Book and cover design
by Michael Schrauzer

CONTENTS

Preface xi

Note for the Second Edition xiv

GENERAL INTRODUCTION 1

PART I: HISTORICAL EIDETIC OF THE SYMBOL 5

CHAPTER I: The Symbol from Antiquity to the Middle Ages 7
  The Greek Origin 7
    Etymology: 7; The Witness of Plato: 9; The Pythagorean Origin: 10; Symbolism and Liturgy: 12
  The Symbol in Greek Judaism 13
    Existence of a Symbolism in Jewish Tradition: 13; The Witness of Philo: 17; Scriptural Attestation of Symbolon: 18
  The Symbol in Greek Christianity 21
    The Vocabulary of Symbolism in the New Testament: 21; The Witness of St Justin and St Irenaeus of Lyons: 23; St Clement of Alexandria: 24; Origen: 26; Theodoret of Cyrus: 28; St Dionysius the Areopagite: 29
  The Symbol in Latin Christianity 33
    A New Meaning of the Word: 33; Symbolum in Early Medieval Literature, Particularly John Scottus: 38; The Twelfth Century and After: 45

CHAPTER II: Symbol and Allegory in Modernity 50
  Their Initial Equivalence 50
  The Goethean Opposition Between Symbol & Allegory 57
  Contemporary Expressions of the Symbol/Allegory Opposition 59

CHAPTER III: The Essence of the Symbol 63
  The Two Poles of the Symbolic Function 63
  The Symbol of Symbols 67
  The Symbol within the Symbol 69
  Conclusion: The Sign of the Covenant 74
    The Cross-Circle of the Symbol: 75

PART II: STRUCTURAL ANALYTIC OF THE SYMBOL 77

CHAPTER IV: The Sign According to Linguistics 79

Epistemic Closure of the Concept 79

Coherence of Language and Coherence of Thought: 79; Science Completes the Concept from the Side of Action: 83; Galileo and Saussure—Two Illustrations of the Epistemic Closure of the Concept: 84; Speculative Openness of the Philosophical Concept: 89

The Linguistic Concept of the Sign 93

The Sign is Primarily a Sign of the Sign: 94; The Saussurean Sign: 94; Refutation and Rejection of the Structural Concept of the Sign: 96; The Function of Communication: 101; Speaking is Not Communicating: 103

CHAPTER V: The Sign According to Philosophy 109

The Semiotic Field 109

Semantic Extraction and the Discovery of Meaning: 109; Unity of the Semiotic Field—Linguistic and Non-Linguistic Signs: 113

General Description of the Sign 129

The Semantic Triangle: 129; Identification of the Signifier: 135; Identification of the Objective Referent: 140; Identification of Meaning, and Discovery of the Intelligible Referent: 146

Historical Remarks 156

Aristotle and the Stoics: 156; The Doctrine of Saint Augustine: 158; The Medievals: 162; The Doctrines of India: 169

CHAPTER VI: The Symbolic Sign 179

Species of the Sign 179

Ground of the Distinction between Species of the Sign: 179; The Inductive Sign and the Institutional Sign: 181

The Symbolic Sign, Transformational Unity of the Inductive and Institutional Signs 186

The Semeion in St John: 186; The Rublev Icon: 191

Semantic Potentiality of the Symbol and Ontology of Reference 194

The Symbol Signifies by Presentification: 194; Semiotic Reference and Symbolic Reference: 197; The Essentially Multiple Orientation of the Symbol: 199; Semantic Unity and Transcendence of the Symbol: 201

Hermeneutics in Accord with the Symbol—Memorial and Anamnesis 204

Institutive Hermeneutics: 205; Speculative Hermeneutics: 207; Integrative Hermeneutics: 213

CHAPTER VII: The General Structure and Organization of the Symbolic Order   217
Diagram of the Symbolic Sign   217
Classification of Symbols   220
  Rejection of the Linguistic Model: 220; Extension of the Symbolic Field: 224; The Nature of the Signifier as Principle of Classification: 226; The Three Fundamental Classes of Elementary Signifiers: 229; The Two Limiting Principles of the Symbolic Field: 233

THE SYMBOL IS A SEMANTIC OPERATOR   237

PREFACE

NO SOONER DOES MAN AWAKEN THAN HIS gaze searches the horizon for that eastern point from which the light will be born. His entire day is lived within this cosmic time, his whole life within this succession of annual cycles. Traversed by the sun, the celestial vault grants him knowledge of the surrounding and sheltering sphere; the inaccessible heights tear him away from his conditioning and awaken in him a sense of the Absolute. The horizon's fourfold division by the equinoctial and solstitial points sign the world with a cross, separating and dividing but also ordering and measuring, revealing the intelligibility of the cosmic wheel. A being both natural and spiritual, man sees in himself that all things have a center, which is in his heart. His vertical body reveals to him the degrees of reality, ascending from stone to spirit, along with the analogical correspondence between them lending unity to the whole. His voice fills time and his movements give it rhythm, performing by ritual mediation the ceaseless action of exodus and return, of creation proceeding from and returning to its Principle. From dawn to dusk, from birth to death, his acts are supported and vivified by ancient Tradition, which through myths celebrated in chant and in liturgical hierodrama, realizes the primordial meaning of the essential moments of each life as of all humanity. By the original Word passed down by the Ancients, he ceaselessly unfolds a commentary on the Book of the World. All things are named and pronounced within him in order that they may be comprehended and integrated within the cosmos's human center, and this in such a way that man, as himself this center, finds his unique place in the heart of multiplicity. Thus, what the light of the sun reveals to his gaze, bringing forth beings and objects out of their nocturnal indistinction and into separative multitude, Tradition and the Word—the sun of the mind—reveals to his intellect, while ritual action brings about the unification of man and world in the unity of sacrifice.

For millennia, man was immersed in this sacred world of religious symbols, in which everything is intelligible speech and all speech a vibrant echo of the Word, the "place" of essences. This is the objective reality of sacred symbolism, and one must first perceive this reality in all its presence and irrefutable obviousness before embarking on any description or analysis.

For 150 years, sacred symbolism has been the object of much study. Religious history, ethnography, sociology, psychology, and philosophy have never lost interest in it. The primary value of this labor has been in the production of an abundant and often profitable literature. Nevertheless, and without exception, far from helping enter into the truth of the symbol, it has served in general to render it more incomprehensible, whatever the illusions of our contemporaries. The truth of the symbol is reached only through a cosmological and epistemological revolution contrary to the strongest mental habits of modern science and philosophy.[1]

One finds the keys to this truth particularly in the work of René Guénon—not that he addressed symbolism *per se*, except in certain places, but because he made exemplary and fundamental applications of it. The study of symbolism was transformed under his influence, as well as under that of A. K. Coomaraswamy, Victor Poucel, Frithjof Schuon, Mircea Eliade, Henry Corbin, and Marcel Jousse. It would be impossible to list here all those who, in Europe, in America, and in Africa, were inspired by their teaching: as particularly representative, we will mention only the work of Titus Burckhardt, Jean Canteins, and Jean Hani, also keeping in mind Jean Chevalier's celebrated *Dictionary of Symbols* or Éditions Zodiaque's admirable *Monde des symboles* [World of Symbols].[2]

Although our work closely follows this tradition, it is distinguished by its method, which is that of philosophy. That is to say, we will begin not from first principles but rather from the data of human experience, past and present, rising by reflexive analysis toward the fundamental ideas rendering it intelligible. This path has imposed itself upon us, as we could not ignore that contemporary thought has been dedicated for half a century to the theoretical problems of language, of sign and symbol. Surely

---

[1] This is the subject of *The Crisis of Religious Symbolism & Symbolism and Reality*, trans. G. John Champoux (Kettering, OH: Angelico Press/Sophia Perennis, 2016).

[2] Now to be completed by Hans Biedermann's *Encyclopedia des Symboles* (Paris: Pochothèque, 1996), presented and expanded for the French edition by Michel Cazenave.

it has reached many conclusions useless for the metaphysician or person of faith. It cannot be denied, however, that it has exercised the greatest influence on the intelligentsia of the West, and even that of the East. It was therefore necessary to take up this challenge and oppose to contemporary thought the model of the symbolic sign as presented to us by sacred cultures and as conceived by traditional philosophy. This is the goal that we have set in writing the present work.

NOTE FOR THE SECOND EDITION

THE PRESENT EDITION REPRODUCES, FOR THE most part, the earlier text—long out of print—published in 1989 by Masonneuve and Larose under the title *Le mystère du signe* [Mystery of the Sign]. The choice of a new title has only to do with the desire to reflect, as accurately as possible, the content of the work. We had considered introducing supplements concerning, in particular, the theory of the sign in Aristotle and the Stoics, the Kantian concept of the symbol (indebted to the work of François Marty), the question of the relation between words and things in Indian linguistic thought (according to the study of Johannes Bronkhorst, *Language et Réalité. Sur un episode de la pensé indienne* [Turnhout: Brépols, 1999]), and more besides. But we abandoned this idea: such supplements, however interesting in themselves, would alter nothing in the theory of the symbolic sign set forth here. We have therefore confined ourselves to modifying only the details: omitting superfluous references; adding essential ones; eliminating obscure, ambiguous, or improper terminology; correcting spelling and transliterations; and rectifying some errors.

GENERAL INTRODUCTION
Two Definitions of the Symbol

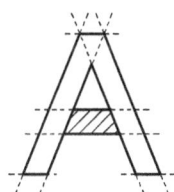AS WE HAVE SAID IN ANOTHER WORK,[1] it is necessary to distinguish two types of definition for any given object: the first, qualitative and metaphysical, considers it in its "Idea" and essential unity; the second, structural and logico-physical, considers it according to the differentiation and articulation of the constituent elements of its empirical existence. Thus, as we said, it is not the same thing to define man as "the image of God" (as does the Bible) and as "a being endowed with reason" (as does Aristotle). It must be understood, of course, that the realization of a theomorphic being in our world entails precisely this two-fold constitution: a living body and a rational soul. Any search for definition must therefore be carried out in two movements, one aiming at a description of the contemplated unity of the Idea, the other striving to analyze a reconstituted articulation of elements. To the first investigation, we give the name "eidetic," since it is relative to the Idea (*eidos* in Greek, of which *eidetikos* is the adjective), the purpose of which is to grasp the essence. The second we name "analytic," the purpose of which is the study of functional structure, as the articulation of the constituent elements of an object is revealed only in light of being decomposed into its most basic elements. These two approaches moreover imply a prior condition of possibility, namely that the object already be given to our consciousness and that we have acquired sufficient experience of it. The name "empirical" is therefore suitable for the science seeking such knowledge, the goal of which is attentively describing the object as it gives itself to the senses and to the understanding. Together, these three sciences constitute philosophical knowledge: the empirical, content with description; the analytic, reaching the concept; and the eidetic, culminating in intuition. The empirical is always first, as without it we would not even know the object under discussion. But the eidetic is not necessarily last: depending

---

[1] *Love and Truth: The Christian Path of Charity*, trans. G. John Champoux (Brooklyn, NY: Angelico Press, 2020), 36–37.

on the circumstance, we might consider it to precede the analytic, especially in that, as a vision of the essence, it has a certain affinity with the descriptive or historical form of the empirical (*historia* in Greek means "inquiry"). Extremes meet.

This is especially the case for the symbol. All analytical theories proposed by modern theorists concerning the structure of the symbolic apparatus, purported to be highly scientific, derive in fact from a certain view of the symbol's essence. Supposedly drawn from the experience of sacred symbolism, they rather reflect the ideological convictions of their authors and are determined by certain preconceptions of the symbolic function, often left implicit because assumed to be obvious. Believing it necessary to develop a "traditional" model of the symbolic sign that could be opposed to contemporary models, we have therefore tried to explicitly formulate its essence.

Where can we find such an essence, the object of our eidetic investigation? Must we inquire into the entirety of the symbolic data, in accordance with the demands of empiricism? This would be an immense and impossible task, and besides, the literature in symbology is abundant and well known. Intending to do the work of a philosopher, then, and not that of a historian or ethnologist, it seems legitimate to seek the essence of the symbol by studying the discourse to which it has given rise: only here can we discover that intuition into its nature which the Ancients possessed. Indeed, if the symbol is an object, it is also a word, and therefore a thought, since it belongs to culture; even in the case of natural beings—trees, rocks, water, and so on—their symbolic dimension reveals itself only under the effect of their cultural "institution," their employment in the symbolic order. The truth of the symbol can therefore be discovered only among the sacred civilizations that have lived in and through it, and thus only appears in light of their immemorial and founding use of it. Any other approach would lead to an elaboration of a novel theory as vain as what has come before. Consequently, it is by listening to what tradition itself says about the symbol—and more, by gleaning the sense it could not help but give this term, consciously or not—that we can grasp its essence. Our eidetics of the symbol is therefore inseparable from a history of the word as given to us by the Western cultural tradition. To this is dedicated the first part of the present work.

* * *

As for the second definition, concerning the structure and function of the symbolic apparatus, the problem is obviously quite different. Such an apparatus is in fact nothing but the means for effectively realizing the end assigned to the symbol by its essence in human culture, just as the ocular apparatus is the means for realizing the visual function. However, just as it is not necessary to understand this apparatus to make use of it, so symbolic activity was practiced long before we inquired into the manner of its operation. A definition of the symbolic apparatus corresponds therefore to a *reflection* on the symbol that can arise only by specific disruptions in its operation, or by a general weakening of the symbolist mentality in all its spontaneous and felicitous immediacy, just as in biology, anatomical and physiological science is dependent upon pathology: structure is revealed only through the process of "deconstruction." Here as elsewhere, the appearance of analytical and structural science (science in the modern sense) is conditioned by the disappearance of an intuitive and vital knowledge, the synthetic and almost instinctive character of which should not make us forget that this knowledge was nevertheless real, though of another order.

Contrary to how we approach its essence, it follows that analysis of the object requires that we turn to a study of the most modern arrangements of the symbolic sign, since it is precisely these which force us to reconstruct the traditional model in opposition. As long as culture existed naturally under the regime of symbolism, such an enterprise would have been pointless and was never attempted.[2] But when there is a crisis of the symbolic function such as the West has never known (think of the destruction of liturgical forms in Roman Christianity), it becomes quite inevitable, insofar as the nature and forms of this *Crisis of Religious Symbolism* can be understood in depth only if one possesses a rigorous concept of the symbolic sign. To this is dedicated the second part of the present work.

---

[2] However, a very elaborated theory of the sign is encountered in the manuals of philosophical scholasticism: Jacques Maritain, *Quatre essais sur l'esprit dans sa condition charnelle* (Paris: Alsatia, 1956), 58–112; and above all, A. M. Rouget, in his "Appendice Technique" to the treatise on the *Sacraments* by St Thomas Aquinas (*Summa Theologica*, III, 60–65 [Paris: Desclée et Cie, 1951], 255–379).

PART I
HISTORICAL EIDETIC OF THE SYMBOL

INTRODUCTION

This study in fact meets two needs. On the one hand, as we said, it gleans a traditional founding definition of the symbol from its history. But on the other hand, it justifies using this word in the first place—after all, many others were available, which enjoy no less antiquity in the West and have meanings almost identical to "symbol." This is the case for "image," "figure," "type," "icon," "allegory," "parable," "example," "reflection," "vestige," "trace," and the like. Yet of all these terms, considering both ancient and modern usage, it would seem that "symbol" is the lesser evil. It is not without its problems, however, the most serious of which is that an expression such as "purely symbolic" can be synonymous with *unreal*, or more precisely, "without referent."[1]

Our lexicological survey in no way claims to be exhaustive nor even to discover new occurrences. We want only to identify and compile a few uses of a term of Greek origin in order to identify their common essence.

---

[1] The question of reference will be examined in Part II.

CHAPTER I

The Symbol from Antiquity to the Middle Ages

THE GREEK ORIGIN[1]

Etymology

THE WORD "SYMBOL" COMES FROM THE Greek *symbolon* through its Latin transliteration, *symbolum*. It derives from the verb *sym-ballein*, as do other words of similar meaning, such as *symbolaion* and *symbole*. There are multiple meanings of the verb *sym-ballein*, but it always has the sense of "being together" or "being with," expressed by the prefix *sym-*, as well as the idea of a "movement," expressed by the verb *ballein*, whence the primary meaning given by dictionaries as "throwing together," "joining," "uniting," "putting in contact." Should we draw the conclusion that the original meaning was topological, as Alleau asserts, citing Pausanias?[2] No. The semantic diffusion of *symbolon* and words of the same family are quite ancient. The same author in a previous

---

[1] In addition to etymological dictionaries, one can consult the following works, each of which contains a more or less detailed history of the word "symbol": the most complete is Max Schlesinger, *Geschichte des Symbols* (Berlin: Leonhard Simion, 1912). See also Frédéric Creuzer, *Religions de l'Antiquité considérées principalement dans leurs forms symboliques et mythologiques*, translated from the German, partly recast, completed and developed by J. D. Guigniaut, 10 parts in 4 volumes (Paris: Treuttel et Wurz, 1825–1851). The French translator profoundly reworked the original text, with Creuzer's agreement it seems, but this is of no consequence, since our purpose is to gather information rather than ideas, and J. D. Guigniaut's erudition is considerable, as can be judged from the note he devotes to the words "symbol" and "myth": t. 1, p. 2, 528–37. Other works include Abbé Auber, *Histoire et Théorie du symbolism religieux* (Paris: Librarie de Féchoz et Letouzey, 1884), t. 1, 4f; René Alleau, *De la nature des symboles* (Paris: Flammarion, 1958), 7–46; Alleau, *La science des symboles* (Paris: Payot, 1976), 29–42; Henri de Lubac, *The Christian Faith: An Essay on the Structure of the Apostles' Creed* (San Francisco: Ignatius Press, 1986), 339–51; Jean Pépin, *Dante et la Tradition de l'Allégorie* (Paris: Vrin, 1970), 15–31.

[2] *La science des Symboles*, 32.

work, *De la nature des symboles*,³ explained that in his opinion, *symballein* could not have the meaning of "binding together," "bringing together," "comparing," "confronting," or "sensing," given the dynamic character of the verb *ballein*. Contrary to the claims of most scholars, then, *symbolon* would not signify those objects (tessera, tablets, rings) of which each contracting party kept a half to serve as a sign of recognition (hence the meaning of "mark," "index," "rallying sign," "emblem," "omen," "contract," "agreement"). Alleau proposes a return to the Greek *synthema* to designate this sense of "mutual link." "The tesserae, the words of agreement, the primary signs of mutual bonds and, in particular, those which belong to the domain of communication between men are *synthemes*, not *symbols*."⁴ The symbol elevates the soul to the sacred and the divine, while the syntheme only designates a mutual bond of an intellectual and social order.⁵

Yet despite the author's assertions,⁶ he is not supported by lexicology. We do encounter *synthema* as signifying a mutual bond, *syntithemi* (from which it derives) meaning "binding," "attaching." But its occurrences are not more numerous than *symbolon*, and overall, its "semantic diffusion" is much smaller.⁷ We can regret this lack of precision in the Greek language in its use of *symbolon*, but we must live with it. And this appears characteristic of the vocabulary of symbolism. Whatever the validity of the distinctions of specialists, none can claim a fixed usage, all being more or less inconsistent.

There is therefore no reason to question the definition of "symbol" given by most scholars: it is a sign of recognition, a "material

---

³ Ibid., 15.
⁴ Ibid., 17.
⁵ Ibid., 21; in fact, *synthema* can also indicate a relation to the sacred and the divine: Damascius, *Problems and Solutions Concerning First Principles*, trans. Sara Ahbel-Rappe (New York: Oxford University Press, 2010), 238.
⁶ "In the examples given by Creuzer and Auber, there is no doubt that the word is inexactly applied to signs of recognition, of mutual social bonds that were *called* "syntema," "syntema," synthemes." Alleau returns to this distinction in *La Science des Symboles* and sees syntheme as purely conventional, as for example in chemical notation. "If one decides to designate oxygen by the letter O, one could equally have chosen the letter G and agreed that G would have the intended meaning in chemical reactions" (50). But G is not the first letter of oxygen! This "pure convention" is therefore obviously motivated.
⁷ Bailly's Greek–French dictionary gives the following survey: *synthema*, three primary and seven secondary meanings; *symbolon*, four primary and nineteen secondary meanings. The cited uses in no way justify Alleau's thesis.

object or a password, by which the initiated could be recognized."[8] Never forget, however, that according to the dynamic meaning of *-ballein*, this sign demands fulfilment, realization; one half of the broken ring calls out to the other, which alone will give it full reality. The symbol is thus already in itself a mutual bond, a connection, a social tie. But this essence produces its effect only insofar as its possessor truly realizes the conjunction signified by the symbol. It has therefore a double role: it guides and orients the search for reunion, and it *guarantees* and *certifies* this reunion when it has finally taken place. It is a sign of recognition because the precise fit of the ring's two halves objectively proves their reunion.

The Witness of Plato

We find in Plato a remarkable passage in which the most fundamental meaning of *symbolon* is employed within a perspective at once mystical and metaphysical. It occurs in the *Symposium* (191d) where Plato gives Aristophanes the following words: "Each of us, then, is a *symbol* of man (*anthropou symbolon*), because each was sliced like a flatfish, two out of one, and each of us is always seeking our own *symbol*."[9] Plato thus utilizes *symbolon* in a "symbolic" sense, transposing (while confirming) its primary meaning. The learned Dr. Guigniaut can therefore write in his study, "The original meaning, the simplest idea of the word *symbol* is *one thing composed from two*. Hence, according to ancient usage, the two halves of a tablet broken by two persons who together contracted a bond of hospitality were called symbols (*symbola, symbolaia, terrae tesserae hospitales*), and these *symbols* were carefully guarded by each of the contracting parties as a pledge of their mutual agreement… Little by little, the word came to designate any kind of pledge … any sign of recognition, any password (*tesserae militares*), any conventional speech … the wedding ring.

---

[8] Lubac, 340.
[9] This is usually rendered as "Each of us, then, is a 'matching half' of a human whole" (trans. Alexander Nehemas and Paul Woodruff, from *Plato: Complete Works*, ed. John M. Cooper and D. S. Hutchinson [Indianapolis: Hackett, 1997], 474). With all due respect to René Alleau, the same use of *symbolon* in the sense of "matching half" is found equally in Aristotle: "Aristotle understands by *symbola* (symbols, *tesserae*) *complementary factors*; for example, the heat of Air, combined with the dry, can form Fire, and the heat of Fire, with the moist, can form Air. The heat of Air and of Fire are *symbola*" (*De la Génération et de la corruption* II.4, 331a23–24, trans. Tricot [Paris: Vrin, 1951], 109, n. 1).

Soon the *symbol* comes to express the *sign* as opposed to the thing signified. Its use in the ancient Greek classics brings it into the sphere of religion, where it comes to express those sorts of relations between men and the gods that are not susceptible of explanation, only interpretation… In popular religion, this word is applied to various aspects of the worship of the gods, but it is more intimately related to the secret doctrine and higher worship practiced in the mysteries. Different emblems and formulas employed by initiates, passwords and signs by means of which they recognized each other—such things bear the name *symbol* or one analogous to it."[10] Of these various meanings, following the text of the *Symposium*, we would like to give some illustrations that can help us better grasp the spirit unifying the semantic field of *symbolon*, perhaps enriching it with a few nuances.

The Pythagorean Origin

It seems that the Pythagoreans or Neoplatonists used this term, though not to the exclusion of others such as *allegoria* ("allegory"), *sema* ("sign"), and *hyponoia* ("secret sign"). This is affirmed by Porphyry and Iamblichus in particular. According to the former, Pythagoras's "utterances were of two kinds, plain (*diexodikos*) or symbolical (*symbolikos*)."[11] He later confirms this, writing that "certain things he declared mystically, symbolically."[12] And Iamblichus tells us, "Those outside, whom I might call the profane, sometimes happened to be present; and under such circumstances the Pythagoreans would communicate only obscurely, through symbols."[13] Plotinus had also previously used the same term to characterize the Pythagorean manner of explanation: wondering how to properly name the One, he reports that "the Pythagoreans symbolically meant the One when among themselves they referred to 'Apollo' as the negation of plurality."[14]

---

[10] Op. cit., 530–33.
[11] Porphyry, *Life of Pythagoras* § 37; in *Pythagorean Sourcebook and Library*, trans. Kenneth Sylvan Guthrie, edited by David R. Fideler (Grand Rapids, MI: Phanes Press, 1987), 130.
[12] § 41; ibid., 131.
[13] Iamblichus, *Life of Pythagoras* § 32; ibid., 111.
[14] V.5.6; *The Enneads*, ed. Lloyd P. Gerson, trans. George Boys-Stones et al. (Cambridge: Cambridge University Press, 2017), 590. This is evidently a symbolic pun, analogous to the Hindu *nirukta*: *Apollon = a–pollon*, literally, "non-multiple."

Nevertheless, if the word *symbolon* enjoys a Pythagorean and Neoplatonic patronage, the reality it designates is much older: the same authors trace it back to the mysteries of Egypt, from which Pythagoras would have returned with it. Porphyry says as much: "In Egypt he lived with the priests, and learned the language and wisdom of the Egyptians, and their three kinds of letters, the epistolographic, the hieroglyphic, and symbolic, whereof one imitates the common way of speaking [this is the kyriological writing referred to by Clement of Alexandria], while the others express the sense of allegory and parable."[15] Iamblichus also develops this in his famous work, *On the Mysteries*:[16] "If you put forward a philosophical question, we will settle this also for you by recourse to the ancient stelae of Hermes, to which Plato before us, and Pythagoras too, gave careful study in the establishment of their philosophy."[17] And later: "first of all, I would like to explain to you the mode of theology practiced by the Egyptians. For these people, imitating the nature of the universe and the demiurgic power of the gods, display certain signs of mystical, arcane, and invisible intellections by means of *symbols*, just as nature copies the unseen principles in visible forms through some mode of *symbolism*, and the creative activity of the gods indicates the truth of the forms in visible signs... Hear, therefore, the intellectual interpretation of the *symbols*."[18] There is therefore a natural and cosmological symbolism corresponding in the cultural order to a traditional or sacred symbolism (sensible forms, words, and gestures) with a noetic or didactic purpose, but also and especially a ritual one: "Of the works of theurgy performed on any given occasion, some have a cause that is secret and superior to all rational explanation, others are like symbols consecrated from all eternity to the higher beings."[19] Cultural and ritual symbols are indeed instituted, but this institution is itself the work of the gods, directly or indirectly, in conformity with the order of things willed by the divine: "Was not this cult established by law at the beginning intellectually, according to the ordinances of the gods? It imitates the order of

---

[15] §12; ibid., 125.
[16] Trans. John M. Dillon and Emma Clark (Atlanta: Society of Biblical Literature, 2003).
[17] *De Mysteriis* §1.2; ibid., 9.
[18] §7.1–2; ibid., 291. Emphasis added.
[19] §1.11; ibid., 47.

the gods, both the intelligible and that in the heavens. It possesses eternal measures of what truly exists and wondrous tokens, such as have been sent down hither by the creator and father of all, by means of which unutterable truths are expressed through secret *symbols*, beings beyond form brought under the control of form, things superior to all image reproduced through images."[20]

Symbolism and Liturgy

It was not only the Pythagoreans and Egyptians who made use of symbolism, even as presented by Iamblichus, which as we have just seen, was a complete and perfectly ordered doctrine. It was present also in the Ancients, as Plutarch declares two centuries before Iamblichus, underlining its essentially ritual purpose: "Among the Ancients, Greeks as well as Barbarians, the science of nature [*physiologia*] was presented under the form of a physical presentation hidden in myths… This is evident in the Orphic poems, the Egyptian and Phrygian legends. But above all, the mind of the Ancients is manifest in the liturgies of initiation into the mysteries and the symbolic rites of the sacrifices."[21]

This last remark is important in clearly affirming the deep affinity between symbolism and liturgy. As we will see, if sacred symbolism is grounded in the natural symbolism of the sensible world, it reaches its true fulfillment and realizes its essence in ritual. In short, true hermeneutics is not the explication of the intellectual meaning of the symbol but a ritual action bringing the symbol into the sacramental order.[22]

---

[20] §1.21; ibid., 80–81. Emphasis added.
[21] Plutarch, *Ex opera de Daedalis Plateensibus* I, edited by Bernardakis, 43, 3–13 (this text exists only in the fragment preserved by Eusebius, cited by Pépin, 184).
[22] This preeminence of the ritual dimension in sacred symbolism is such that it even draws symbolism used for didactic purposes into its orbit. Myths must not only be the object of an exegesis revealing their abstract meaning: they are in themselves—through their recitation, independent of any rational comprehension—a ritual act, a true invocation, in that they imbue memory and language with a sacred form inherently endowed with divine and deifying virtue. Proclus asserts precisely this concerning the Platonic myths: "The good that belongs to [these myths] is not educational but rather mystical." They constitute "the hieratic and symbolic evocation of the divine" (*Commentary on Plato's Republic* I.80; in *Volume 1: Essays 1–6*, ed. & trans. Dirk Baltzly et al. [Cambridge: Cambridge University Press, 2018], 84). As Trouillard writes, "there is a secret virtue in them which, like an initiation, leads the suitably prepared soul to the divine" (Proclus, *Eléments de Théologie*

The Symbol from Antiquity to the Middle Ages   13

All things considered, the few examples that we have given suffice to show that *symbolon* (and its derivatives) was for the Greeks able to characterize the "iconic" nature of the sensible world, the esoteric meaning of sacred cultural forms revealed by the appropriate hermeneutics,[23] and the mystical and divine dimension of liturgy and sacrifice.

But it is not the only such term, as we often find "allegory," "allegorical," and "allegorically" employed for the same purposes. We will now briefly examine this point by treating some Jewish and Christian texts written in Greek.

THE SYMBOL IN GREEK JUDAISM

Existence of a Symbolism in Jewish Tradition

Philo of Alexandria (20 BC–50 AD) seems to have first explicitly formulated a doctrine of the symbolic interpretation of the Scriptures. He gave it the name *allegory*, borrowing this term from the grammatical vocabulary of Greek rhetoric. But does this mean that such interpretation was absent from Palestinian Judaism and known only to the Alexandrian,[24] under the influence

---

[Paris: Aubier, 1965], 41). We should not forget—and we will return to this point—that the reading of the Bible, both Old and New Testaments, was considered a sacrament at the time of St Augustine.

[23] Note, for example, that a (lost) treatise of Proclus devoted to the allegorical exegesis of myths was entitled *Peri ton muthikon symbolon* (H. D. Saffrey and L. G. Westerink, "Introduction," in *Proclus: Théologie platonicienne*, vol. 1, trans. Saffrey and Westerink [Paris: Belles Lettres, 1968], lvii). *Symbolon* and *symbolikos* are technical terms Proclus uses to designate Plato's mode of mythical exposition. In *Platonic Theology* I.4, he distinguishes four modes of exposition: "sometimes according to a deific energy, and at other times dialectically... sometimes he symbolically announces their ineffable peculiarities, but at other times he recurs to them from images" (*The Six Books of Proclus, the Platonic Successor, on the Theology of Plato*, trans. Thomas Taylor [London: A. J. Valpy, 1816], 10). As an example of divine inspiration, he gives the *Phaedrus*, and of dialectic, the *Sophist*. For the symbolic, he gives the *Gorgias*, which "is indeed not only a fable, but a true narration." And he continues, "in the *Symposium*... and in the *Protagoras*... he conceals in a *symbolic manner* the truth respecting divine natures" (11, altered). Images take the form of mathematical, physical, or ethical examples. He specifies later that "he who desires to signify divine concerns through symbols is Orphic and in short, accords with those who write fables concerning the Gods" (12). The difference between *image* and *symbol* is roughly equivalent to that between natural and cultural symbols.

[24] In the study of the Jewish religion in the three centuries before Christ and those following, we can distinguish two kinds of Judaism: those Jews

of Hellenism and the allegorical exegesis of the Homeric texts practiced by the Stoics? An important question, both in itself and as it relates to the exegesis of Saint Paul, especially since he gave scriptural support to Christians using the term *allegoria* in designating the symbolic interpretation of the Bible.

Many scholars, particularly Pépin,[25] favor a Greek origin for Jewish allegory, given its absence in Palestinian and abundance in Hellenized Judaism. If allegory is essentially understood to be the process of interpretation developed by the Stoics, which views the gods and religious myths as personifications of natural forces (physical allegory) or figurative representations of psychological truths (moral allegory)[26] and purports to rationalize naïve expressions ignorant of their own content, it is certain that such "philosophical" allegory is deeply foreign to the faith of Israel. But if *allegoria* is taken as a synonym for *symbolon*, then it is evident that the spiritual and mystical interpretation of the Scriptures far antedates the encounter between Alexandrian Judaism and Greek philosophy. Truthfully, though, the alternative is untenable because simply impossible: sacred symbolism is the essence of all religious expression without exception, and there is no need to support this with historical evidence.[27]

Revelation itself affirms (symbolically) the reality of its double meaning. YHWH says to Ezekiel, "Open thy mouth, and eat that I give thee. And when I looked, behold, an hand was sent unto me; and, lo, a roll of a book was therein; And he spread it before me; and *it was written within and without*."[28]

---

who remained in Palestine, and those of the *diaspora* who spread throughout the Mediterranean Basin, assimilating Greek culture along with the language, which served as a *lingua franca*. The Greek versions of the Torah, with the Septuagint (third century BC) being the most famous, were born in the heart of this Hellenized *diaspora*, which had Alexandria as its intellectual center. There may also have been Latin (and therefore pre-Christian) versions, as the Jewish communities in Rome were also significant. (Jean Daniélou, *A History of Early Christian Doctrine Before the Council of Nicaea, Volume 3: The Origins of Latin Christianity*, trans. David Smith and John Austin Baker [London: Darton, Longman, & Todd, 1977], 6ff.)

[25] *Mythe et Allégorie*, 225ff.

[26] See the faithful explanation given by Cicero in his *De natura deorum* II.28.70–71; and also J. Pépin, *Mythe et Allégorie*, 126ff.

[27] Yet a scholar of Hebrew once assured us that the Jewish revelation excludes all symbolism!

[28] Ezek. 2:8–10.

The Symbol from Antiquity to the Middle Ages

This injunction to eat a text written within and without (which is itself symbolic) — seeking to understand a message possessing both a manifest, visible meaning and an invisible, mysterious one — was essentially put into practice by the prophets. They reinterpreted certain fundamental and founding events in the sacred history of Israel (such as Adam and Paradise, the Flood, and the Exodus), transforming them into symbolic and sacred figures, into "types" in the Pauline sense, in which can be discerned, more or less clearly, not only the destiny of Israel but also that of the human soul. The very sequence of the texts of Holy Scripture presents what comes later as a hermeneutical reworking of what is primitive and archetypal. The work of specialists therefore leaves us in no doubt as to the existence of a "typology" proper to the Old Testament.[29]

Independent of the witness presented by Holy Scripture, the study of Palestinian Jewish exegesis leads to the same conclusions. In a study examining Talmudic exegesis as practiced "in the Academies of Palestine and Babylon," Fr Bonsirven observes, "allegorical interpretation was actually rare among the rabbis,"[30] though he specifies that this is true only if we understand allegory in the strict sense. If within allegory we include "parable or symbol," however, we can then say that Scripture is entirely allegorical: "Everywhere we get the same impression: it is less allegory per se than the *elementary forms* of allegory, namely metaphorical or symbolic interpretations."[31]

The existence of a symbolic exegesis of Palestinian origin is also now attested by the discovery of the Dead Sea Scrolls in Qumran. The fragments found there reveal an exegesis that "normally made use of typology, especially with regard to the figures of Adam and Moses."[32]

---

[29] Among other works, see Jean Daniélou, *From Shadows to Reality: Studies in Biblical Typology*, trans. Dom Wulstan Hibberd (London: Burns & Oates, 1960), 11–21, 153ff, etc. See also, by the same author, *History of Christian Doctrines Before Nicaea: Volume 1: The Theology of Jewish Christianity*, trans. John A. Baker (London: Darton, Longman, & Todd, 1964), 87ff.

[30] Joseph Bonsirven, "Histoire de l'exégèse juive," in *Dictionnaire de la Bible: Supplement*, t. IV (Paris: Letouzey et Ané, 1949), col. 561–69.

[31] Ibid., col. 566. We note in passing the terminological imprecision of this text, if we recall that allegory, for Quintilian and therefore in the proper sense, is an "extended metaphor."

[32] Daniélou, *The Theology of Jewish Christianity*, 87.

Finally, and not to speak of the major work of Philo of Alexandria[33]—who, though Greek in form remains profoundly Jewish in substance, and to whom we will refer later—we should mention here the Kabbalistic witness. The Kabbalah could obviously be seen only as a collection of texts appearing in Germany, France, and Spain toward the middle of the 12th century, in which case it would constitute a relatively late phenomenon and have no validity as proof of a symbolism proper to Judaism. But if it is seen as the esoteric doctrine of mystical Judaism, as did the Kabbalists themselves, then it is as ancient as revelation and dates back to Paradise. Independent of this primordial origin, which necessarily eludes historical method, it can nevertheless not be doubted that there existed a geographically Palestinian Jewish gnosis, interested primarily in the mystical and metaphysical meaning of Creation (the doctrine of *Bereshit*) and Ezekiel's vision of the celestial chariot (the doctrine of *Merkaba*). Both existed between the first and second centuries, "above all in the circles of the Talmudists," which is why "the historian of religion is entitled to consider the mysticism of the Merkabah to be one of the Jewish branches of gnosis."[34] To these should be added the *Sefer Yetzirah* (Book of Creation), which dates from the same period and received commentary from the medieval Kabbalists. In particular, this book contains the first formulation of the famous *Sefirot*, the ten primordial "numbers."[35] However, as before, it is difficult to describe this kabbalistic exegesis as allegory, as it was "strictly symbolic." It describes "the hidden process of divine life, as it unfolds in the manifestations and emanations of the *sefiroth*."[36]

Three conclusions seem to emerge from these brief considerations: first, there is a properly Jewish symbolism, which in both essence and form owes nothing to Hellenism. Second, there is no

---

[33] Cf. in particular Maurice de Gandillac, "Compte rendu critique de *Mythe et allégorie*," *Revue philosophique*, January–March 1961, 59–65.
[34] Gershom Scholem, *Origins of the Kabbalah*, trans. Allan Arkush (Princeton, NJ: Princeton University Press, 1987), 19, 21 [altered].
[35] Ibid., 35. The systematization of the primordial numbers in the form of the *sefirotic tree* will "appear" only later, in the *Zohar*. On the doctrine of the sefirotic tree, see Leo Schaya, *The Universal Meaning of the Kabbalah*, trans. Nancy Pearson (Hillsdale, NY: Sophia Perennis, 2005).
[36] Scholem, *On the Kabbalah and Its Symbolism*, trans. Ralph Manheim (New York, NY: Schocken Books, 1965), 52. Scholem then cites the opinion of Nahmanides, for whom "the symbol became meaningful only through the actual enactment of the commandment" (53).

fundamental difference between *allegoria* and *symbolon*, as Pépin rightly insists. However, third, and as will soon be seen, this is possible only on condition that *allegoria* is referred to *symbolon* rather than the reverse, as Bonsirven says, insofar as *allegoria* will never quite lose its relation to speech, while due to its Pythagorean origin, *symbolon* remains redolent of living mystery and esoterism.³⁷

The Witness of Philo

We come to the writings of Philo of Alexandria, where the word "symbol" appears most clearly. This is all the more remarkable given that Philo was in fact the first, not to practice, but to have formulated the doctrine of allegorical interpretation, using the word *allegoria* abundantly in doing so, even using it for the name of one of his essential works, *Allegorical Interpretation*.³⁸ He writes, "These explanations of the sacred scriptures are delivered by mystic expressions in allegories."³⁹ But in another work, still on

---

³⁷ It is doubtless not without interest that the word *allegoria* probably originates much more recently than does *symbolon*. Pépin cites Plutarch of Chaeronea on the subject (*Mythe et Allégorie*, 87), who declares that what was once called *hyponia* ("hidden meaning") is today called *allegoria* (*How the Young Man Should Study Poetry* 19e; in *Moralia*, vol. 1, trans. Frank Cole Babbitt [Cambridge, MA: Harvard University Press, 1927], 101). The word is absent from the Platonic corpus, which knows *hyponia* and, as we have seen, *symbolon*. Was the word indeed invented by grammarians in the first century BC? The numerous examples assembled by Pépin (*Mythe et Allégorie*, 88ff) suggest as much. Henri de Lubac, citing Cicero (*Orat.*, c. xvii), attributes the creation of *allegoria* to the grammarian Philodemus of Gadara around 60 BC (*Medieval Exegesis: The Four Senses of Scripture*, vol. 2, trans. E. M. Macierowski [Grand Rapids, MI: Eerdmans, 2000], 1). We will at least reproduce here the definition of allegory given by the Stoic (Pseudo-)Heraclitus of Pontus, a contemporary of Augustine: "For the moment, it is probably essential to give a little technical account of allegory, quite briefly. The word itself, which is formed in a way expressive of truth, reveals its own significance. For the trope which says [*agoreuon*] one thing but signifies something other [*alla*] than what it says receives the name 'allegory' precisely from this" (*Homeric Problems* V.1–2; eds. & trans. Donald A. Russell and David Konstan [Atlanta, GA: Society of Biblical Literature, 2005], 8). To this text can be added the commentary of Félix Buffière: *Les Mythes d'Homère et la pensée grecque* (Paris: Belles Lettres, 1973), 45ff; and *Héraclite: Allégories d'Homère*, ed. & trans. Félix Buffière (Paris: Belles Lettres, 1962), esp. 91.
³⁸ *The Works of Philo: Complete and Unabridged*, trans. C. D. Yonge (Peabody, MA: Hendrickson, 1993), 25–79. Émile Brehier's study of the origins of Philo's allegorical method causes him to conclude with a Jewish source: "We are here on the way to a purely Jewish tradition" (*Les Idées philosophiques et religieuses de Philon d'Alexandrie*, 3rd ed. [Paris: Vrin, 1950], 54).
³⁹ *De vita contemplativa* § 78; ibid., 705.

the subject of exegesis, Philo expresses himself as follows: "The seventh day is accounted sacred, on which [the Essenes] abstain from all other employments, and frequent the sacred places that are called synagogues, and there they sit according to their age in classes, the younger sitting under the elder, and listening with eager attention in becoming order. Then one, indeed, takes up the holy volume and reads it, and another of the men of the greatest experience comes forward and explains what is not very intelligible, for a great many precepts are delivered *by means of symbols, as the old fashion was.*"[40] For "the expressed narrative is the *symbol* of a hidden thought that must be examined."[41] Philo distinguishes three degrees of scriptural understanding: the letter, the clear light of truth, and allegory, which is midway between the literal and the contemplative. As he explains, "the things which are expressed by the voice are the *symbols* of those things which are conceived in the mind alone."[42] And when engaged in allegorical practice rather than theory, Philo does not hesitate to use the word *symbolon* or its derivatives. This is how he explains that Abraham "is a *symbolical* expression for the active intelligence"[43] or, speaking of the Tabernacle, "there were seven candles and seven lights, beings *symbols* of those seven stars which are called planets by those men who are versed in natural philosophy."[44] The word "symbol" can therefore clearly be applied as much to the words of Scriptures as to the things of which it speaks.

Scriptural Attestation of Symbolon

The word *symbolon* was not the sole property of Greek philosophy. It had some scriptural endorsement (unlike *allegoria*) in that it once appears in a book of the Bible, the Wisdom of Solomon. This text, composed in Greek by a Jewish scribe from Alexandria in the first century BC, can be found in the Septuagint between Job and Ecclesiasticus. It is generally believed to have

---

[40] *Quod omnis produs liber sit* § 81–82; ibid., 690 [altered, emphasis added].
[41] *De praemiis et poenis* § 6 [Tr: Translated from the French].
[42] *De Abrahamo* § 119; ibid., 421 [altered]. In what we have called the "three degrees of understanding" should not be seen the prefiguration of the three (or four) senses of Scripture first seen in Origen. Philo's perspective is different: the third degree is not a "sense," but the grasping of realities "as if at noonday" with no more of the "double shadow" of words and allegory.
[43] *De Abrahamo* § 99; ibid., 419 [altered].
[44] *De vita Moysi* § 103; ibid., 500.

been admitted into the scriptural canon by the Jews in Alexandria but refused by those in Palestine, as it was written in a language other than Hebrew. But this commits the sin of anachronism: no authority had officially proclaimed a list of inspired books at this time. We know that tradition has added to the Torah, the Law (Pentateuch) written by Moses to the chosen people, not only the words of the Prophets (hence "the Law and the Prophets" of which Christ speaks) but also a third category of writings, the *Hagiographa* or Writings. We must place the Wisdom of Solomon among the latter. However, the list of these Writings varied according to usage and synagogal communities. It is certain that in Palestine, where Scripture was read in Hebrew and Aramaic, there was a tendency to ignore texts written in Greek used by the Jews in Alexandria. It was only around 90 AD, at the synod of Jamnia, that Jewish authorities fixed the list of authentically inspired books, owing to anxieties about preserving the Jewish faith from any Essene or Christian contamination. But neither in Palestinian Judaism, which sometimes continued to use rejected books (e.g., Ecclesiasticus), nor *a fortiori* in Alexandrian Judaism did these decisions truly alter established practice. The proof of this is that the first Christians received the Canon of Scripture bequeathed by Greek tradition as authentic and directly revealed, and this canon included the Wisdom of Solomon. Neither among Christians was there some solemn and public decision on this subject in the first two or three centuries. And if discussions arose concerning the canonicity of the Wisdom of Solomon or Sirach, these were due to a foreign and "lateral" influence on the tradition received from Greek Judaism in apostolic times, and not due to these books' "secondary intrusion into the traditional Jewish canon."[45]

This brief account was necessary in order to better show the exceptional importance of the encounter between Judaism and Greek culture for the history of religions and of Western civilization. Doubtless it could use fuller development, especially in a time such as ours when the tendency is rather to "Judaize" the history of Christian origins. Already fifteen hundred years ago, the Hieronymian version of the Bible sought the *veritas hebraica*.

---

[45] Cf. Pierre Grelot, *Bible et Théologie: L'Ancienne Alliance, L'Écriture Sainte* (Paris: Desclée, 1965), 124–41.

But in so doing, we forget that millions of Jews and Christians have for centuries venerated a Bible written in Greek, and that this version seemed to them no less sacred and inspired than the Hebrew. Greek thus became as it were the property of the Jewish and Christian revelations. The language of Homer and Plato, whether we like it or not, was grafted onto the branch of Jewish culture and definitively established itself as the vehicle of the Abrahamic and Christian message.[46]

In this sense, we can say that *symbolon* receives scriptural support and becomes an integral part of the language of revelation. Indeed, The Book of Wisdom declares, "they were troubled for a small season that they might be admonished, having a *symbol* of salvation [*symbolon soterias*], to put them in remembrance of the commandment of thy law. For he that turned himself towards it was not saved by the thing that he saw, but by thee, that art the Saviour of all" (16:6–7).[47] The scribe alludes here to the episode with the Brazen Serpent spoken of in Numbers. The Jews, tired of wandering in the desert, murmur against YHWH, who punishes them by sending blazing serpents. Repenting, they beg Moses to intercede for them. God accepts Moses's prayer and tells him, according to the Septuagint version, "Make thyself a serpent and set it as a sign (*semeion*), and whoever is bitten and looks upon it shall live."[48] It is interesting to note that the Hellenistic scribe, who read the Bible in the Septuagint version and so for whom the

---

[46] Historians of religion sometimes seem to have only one scientific category: influence. They will say that Philo the Jew and Paul the Jew were influenced by Hellenism and Greek thought, or weren't, or were to some degree. Others will say, with the current trend, that in them a Jewish soul expresses itself in a Greek style, as if it were a mortal sin to admit that there is truth in Plato. But the very concept of influence must itself be submitted to philosophical critique. There are obviously cultural phenomena that fall into this category, but there are many others where it is simply not applicable. If Philo or St Paul use elements from Greek culture, perhaps this was because they recognized in them the pure and simple Truth, which is neither Jewish nor Greek, but universal. There is therefore no need to clear them of suspicion for having succumbed to the illusory and corrupting prestige of "pagan" culture. For St Paul, the only fact of which "pagan" wisdom was ignorant was the incarnation of God in Jesus Christ. Other than that, it seems doubtful that he thought about his mode of expression in terms either of influence or its resistance.

[47] The Vulgate, taking up the older version of the *Vetus latina* (2nd century), translates *symbolon* by *signum* [altered].

[48] Num. 21:8. According to the Hebrew, "hang it on a post." *Semeion* could also be translated "(military) standard." [Tr: Translated from the French.]

word *semeion* is backed by Scripture, does not reuse this term but substitutes *symbolon*: he speaks of a *symbol of salvation*. We think the reason for this preference is that the religious and concrete significance of *symbolon* for a Jew steeped in Greek culture made it more pregnant than *semeion*.

But the story does not end there. However unique the scriptural occurrence of the word "symbol," it is in a way taken up and authenticated by the use Christ makes of the Brazen Serpent, inviting his disciples to see in it a figure of the Son of Man: "And as Moses lifted up the serpent in the wilderness, even so must the Son of man be lifted up: that whosoever believeth in him should not perish, but have eternal life."[49] Thus, just as in the Torah, the bites of poisonous snakes are healed by contemplating a non-poisonous snake, but, says the Alexandrian scribe, this is because it is the "symbol of salvation," the sign of the Savior's virtue. In the same way, Christ—saving serpent hung on the cross, sign of redemption—heals by the blood of his wounds that original wound wrought by the deceitful serpent. This interpretation, common to many Fathers of the Church (such as St Ambrose, Theodoret, and St Augustine) as well as St Thomas, is all the more remarkable in making *symbolon* not only a sign and type (the serpent representing Christ) but a rite and a sacrament, which agrees with the conclusions already drawn from Greek literature outside of Judaism and Christianity.

THE SYMBOL IN GREEK CHRISTIANITY

The Vocabulary of Symbolism in the New Testament

The body of writings designated by the Church as the New Testament does not contain the word *symbolon*. On the other hand, there are many terms with similar or even identical meanings. One of these—*allegory*, used once by St Paul—was destined for great fortune.[50] As for the others, it is not necessary to list them all in a survey dedicated only to *symbolon*, but we will mention the following terms as an indication: *eikon*, "image," used 23 times; *charakter*, "mark," used once; *morphe*, "form," "image," used 3 times;

---

[49] Jn. 3:14–15. Incidentally, note that the serpent is not necessarily a symbol of evil, neither for Moses, nor for Christ, nor for Christian exegesis.
[50] It in fact occurs in the verbal form, *allegoroumena*, which the Vulgate translates as *per allegoriam* (Gal. 4:24).

mysterion, "mystery," "sign," "sacrament," which the Vulgate translates as either *mysterium* or *sacramentum*, 28 times; *omoioma* or *omoiosis*, "likeness," 6 times and once, respectively; *parabole*, "parable," used in the Septuagint to translate the Hebrew *machal*, with the sense equally of "figure" and "symbol," 50 times; *paroimia*, which St John prefers to "parable" and with the same sense, 5 times; *semeion*, "sign," 70 times; *schema*, "figure," twice; *typikos*, "in type," once; *typos*, "figure," "prophetic image," 15 times.[51]

Of all these, none prevailed to the point of eliminating the others, nor, more remarkably, did any oust *symbolon*, which enjoyed no New Testament support. *Allegoria* or *typos*, which many (primarily Pépin, and also Daniélou) would want to make the official designations for Christian symbolism, are the terms most often used in competition with *symbolon*. We will see precisely this in our investigation of the Greek literature of Christianity. Certainly, the following will be incomplete and depend quite a bit on the chance of our reading, since no systematic analysis exists of the occurrences of *symbolon* in Christian literature. But it will nevertheless be sufficiently demonstrative, even occasionally surprising.[52]

---

[51] *Mythos* ("myth," "fable") is always used pejoratively by St Paul (four times) and St Peter (once). Our totals are drawn from Sr Jeanne d'Arc OP, *Concordance de la Bible: Nouveau Testament* (Paris: Cerf/Desclée, 1970). We will return to the term *semeion* (by far the most used) when we treat the symbolic sign.

[52] It could be objected that the New Testament was canonically formed too late for its language to have had an influence on the first Christian writers. We must, however, distinguish between the canonical definition of the New Testament *corpus*, little attested before the second century, and the dates of composition for the texts that compose it. On the second point, the most recent trend in exegetical science goes against the current of assertions that still pass today for the "assured results of higher criticism," in particular by Bultmann and the post-Bultmannians. It appears that the four gospels were written during the first century, and certainly before 70 AD, despite received opinion declaring them much later (Louis Bouyer, "Un tremblement de terre dans la critique du Nouveau Testament," *Nova et Vetera*, v. 4, Oct–Dec 1977, 307–12; John A. T. Robinson, *Redating the New Testament* [Eugene, OR: Wipf and Stock, 2000]). These conclusions are confirmed by the work of the great Hebraist Fr Jean Carmignac, who summarized his findings in a small book, *The Birth of the Synoptic Gospels*, trans. Michael J. Wrenn (Chicago: Franciscan Herald Press, 1987). On the first point, it should be remembered that St Justin, for example, was fully aware of our four gospels, which he calls "the Memoirs of the Apostles." On knowledge of the New Testament among the Apostolic Fathers, see J. N. D. Kelly, *Early Christian Doctrines* (San Francisco: Harper One, 1978), 56–60.

The Witness of St Justin and St Irenaeus of Lyons

We will first gather the attestations of St Justin (first half of the second century) who was, if not the oldest of the Apologists, at least the first "Christian philosopher" in history, as well as the first writer to have used *symbolon* as a synonym for *typos*.[53] Symbolic interpretation of the Scriptures for Christians consists essentially in seeing in the words and actions of the Old Testament the veiled announcement and prefiguration (indecipherable for the Jews) of the doctrine of Christ. The word *typos*, used by St Paul, traditionally defines this symbolic relationship between past and future. Justin makes copious use of it and even formulates the following hermeneutic rule: "The Holy Spirit sometimes caused something that was to be a type [*typos*] of the future to be done openly, and on other occasions He spoke [*logoi*] of things of the future as though they were actually taking place, or had already taken place. Unless readers are familiar with this manner of speaking, they will not be able to grasp the full meaning of the Prophet's words."[54] But he does not hesitate to speak equally of symbols: "If I were to enumerate all the other Mosaic precepts, my friends, I could show that they are types, symbols, and prophecies [*tupous kai symbola kai katangelias*] of what would happen to Christ and those who were foreknown as those who would believe in Him, and similarly of the deeds of Christ Himself."[55] If Justin permits himself this assimilation of *typos* and *symbolon*, we think him amply supported by the *symbolon* in the Book of Wisdom, as suggested in the following: "According to you, even Moses would be judged a violator of the Law, for he, after ordering that no image of any of the things in heaven or on earth or in the sea should be made, personally constructed a brazen serpent and set it up as a sign, commanding those who had been bitten by the serpents to gaze upon it. . . . Shall we, therefore, accept such stupid interpretations of these things as given by your teachers, instead of regarding them as *symbols*?"[56] The paschal lamb is also

---

[53] Jean Daniélou, *A History of Early Christian Doctrine Before the Council of Nicaea, Volume 2: Gospel Message and Hellenistic Culture*, trans. John Austin Baker (London: Darton, Longman, & Todd, 1973), 203.
[54] *The Dialogue with Trypho* § 114.1; in *The Writings of Saint Justin Martyr*, trans. Thomas B. Falls, DD (Washington, DC: Catholic University of America Press, 1948), 323–24. See also, among others, § 40.
[55] § 42.4; ibid., 211.
[56] § 112.1–2; ibid., 320–21.

a *symbolon* of Christ, the twelve bells of the High Priest's robe are the *symbolon* of the twelve Apostles, and so on.[57] Moreover, *symbolon* is not only the equivalent of *typos*, since Noah and his companions are the *symbolon* of the Eighth Day.[58]

Yet there is one term Justin never uses: *allegoria*. We can no doubt assume that the "scholarly" origin of this term, its literary and abstract character, rendered it relatively unsuitable for religious use.[59] Religious symbolism implies a quasi-existential relation between the symbol and the reality designated, which is not entirely the case for *allegoria*, at least not in its strictly technical sense: "Justin, therefore, champions a realist interpretation of the prophets, in keeping with the factual quality of the Incarnation, just as his typology is essentially an interpretation of history. He will have nothing to do with an allegorism which seeks to dissolve history into myth."[60]

Sts Irenaeus of Lyons and Melito of Sardis knew the distinction between (prophetic) words and (figurative) events, almost always using the Pauline expressions *typos* or *allegoria*.[61] Yet the meaning of *typos* is hardly different from that of *symbolon*. This is shown by the example of Ptolemaeus, a Christian gnostic and disciple of Valentinus opposed by St Irenaeus, who in the *Letter to Flora*, devoted to the meaning of the Old Testament, discerns in the Scriptures a "typical and symbolic" element established in imitation of spiritual and transcendent realities.[62]

St Clement of Alexandria

Clement's work offers a rich harvest of designations for symbolic expression: *typos, mysterion, ainigma, semeion, allegoria*, but also *symbolon* and its derivatives, which are used technically to designate this mode of expression in its greatest generality, to define its *genre*. The most interesting occurrences are mainly to be found in Book V of the *Stromata*, dedicated to the exposition of symbolic gnosis: "it was not only the most highly intellectual

---

[57] § 41.1–3, § 42.1, and also § 86.1; ibid., 209–11, 285.
[58] § 138.1; ibid., 360.
[59] Daniélou, *Gospel Message and Hellenistic Culture*, 204.
[60] Ibid., 214.
[61] St Irenaeus of Lyons, *Adv. Haer.* I.3.6 (*allegoria*); IV.14.3, 21.3 (*typos*). The citations from St Melito of Sardis are given by Daniélou, *Gospel Message and Hellenistic Culture*, 234–36.
[62] Ibid., 222.

of the Egyptians, but also such of other barbarians [and therefore also Judeo-Christians] as prosecuted philosophy, that affected the *symbolical style* [*symbolikos eidos*]."[63] The major portion of this text is moreover dedicated precisely to the presentation of different aspects of this symbolic genre.[64] This is confirmed by the beginning of Book VI of the *Stromata*, which summarizes what has just been developed: "For since we have shown that the *symbolical style* was ancient, and was employed not only by our prophets, but also by the majority of the ancient Greeks, and by not a few of the rest of the Gentile Barbarians, it was requisite to proceed to the mysteries of the initiated."[65] That the symbolic genre is the one containing the different modes of figurative expression is evident in the famous passage on Egyptian writing:[66] Clement distinguishes three types of writings (epistolographic, hieratic, and hieroglyphic), dividing the third in two categories, which he names *kyriological* (abbreviated) and *symbolic* (figurative). Symbolic writing further comprises three kinds according to whether it proceeds by direct imitation, by metaphor, or by allegory and enigma.

However, it cannot be said that Clement restricts himself to a strict vocabulary, that allegory and metaphor are always the species of which symbolism is the genus. As he writes, "All then, in a word, who have spoken of divine things, both Barbarians and Greeks, have veiled the first principles of things, and delivered the truth in *enigmas*, and *symbols*, and *allegories*, and *metaphors*, and such like tropes."[67] Elsewhere, in speaking of the Platonic myths, he seems to understand by *symbol* the expressive figure as such, and by *allegory* the process of its employment: "Even those myths in Plato... are to be expounded allegorically, not absolutely in all their expressions, but in those which express the general sense. And these we shall find indicated by *symbols* under the veil of allegory."[68]

As to the grounds requiring the use of *symbol*, Clement's writings confirm what has already been said concerning its relationship

---

[63] *Stromata* V.8; in *The Ante-Nicene Fathers*, vol. 8, eds. Alexander Roberts and James Donaldson (Grand Rapids, MI: Christian Classics Ethereal Library, 2005), 454.
[64] André Méhat, *Études sur les Stromates* (Paris: Seuil, 1966), 278.
[65] *Stromata* VI.2; ibid., 481.
[66] V.4; ibid., 449.
[67] Ibid.
[68] V.9; ibid., 458.

to the sacred, the mysterious, and the esoteric. This esoterism[69] concerns not only religion but also philosophy: "life would fail me to adduce the multitude of those who philosophize in a *symbolical* manner."[70] "Very useful, then, is the mode of *symbolic interpretation* for many purposes; and it is helpful to the right theology."[71] The veil of the symbol intrigues us, inciting us to search: "For many reasons, then, the Scriptures hide the sense. First, that we may become inquisitive, and be ever on the watch for the discovery of the words of salvation." But the text goes on to state the negative justification for all esoterism: "Then it was not suitable for all to understand, so that they might not receive harm in consequence of taking in another sense the things declared for salvation by the Holy Spirit."[72] It is therefore not only a matter of preserving holy things from profanation but also, and above all, of preserving the ignorant from the dangers represented by the revelation of gnosis.[73]

Origen

Turning now to the great Origen, we do not find in him a less frequent use of the word *symbolon* and its derivatives. Yet Origen stands as the undisputed master of allegorical exegesis,

---

[69] The words *esoteric* and *exoteric* are found in Clement: *Stromata* V.9; Roberts and Donaldson, 459.
[70] V.9; ibid., 457.
[71] V.8; ibid., 455.
[72] VI.15; ibid., 509.
[73] For Clement, the esoterism of gnosis does not consist only in its symbolic veiling. It is also a secret knowledge transmitted orally by Christ to the Apostles — at least some of them, in particular Peter, James, John, and Paul — and by the Apostles to some Christians, up through Clement himself. This gnosis, which is a *tradition* (*paradosis*), "revealed by the Son of God," "has descended by transmission to a few, having been imparted unwritten by the apostles" (*Stromata* VI.7; Roberts and Donaldson, 494). "They [Clement's masters, holders of gnosis] preserving the tradition of the blessed doctrine derived directly from the holy apostles, Peter, James, John, and Paul, the sons receiving it from the father (but few were like the fathers), came by God's will to us also to deposit those ancestral and apostolic seeds" (I.1; Roberts and Donaldson, 301). Such a doctrine is moreover not specific to Clement: "The idea of a secret teaching, given by Christ to the Apostles to be transmitted orally to select individuals, was common at the end of the second century" (Daniélou, "Les Traditions secrètes des Apôtres," *Eranos Jahrbuch* 31 [1962], 199; he concludes that "there is no reason to challenge Clement's witness" [214]). But in the opinion of André Méhat (heard from him directly), if there was indeed a doctrinal esoterism, "there is not the slightest trace in Clement of a gnostic *sacrament*."

who (having been misread) has been considered to abuse it outrageously.[74] And though it is obvious that we find abundant use of *allegoria* in his writings, it must first be observed that Origen's vocabulary is actually quite varied: without being exhaustive, we can find not only *allegoria*, but also *mysterion, parabole, problema, symbolon, tropologia, typos, hyponoia*, etc. On the other hand, Origen's use of these terms is flexible enough for us to consider them interchangeable in his work. Finally, he is clearly aware of the "problem of hermeneutics" and that allegory is an exegetical method whose value depends on use. Moreover, not only can pagan *allegoria* be criticized,[75] but also that of Christian Gnostics, who "take refuge in allegories and new interpretations" when encountering a surprising passage in the Gospel.[76]

That said, I think we must maintain that for Origen, the semantic field of *symbolon* is more extensive than that of *allegoria*. The latter almost exclusively refers to either a mode of expression or a mode of Scriptural interpretation, whereas *symbolon* and its derivatives can apply not only to such an interpretation or expression,[77] but also to concrete fulfillment, which is usually not the case for *allegoria*. Thus the Eucharistic bread is qualified as *symbolic* without any "derealizing" intention: "it is not the material of the bread but the word which is said over it which is of advantage to him who eats it not unworthily of the Lord. And these things indeed are said of the typical and symbolical body [*peri tou typikou kai symbolikou somatos*]."[78] Similarly, Origen explains the naming of the "Eucharistic" bread, maintaining that "we have a *symbol* of our thanksgiving to God in the bread," a symbol of our gratitude.[79] But the symbolic nature of sacred realities is not found only among Christians, having already existed

---

[74] On Origen's exegesis, refer to the classic work by Fr Henri de Lubac, *History and Spirit: The Understanding of Scripture According to Origen*, trans. Anne Englund Nash (San Francisco, CA: Ignatius Press, 2007).

[75] Cf. the texts assembled by Pépin, *Mythe et allégorie*, 453–62.

[76] For example, "Homily 16"; in *Homilies on Luke*, trans. Joseph T. Lienhard, SJ (Washington, DC: Catholic University of America, 1996), 67. It concerns the "unjust steward."

[77] *Contra Celsum* V.30; ed. & trans. Henry Chadwick (Cambridge: Cambridge University Press, 1980), 287.

[78] *Origen's Commentary on the Gospel of Matthew* XI.14; in *The Ante-Nicene Fathers*, vol. 9, ed. Allan Menzies (Grand Rapids, MI: Christian Classics Ethereal Library, 2005), 443.

[79] VIII.57; Chadwick, *Contra Celsum*, 495.

among the Jews: "we [previously] gave a partial account of the holy and peculiar society of the Jews at the time when it exhibited to them the *symbol* of the city of God, and of His temple, and the sacerdotal worship in it at the altar."[80] Finally, it is equally remarkable that even when an adequate term is provided by Scripture, Origen tends to gloss it with *symbolon*. He thus affirms the equivalence of *symbolon* and the Johannine *semeion*: "nothing miraculous happens in Scripture that is not also a sign (*semeion*) and symbol of something else beyond the literal occurrence."[81]

To summarize — and this is one of the surprises referred to earlier — Origen, the great doctor of allegory, that impenitent allegorist, in some of his works uses *symbolon* more often than *allegoria*. Thus in his longest work, *Contra Celsum*, there are 34 occurrences of *symbolon* with its derivatives and only 12 of *allegoria*, nearly three times fewer![82]

Theodoret of Cyrus

Before coming to the master of Christian symbolic theology, we will cite another writer, one of the most fecund in all Greek patristic literature and a good witness for common usage in the fourth and fifth centuries — Theodoret of Cyrus (393–458).

Although he belonged to the Antiochian school, traditional rival of the Alexandrian, we find in him a quite "Origenian" use of *symbolon*. He evidently knew the term's Pythagorean source: "[Pythagoras's] style is enigmatic and abstruse — indeed he has offered his views in the form of symbols."[83] But he also speaks willingly of symbolism in the case of the Eucharistic bread, without placing realist intention in doubt. In a didactic treatise written in the form of a dialogue, he expresses himself as follows:

> *Orthodox.* Then tell me, what is symbolized by the sacramental symbols [*mystika symbola*] that are offered to the Lord God by those who offer sacrifice?

---

[80] V.42; ibid., 297.
[81] XIII.452; in *Commentary According to the Gospel of John: Books 13–32*, trans. Ronald E. Heine (Washington, DC: Catholic University of America, 1993), 164.
[82] These figures come from the index established by Marcel Borret in the fifth volume of his edition of *Contra Celsum*, included in the "Sources Chrétiennes" series.
[83] "Discourse 8: On the Cult of the Martyrs" §1; in *A Cure for Pagan Maladies*, trans. Thomas Halton (Mahwah, NJ: Paulist Press, 2013), 170 [altered].

> *Eranistes.* The Lord's body and blood.
>
> *Orthodox.* The real body or one that is not real?
>
> *Eranistes.* The real one.

And he concludes a little later: "just as the symbols of the Lord's body and blood are one thing before the priestly invocation, [they] are transformed and become something else after the invocation."[84] The word *symbolon* therefore applies for him as much to a text with a hidden meaning as to a sacred reality filled with the divine presence.

St Dionysius the Areopagite

This use of *symbolon* is found eminently in Dionysius the Areopagite, whom we have called the master of Christian symbolic theology. This is due first to the profundity and beauty of his doctrine, making him one of the pinnacles of Christian thought—so much so that the metaphysics of sacred symbolism is present as a whole within his work, and we could content ourselves with citing him alone if developments in culture and mentality did not make a longer journey necessary. Second, because he announces in *The Divine Names* a treatise, now lost, to be entitled *The Symbolic Theology*, to which he refers in *The Celestial Hierarchy* and *The Mystical Theology*.[85] And finally, it is not only the Dionysian *doctrine* that belongs essentially to sacred symbolism but also its *manner of presentation*, which can be explained only in virtue of its symbolic meaning. We are alluding here to the controversial question of the authorship of the Areopagitic writings, which we will now discuss briefly.

"With Denys we have a unique case in theology, indeed in all intellectual history. A man of the foremost rank and of prodigious power hid his identity not only from centuries of credulity but also

---

[84] *Eranistes* II.151–52; trans. Gerard H. Ettinger SJ (Washington, DC: The Catholic University of America, 2003), 131–32.

[85] *Divine Names* IV.5 (700d); in *Pseudo-Dionysius: The Complete Works*, trans. Colm Luibheid (Albany, NY: Paulist Press, 1987), 74. Most scholars once considered the non-extant treatises mentioned by Dionysius to be fictitious. But René Roques (with hesitation) and Hans Urs von Balthasar (more clearly) come out in favor of their loss (Roques, *Dictionnaire de spiritualité*, t. III, col. 257ff; Roques, *Structures théologiques: De la gnose à Richard de Saint-Victor* [Paris: Presses Universitaires de France, 1962], 128–32; Balthasar, *The Glory of the Lord: A Theological Aesthetics, Volume 2: Studies in Theological Style: Clerical Styles*, trans. Andrew Louth et al., ed. John Riches [San Francisco: Ignatius Press, 1984], 154ff).

from the critical acumen of the modern period."[86] This remark perfectly epitomizes the Dionysian question.[87] To this must be added the following argument, which we consider irrefutable: it is impossible to reconcile the hypothesis of a forger wishing to cloak his works in the mantle of another's renown with the nobility and sanctity which radiate from such an incomparable work, though this is an argument that will appear naïve or subjective only to minds affected by "spiritual 'color blindness.'"[88] True, it is extremely difficult to accept that the text of the *Corpus*, as it has come down to us, comes from the pen of the convert of Saint Paul.[89] This is why Balthasar suggests viewing the "Dionysian veil," with which the author of the *Corpus* covered himself, as a symbolic necessity: the transposition of the author and his interlocuters to the apostolic era expresses the profound "truth" of the work, is its true "signature," because it signifies the primordial and as it were timeless character of the contemplation it teaches, beyond disputes and discussions. But if "Dionysius the Areopagite" is indeed a "hieronym," such that the individual disappears behind the sapiential function he must — and did — assume in the history of Christianity, we must still wonder why

---

[86] Balthasar, *The Glory of the Lord*, v. II, 144.
[87] On the recent state of this question, see René Roques, *Structures Théologiques*, 63–115. In favor of the Dionysian authorship of the *Corpus*, refer to the work of Natya Josiana Foatelli, *Denys l'Aréopagite et le Mystère Dionysien*, Revue Atlantis no. 261, January–February 1971, 146–234.
[88] The expression is Balthasar's (op. cit., 146).
[89] The difficulties can be reduced to three: (1) the inexplicable silence of Christian literature on texts that are nevertheless virtually apostolic; (2) the developed state of the ecclesial and monastic liturgy mentioned in the corpus; and (3) the close affinity of the end of *The Divine Names* IV with Proclus's *De Malorum subsistentia*. None of these arguments is truly decisive. The Neoplatonic connection had already been noticed by St Thomas Aquinas, who, as we know, was the first to recognize the *Liber de Causis*, attributed to Aristotle, as a compilation of Proclus's *Elements of Theology*, recently translated by William of Moerbeke. Did Thomas consider Proclus a plagiarist of Dionysius? Roques says he did (op. cit., 64), while Balthasar denies this, supposing that for Thomas, Dionysius is later than Proclus (op. cit., 151). St Thomas indeed writes that "Dionysius, however, corrects this position when they [the Platonists] assert that the different separate forms, which they call 'gods,' exist in succession, so that one would be *per se* goodness, another *per se* being, another *per se* life, and so on with regard to the others" (Prop. 3.20; in *Commentary on the Book of Causes* [*Super Librum De Causis Expositio*], trans. Vincent A. Guagliardo OP et al. [Washington, DC: Catholic University of America, 1996], 22).

The Symbol from Antiquity to the Middle Ages 31

this name and not another which could equally be found in the New Testament. We see no other plausible answer than to accept that the theological inspiration testified to by the *Corpus* appearing in 533 indeed goes back to Dionysius the Athenian, who believed in the resurrection of Jesus Christ proclaimed by Paul the Jew before the Areopagus one autumn day in 50 AD.

The *Corpus Areopagiticum* thus comes to us wholly as a symbol. No wonder then that it offers the most numerous occurrences of the term in all Christian literature. Certainly, Dionysius uses other words to signify the symbolism of the cosmos, of Scripture, or of the sacraments (*eikon, typos, theoplastia,* and so on), but there is one that he never uses and is sought in vain through the whole expanse of the *Corpus*: *allegoria*.[90] Its omission can only have been intentional, especially if we consider its Pauline endorsement and diffusion in Hellenistic literature. The only conceivable explanation relates, as already noted, to the rhetorical and grammatical origin of this term and therefore to its being evidently too profane to be allowed in a discourse which is at once, and inextricably, metaphysical speculation and hymnic liturgy. Only the word *symbolon* can adequately render these mysterious realities that are at once "immediate theophanies"[91] and sacramental celebration, because sacred intellection is a rite, and rite an intellection: "that love toward humanity cover[s] the truths of the mind with things derived from the realm of the senses. And so it is that the Transcendent is clothed in the terms of being, with shape and form on things which have neither, and numerous *symbols* are employed to convey the varied attributes of what is an imageless and supra-natural simplicity."[92] This is why Roques can write, "Dionysius understands by *symbolon* not only the sign of a divine reality but this reality itself. This precision is very important for the study of the sacraments."[93] Thus, in the third chapter of *The Ecclesiastical Hierarchy*, Dionsyius almost always uses *symbolon* or the plural *symbola*, taken absolutely, to designate the sacraments, and particularly the Eucharist.[94] In such a perspective,

---

[90] In this respect, Gandillac's beautiful translation can be misleading: *Œuvres complètes du Pseudo-Denys* (Paris: Aubier, 1943).
[91] Balthasar, op. cit., 179.
[92] *Divine Names* I.4 (592b); Luibheid, 51.
[93] *L'univers dionysien* (Paris: Aubier, 1954), 104.
[94] 424b–445c; op. cit., 208–23.

the *symbolon* is truly the place where the unity of signifier and the reality signified is realized, a dynamic rather than static unity, such that the *symbolon*, properly known and contemplated, leads the illumined soul towards the archetype revealed within it. The movement of revelatory emanation and apophatic return to the One, characteristic of all Dionysian thought, is eminently valid for the *symbola*: neither an idolatry of the created, nor an idealism despising the sensible, but rather, within symbolic realities, a perpetual movement of revelation and incorporation, revealing by incorporating and incorporating by revealing.

This conception (or vision) of the *symbolon* is so strong that it drags into its orbit all neighboring terms, which thereby participate in the continuous circularity of its twofold dynamic. Thus *typos*—which as we have seen, seems the most characteristic of Christian hermeneutics—while present in Dionysius, means hardly more than *symbolon*. He is not entirely unaware of the typology which sees in the Old Testament a prophetic image, a figure (*typos*) of the truth (*aletheia*) revealed in the New.[95] But in general, *typos* is seen much more in its permanent vertical relation to the *archetypes* than in its temporal horizontal relation to salvation history: "It is the mark, the imprint, the seal of an archetype, rather than the prefiguration and announcement, in history and according to history, of an antitype to come."[96] But is not everything a symbol, with time itself revealing *aletheia* to us only in the form of *typos*?

We can therefore conclude our investigation by affirming that *symbolon*, if it is not alone in expressing the idea of cosmic, scriptural, and ritual symbolism, is used as much as any other, even tending occasionally toward a certain hegemony integrating *typos*

---

[95] *Ecclesiastical Hierarchy* III.3 (432b); ibid., 213. By way of comparison, here is the terminological frequency of the vocabulary of symbolism in the Dionysian *Corpus*, according to the index by Dom Phillipe Chevallier et al.: *symbolon*, 64; *eikon*, 62; *symbolikos* (adj.), 20; *typos*, 14; *symbolikos* (adv.), 6; *typikos*, 1; *allegoria*, 0; *hyponoia*, 0. (*Dionysica*, vols. 1–2 [Paris: Desclée de Brouwer et Cie, 1937–1950]).

[96] Roques, *Structures théologiques*, 186. Is this Dionysian interpretation of typology truly foreign to the theology of the Fathers? Does not the reduction of Christian symbolism to a specifically historical typology, as Daniélou often tends to do, constitute an error of perspective? Is this not the projection of a modern category (history) onto a cultural mentality that dismisses it—in order, moreover, to rehabilitate it for contemporary eyes? In any case, we should know that it is not possible to conduct such analyses without a *philosophical* critique of the concepts of history and of historical consciousness.

The Symbol from Antiquity to the Middle Ages

into its semantic orbit and casting *allegoria* back into the profane order of rhetoric and grammar. Essentially linked to the sphere of the sacred and religious, it is inseparable from ideas of mystery, esoterism, and sacrament.

THE SYMBOL IN LATIN CHRISTIANITY

A New Meaning of the Word

Latin evidently knows a transliteration of the Greek *symbolon* as *symbolum*, as well as *symbola* (from *symbole*) and the form *symbolus* (from *symbolos*), which it is not always possible to distinguish from the neuter. In addition to the sense of "communal meal" for *symbola* (attested particularly by the Vulgate in Proverbs 23:21), dictionaries[97] essentially confirm the etymological meaning of the Greek: the idea of a sign of recognition, which we recalled at the outset. Thus, in Plautus for example, *symbolum* or *symbolus* equate to the *tessera hospitalis*, that token of hospitality whose exchange allows mutual identification between those who meet.[98] But the sense of "figurative expression of a superior reality" is encountered only belatedly and in the technical Latin of the grammarians, under the forms *symbolice* (attested by Aulus Gellius in the second century) and *symbolicus* (by Charisius in the second half of the fourth).[99] This fact is due perhaps to the non-symbolic mind of the Romans, whereas to the contrary *symbolum* as sign of recognition satisfied their taste for the concrete and juridical. Yet we can also think that the Latin *signum* allowed all the uses of the Greek *symbolon* and therefore to some extent countered the diffusion of this foreign word.

The Latin Christian writers evidently conformed to this usage, at least so long as the constraining force of Latin culture lasted in the first centuries, using *signum* for what the Greeks called symbol. The most famous example is that of St Augustine, who formulated a true theory of the sign, in fact the first to date, in which *signum* ceased to be only the verbal sign and was applied to the symbolism of the cosmos generally. However, we find in Tertullian at least two metaphorical uses of *symbolum*, "referring

---

[97] Félix Gaffiot, *Dictionnaire Latin-Français*, s.v.; and Albert Blaise, *Dictionnaire Latin-Français des Auteurs chrétiens*, s.v.
[98] Plautus, *Bacchides*, 263; *Pseudolus*, 55; *Poenulus*, 1047–1048; etc.
[99] Gaffiot, s.v.; and Blaise, s.v.

to its original meaning as a seal which guarantees a contract."[100] "God grants us the symbol of death,"[101] he writes metaphorically of baptism. Elsewhere he asks "under what *symbol*"[102] one must receive the testimony of the Apostle Paul, which is to say, what is the mark, the sign of recognition allowing its authentication? But these attestations are, on the whole, extremely rare.

It was in the middle of the third century with St Cyprian—an assiduous reader of Tertullian, from whom he was separated by some sixty years—that a new meaning appeared for the first time in Christian literature of the word *symbolum*, a word called to great fortune, by which he designates what we call the Creed. Speaking of the Novatian schism,[103] St Cyprian writes, "if anyone objects—to say that Novatian holds the same law as the Catholic Church holds, baptizes with the same *symbol* with which we baptize ... let whoever thinks that this must be objected know first that there is not one law of symbol for us and the schismatics."[104] Taken in this sense, the term becomes the official designation for the rule of faith recited at baptism, and there are countless attestations of this. Rather than list them all, it is more interesting for our purposes to examine the grounds for using *symbolon* in this sense. Many scholars believe that this meaning is foreign to the question of symbolism and deplore the fact that it prevailed almost exclusively among the Latins.[105] We disagree: the grounds justifying the expression *symbolum fidei* are important insofar as they do imply a certain symbolism. Moreover, we will see that the "symbolist" sense of the term is not so rare as is widely asserted.

---

[100] De Lubac, *The Christian Faith*, 340–41. One also finds here *symbola* in the sense of "the process of a common reckoning" (*Adversus Valentinianos* XII [PL 2:562a]; in *Ante-Nicene Fathers*, vol. 3, ed. Allan Menzies DD [Grand Rapids, MI: Christian Classics Ethereal Library, 2006], 510).

[101] *De Poenitentia* VI (PL 1:1238b–1239a); ibid., 661.

[102] *Adversus Marcionem* V.1 (PL II 562a); ibid., 430.

[103] This refers to disciples of Novat, the leader of a group of African heretics. Toward the year 250, they allied themselves with the *Novatianists*, disciples of the illustrious Roman theologian Novatian who, having been consecrated a bishop, caused the first schism in the history of Christianity. All these schismatics were thereafter referred to as Novatianists.

[104] Letter 69.7; in *Saint Cyprian: Letters (1–81)*, trans. Sr Rose Bernard Donna CSJ (Washington, DC: Catholic University of America, 1964), 249.

[105] Such is the opinion, for example, of Gerhart B. Ladner, in a study published by the American journal *Speculum: A Journal of Medieval Studies*, entitled "Medieval and Modern Understanding of Symbolism" (vol. 54, no. 2, April 1979, 223–56).

First, we note that St Cyprian could rely on Tertullian to speak of the baptismal "symbol," since the latter calls it *tessera* or *contesseratio hospitalis*,[106] and as previously observed, the Latin *tessera* (small cube, token) is equivalent to the Greek *symbolon*. On the other hand, the symbolic "etymologies" given by the Christian authors to justify the designation of *Symbol* themselves constitute a veritable constellation of symbols which echo and complement each other without repetition.

The *symbolum* St Cyprian speaks of is attested in the form *symbolum apostolorum* (Symbol of the Apostles) for the first time in a letter to the Pope by St Ambrose.[107] However, its apostolic origin was known much earlier, as St Irenaeus speaks already of a "rule of faith which the apostles handed down to the leaders of the Church."[108] And this rule of faith was received by Irenaeus from priests who were themselves taught it by the Apostles.[109] It seems to follow from Irenaeus's statements[110] that the rule of faith was transmitted orally and covered by the discipline of the arcane: as Ambrose writes, "this I desire you to be warned of, that the Symbol is not to be written down... Wherefore? So we have received, that it is not to be written down... Say over the Symbol to yourself inwardly... lest you form a habit, and when you are accustomed to saying it over aloud where there are some of the faithful, you come to saying it among catechumens or heretics."[111]

Now, according to the tradition reported by Rufinus,[112] the Apostles came together to compose the Symbol, and it is even explained (somewhat later, around the sixth century) that each of the twelve Apostles pronounced in turn one of the twelve

---

[106] *De praescriptione* XX; op. cit., 252. Tertullian says that the different Churches can be *contesseratae* thanks to this *tessera* (De Lubac, op. cit., 341).
[107] Letter 44 (PL 16:1125b); in *Saint Ambrose: Letters*, trans. Sr Mary Melchior Beyenka OP (Washington, DC: Catholic University of America, 1954), 227.
[108] *Adversus Haereses* III.4.1–2 (PG 7:549) [TR: Translated from the French].
[109] *Proof of the Apostolic Preaching* § 3; trans. Joseph P. Smith SJ (Westminster, MD: The Newman Press, 1952), 49. Irenaeus was the disciple of Polycarp, himself a disciple of John.
[110] He writes, "if the Apostles had not left any writing behind, we would still need to follow the rule of faith"; Lubac, op. cit., 20ff.
[111] *The Explanatio symboli ad initiandos* § 12; trans. Dom R. H. Connolly (Cambridge: Cambridge University Press, 1952), 26–27.
[112] *Commentarius in symbolum Apostolorum* § 2 (PL 21:337a); *A Commentary on the Apostle's Creed*, trans. J. N. D. Kelly DD (Westminster, MD: The Newman Press, 1955), 29–31.

articles of the Creed.¹¹³ All the elements are thus brought together to justify the use of the word *symbolum*: Etherius, the bishop of Osma, writes in 784 that "there were twelve disciples of Christ and teachers of nations; as they were all one, they thus composed one symbol. Each of them spoke a word, and these words agreed in a single faith, and there were only twelve words or articles."¹¹⁴

The *Symbolum Apostolorum* is therefore a symbol "for a number of excellent reasons," as Rufinus declares: "*Symbol* in Greek can mean both 'token' [*indicium*] and 'collection' [*collatio*], that is, a joint whole to which several persons contribute. This is what the Apostles did in the case of our formulary, each contributing the clause he judged fitting. At the same time, it gets the name 'token' or 'watchword' [*signum*] from the fact that in those days, as the Apostle Paul vouches and as is testified in Acts, numerous vagabond Jews [were] posing as apostles of Christ... but their message did not conform to the traditional outline. The Apostles therefore prescribed the creed as a badge [*indicium posuerunt*] for distinguishing the man who preached the truth about Christ in harmony with their rule."¹¹⁵ Finally, continues Rufinus, just

---

¹¹³ Lubac, op. cit., 34.

¹¹⁴ PL 96:1026. The article attributed to each apostle varies according to the list of apostles adopted. This question is also of interest for the iconography of the apostles in the Middle Ages (Cf. Charles-Auguste Auber, *Histoire et théorie du symbolisme religieux avant et depuis le christianisme*, t.3, 143, which criticizes the attributions of Durand de Mende's *Rational*).

¹¹⁵ *Commentarius in symbol. Apostol.* § 2 (PL 21:337–38); op. cit., 30. This text is taken literally by Isidore of Seville, in *De Ecclesiasticis officiis* II.23 (PL 83:816). Similarly, in his encyclopedic work, *The Etymologies*, he is content to summarize Rufinus's account: "The word 'creed' (*symbolum*) from Greek means 'sign' or 'token of recognition,' for the apostles, about to disperse for preaching the gospel among the nations, proposed the creed for themselves as a sign or guidepost for preaching... This symbol of our faith and hope is not written on papyrus sheets and with ink, but on the fleshly tablets of our hearts" (VI.57–58 [PL 82:257a–b]); *The Etymologies of Isidore of Seville*, trans. Stephen A. Barney et al [Cambridge: Cambridge University Press, 2006], 149–50, altered). It would be useful to compare the etymological method of Isidore of Seville with the *nirukta* of Hindu tradition. The process is entirely identical, breaking down the word to be explained into a certain number of "word-elements" that reveal its true meaning. It is therefore not what we understand by etymology today, but a symbolic explanation fixing in the memory and intellect the intelligible essence of the word. *Nirukta* is one of the sciences of the *Veda* (*Vedanga*). We find here and there what Gérard Genette proposed to call "cratylism," in homage to Plato (*Mimologics*, trans. Thaïs E. Morgan [Lincoln/London: University of Nebraska, 1995], 5). On *nirukta*, cf. René Daumal, *Bharata: L'origine du Théâtre, La poéseie et la musique en Inde* (Paris: Gallimard, 1970), 86.

as in civil wars, where members of each side are recognized by a sign, the same is true for Christians: questioned about their quality, they answer only with the Symbol, the text of which can never be written and so is truly a "password." From then on, even scattered for the purposes of preaching, Christians keep the unity of the faith present in their hearts, realizing a sort of anti-Babel. Whereas the sons of Noah, having erected their tower of pride, could no longer understand one another, Christians remain united even in dispersion because they have built the tower of faith.

We can see that the Creed is an authentic *symbolon*. As a sign of recognition for initiates alone, it exercises the fundamental functions of any true symbol: it "gathers what is scattered," forms multiplicity into unity, maintains proximity in separation, unites earth to Heaven after their division at the Tower of Babel. The double meaning that Rufinus sees in the word is actually quite judicious: the *symbolum* is a sign by its nature and a gathering by its function. It is a sign, that is (1) a sensible and objective mark, thus (2) a distinctive sign, and therefore (3) a sign of recognition. It is a gathering because (1) it is the work of the many united in a common work, (2) it expresses the communion in the truth of those who bear it alive in their hearts, and (3) it calls and incites those who are scattered to come together. Or again, and in an exact correspondence, we have (1) the multiple unified *within* the symbol, (2) the symbol expressing and maintaining unity *within* the multiple, and (3) the multiple focused and drawn back *by* the symbol. This triple function is fundamental and could be related to the whole metaphysics of symbolism. Indeed, from the point of view of being, the symbol is the many in the one; from that of knowledge, it is the one in the many (in the multiplicity of knowing subjects); and from that of action (its ritual realization), it is the multiple returned to the one.

Such is the profound symbolism of the *Symbolum Apostolorum*, the recitation of which is required of the candidate for baptismal initiation. All Latin Christian literature will but take up and comment on this symbolism, and so it is therefore unnecessary to provide further examples. But far from being foreign to the general question of symbolism, the Creed clearly constitutes a particular realization of it, certainly preponderant (at least for a while) though by no means exclusive, as we will now see.

Symbolum in Early Medieval Literature, Particularly John Scottus

The use of *symbolum* to designate the sensible representation of a higher reality never disappeared. We find many occurrences in the fourth century among writers of the first rank as well as the *minores*.

Firmicius Maternus was a Sicilian convert to Catholicism, passionate about astrology, devoting to it the most complete study in Latin literature. Shortly after, he wrote a violent pamphlet against pagan religion, *De errore profanorum religionum*, which attests to the aforementioned equivalence between *signum* and *symbolum*. Concerning the Eleusinian Mysteries, he writes, "I should like to explain what signs or symbols the wretched human throng uses for purposes of recognition in the superstitious cults themselves."[116]

In his commentary on the Psalms, St Hilary of Poitiers, the Athanasius of the West, expounds an eminently classical teaching on the typological meaning of the Old Testament in relation to the New, "so that our understanding of God cannot be one thing in the writings of the prophets and another in the Gospels... And indeed our fathers were under the cloud in Moses, were baptized in the Red Sea, they were satisfied by the manna falling from heaven, they were quenched with the water they received from the rock, which is Christ: all these things accomplished for their salvation, also constituted in themselves a symbol of our salvation."[117]

Zeno of Verona, a bishop of African origin living toward the end of the 4th century, similarly uses the expression *in symbolis* to indicate that the Old Testament expresses itself allegorically.[118] These equivalences testify to the resilience of *symbolum* as much to fluctuations of vocabulary. We must wait until the ninth century to encounter the earliest writer (to our knowledge) who attempted a classification of this vocabulary, excepting certain remarks by

---

[116] *De errore profanorum religionum* § 18 (PL 12:1022a); *The Error of the Pagan Religions*, trans. Clarence A Forbes DD (New York, NY/Paramus, NJ: Newman Press, 1970), 80–81. In § 22, concerning Isis and Osiris, he proposes to exhibit "another symbol" of the pagans so that their crimes would be manifested (PL 12:1032; *ibid*, 93).

[117] *Tractatus in LXVII Psalmam* § 9 (PL 9:448b). Some manuscripts contain the variant *figura*, which conforms more to Latin usage. Was this use of *symbolum* (or *symbola*) influenced by St Hilary's four-year (356–360) sojourn in the East? Presumably, since the *Tractatus in Psalmos* is later than 364 (Fulbert Cayré, *Manual of Patrology and History of Theology*, trans. H. Howitt [Paris/Tournai/Rome: Desclée & Co, 1936], t.1, 364).

[118] *Sermones seu Tractatus* 1.3 (PL 11:349b).

The Symbol from Antiquity to the Middle Ages 39

Clement of Alexandria mentioned above: John Scottus,[119] one of the four great representatives of Christian Neoplatonism (alongside Dionysius the Areopagite, Meister Eckhart, and Nicholas of Cusa).

The doctrine of symbolism presented by the Eriugenian writings presents at once great profundity and extreme subtlety. Indeed, the whole of his theological structure emerges as a metaphysics of the symbol, as a *theophanic ontology,* or rather an "exemplarist monism," to use the expression of Dom Maïeul Cappuyns.[120] For this reason, a precise idea of his doctrine cannot be given absent an explanation of the system in its entirety.[121] We will simply make a few observations.

The great Irishman was a reader and translator of the Areopagitic corpus. It is therefore not surprising that he uses the word *symbolum* extensively, although "he equally uses the word *allegoria* and its derivatives, as well as *mysterium, typice, spiritualiter, sacramentum, secundum intelligibilem sensum,* and others."[122] The word *symbolum* is applied to all that can be the sign of a superior reality, whether a scriptural sign or a sensible reality. Commenting on the way in which, according to Dionysius, Scripture initiates us into divine illuminations "symbolically and anagogically," John Scottus explains that by "symbols" must be understood "signs similar to sensible things, sometimes pure and sometimes dissimilar and confused," realizing their meaning "through anagogy (that is, through the ascent of the mind into the divine mysteries)."[123] He continues, "these visible forms that man contemplates, either in the nature of things or in the most holy mysteries [*sacramenta*] of divine Scripture, it is not for themselves that they were produced, that they are to be desired, that they were communicated to us, but they are imaginations of the invisible Beauty, by which

---

[119] We know now that this is the name that must be attributed to him, *Scottus* in this period meaning "born in Ireland" and therefore forming a pleonasm with "Eriugena." Cf. Édouard Jeauneau, "Introduction," in Jean Scot, *Homélie sur le Prologue de Jean* (Paris: Cerf, 1969), 9–10.

[120] *Jean Scot Erigène: sa via, son oeuvre, sa pensée* (Paris: Desclée De Brouwer, 1933), 385.

[121] The major work of John Scottus, *On the Division of Nature* (*Periphyseon*) is being translated and annotated by Francis Bertin with Presses Universitaires de France. Three volumes of this monumental effort have so far appeared: in 1995, Bks I & II (459 pp), and Bk III (307 pp); in 2000, Bk IV (295 pp).

[122] Dom Cappuyns, 295.

[123] *Super Hierarchiam caelestem* §2 (PL 122:132d). This is a commentary on Dionysius's treatise, *The Celestial Hieararchy* I.2.

divine Providence brings back the souls of men towards the pure and invisible Beauty itself, towards this Beauty of the Truth that loves and to which tends all that loves, whether he knows it or is unaware of it."[124]

Such is the basis of the Eriugenian doctrine of symbolism. "The eternal light reveals itself in a twofold manner through Scripture and through creature."[125] These are the two "veils" which at once manifest and diminish the cosmic irradiation of the "Father of Lights."[126] Scriptural or not, symbols function as sensible realities that call us by anagogical recollection toward spiritual and divine realities, also playing the role of esoteric discrimination: "The profane," he says, "understand the symbols carnally and grossly... so that in all manifestations [of Scripture] one seeks nothing mystical or allegorical, but accepts them, so to speak, in their nakedness as a simple history of events which occurred naturally."[127] Note that none of these texts offers an example of specialization for the word "symbol."

However, in our author's final work, the *Commentary on the Gospel of John*,[128] indeed in the last pages of a work perhaps interrupted by his death, we do encounter such a terminological specialization. John Scottus makes a distinction between *mysteria* and *symbola* by means of the distinction between two sorts of allegory, "allegory of fact and of speech" and "allegory of speech and not of fact." "In the proper sense," he declares, "the mysteries are delivered to us [in Scripture] according to allegory of fact and of speech [*allegoria facti et dicti*], that is to say: the mysteries are of fact according to the actions performed, and they are of speech insofar as they are recounted."[129] Thus there is "mystery" when

---

[124] PL 122:138. Faced with these texts, it is somewhat regrettable that Hans Urs von Balthasar granted so little space to John Scottus in his theology of Beauty: *The Glory of the Lord, A Theological Aesthetics: Volume 4: The Realm of Metaphysics in Antiquity*, trans. Brian McNeil CRV et al., ed. John Riches (San Francisco: Ignatius Press, 1989), 343-55.
[125] *Homily on the Prologue to the Gospel of St John* XI (PL 112:289c); in *Voice of the Eagle: The Heart of Celtic Christianity*, trans. Christopher Bamford (Great Barrington, MA: Lindisfarne, 2000), 88.
[126] *Super Hier. Cael.* (PL 122:136c).
[127] Ibid. (PL 122:147a-b).
[128] Introduction, critical text, translation, notes, and index by Édouard Jeauneau, *Commentaire sur l'évangile de Jean*, SC 180 (Paris: Cerf, 1972).
[129] VI.5 (PL 122:344d); our translation, as literal as possible, has not the elegance of Jeauneau's.

the "scriptural speech" corresponds to a "historical fact," and allegory relates them. "In both Testaments, the mysteries were performed according to history and recounted according to the letter." For example, in the Tabernacle of Moses, "the mysteries of baptism, of the body and blood of the Lord, of holy chrism" are accomplished in reality and recorded in scripture. "Symbols, on the contrary, are only what, though not accomplished, are stated as if accomplished, in view of instruction alone."[130] Parables, for example.

For Jeauneau,[131] "The definitions of the two types of allegory are clear. True allegory must affect not only words (*dictum*) but also facts recounted by words (*factum*): it is 'allegory of fact and of speech' (*allegoria facti et dicti*). The other allegory bears only on words: it is 'allegory of speech and not of fact.' The examples given for both types of allegory perfectly illustrate these definitions."[132] But it is precisely these examples, some of them at least, along with other oddities of the Eriugenian text, which create apparent difficulty. It therefore seems impossible to oppose *symbolum* and *mysterium* as false and "true" allegory—ridiculous indeed that we should find here, inverted, the familiar modern opposition between allegory and symbol!

It must first be observed that this terminological distinction is without any effect for the entire Eriugenian corpus, not even in the *Commentary* in which it is first stated, at the very end of the text—not even in the sentence *immediately preceding* its statement, which explains concerning the multiplication of loaves and fishes that "by the five loaves are evoked the *symbols* of the five senses or of the five books of Moses, and by the fishes, the two Testaments."[133] Yet this miracle did take place, and moreover, a few pages later the miracle is again recalled and described as a "historical narrative" (*secundum res gestas*).

On the other hand, after giving some examples of allegory "of speech and not of fact," John Scottus concludes: "This form [of allegory] is recognized in almost all the parables; it is properly called symbolic, although Holy Scripture is accustomed to

---

[130] Ibid. (PL 122:345b).
[131] Along with others. Henri de Lubac, for example: cf. *Medieval Exegesis*, v. II, 88.
[132] Jeauneau, 399.
[133] Ibid. (PL 122:344d).

presenting symbols as mysteries and mysteries as symbols, due to a certain similarity and resemblance."[134] This is a difficult passage, but it clearly indicates that we are not here dealing with a terminological question, as is implied by Jeauneau's translation: "Scripture has the habit of *calling* 'symbol' what is a mystery and 'mystery' what is a symbol,"[135] even though Scripture really never (except once) uses the word "symbol."

In fact, if we meditate attentively not so much on John Scottus's examples as on his explanations, we realize that this distinction is in no way intended to distinguish two forms of allegory, even less to assert the superiority of twofold allegory over single; on the contrary, as we will see, symbolic allegory is given primacy.

The distinction between the two allegories, in fact, is not raised for its own sake. Given its patristic antiquity,[136] going back to St Augustine, it serves rather to support the distinction between *symbola* and *mysteria*, each considered within the scriptural text and no longer in the "book of creation." And this distinction is made not only with respect to the objects distinguished (which scriptural passages are mysteries and which are symbols) but also, and above all, with respect to their respective spiritual functions — that is to say, the effect each produces on the human mind, precisely why the Holy Spirit has presented them in Scripture. In other words, we must consider not only their natures but also their respective ends.

With respect to nature, John Scottus evidently wishes above all to draw attention to the fact that not all passages in Scripture have a historical sense, although Scripture is not in the habit of distinguishing these from the others. For example, Scripture presents the story of Paradise and the Fall in the same way that it recounts the crossing of the Red Sea, as history. However, to understand the former, which has no historical reality[137] (in the ordinary sense), we must engage in allegory of speech, not of fact. But this in no way implies that what is said is devoid of referent, that it designates nothing real. Far from it, yet the reality designated is of another order than the historical: it belongs to the metaphysical

---

[134] "*Symbola pro mysteriis et mysteria pro symbolis... ponere*" (PL 122:345d).
[135] Jeauneau, 357.
[136] Op. cit. (PL 122:345a).
[137] John Scottus here follows Origen. *Periphyseon* IV.16 (PL 122:818b–c); in *Periphyseon: The Division of Nature*, trans. I. P. Sheldon-Williams and John J. O'Meara (Montréal: Béllarmin, 1987), 473.

and spiritual. This is proven by the example of a symbol given by John Scottus in his Gospel commentary: "In the Principle was the Word, and the Word was with God, the Word was God. This is only speech, in which we know of no accomplished fact."[138] Can it be doubted for a single moment that, for John Scottus, this speech causes us to know a Reality incommensurable with any common historical fact? Which is more important: the mystery of the crossing of the Red Sea or the immanence of the Son in the Principle, his relation to the Father and his identity with God?

Moreover, a little reflection suffices to convince us of this. Mystery is not distinguished from symbol from the perspective of allegory, insofar as this would be a process of explanation: both are presented as stories, and both require interpretation. *Allegoria* is always the *allegoria* of a *dictum*. What alone distinguishes them is that, in one case, this *dictum* refers to a historical *factum*, such that the *allegoria* of the *dictum* is also an *allegoria* of the historical factum; in the other case, it does not. The only remaining question, therefore, is why Scripture presents us with these two forms of allegory, with both mystery and symbol.

Returning to the miracle of the multiplication of loaves and fishes, John Scottus takes this as a *symbol of the distinction between mystery and symbol*, the loaves symbolizing mysteries and the fish, symbols. This interpretation is motivated by the fact that the loaves are five in number, like the five senses, indicating all that can be apprehended in the sensible world and therefore everything having historical existence—these are the mysteries. The fish are only two in number, like the Scriptures, which can only be apprehended by sight and hearing. Loaves and fishes, mysteries (sacraments) and symbols, these are mediated by the disciples (the Church and its ministers) to all Christians, that their hunger might be satisfied. But Scripture also tells us that they "filled twelve baskets with the fragments of the five barley loaves," and this on the order of Christ to "gather up the fragments that remain." He did not say this of the fish. John Scottus concludes from this that, on the one hand, the loaves were *broken*, and so we speak of fragments; while on the other hand, the crowd of men seated on the grass did not eat everything, but others collected the *surplus*. He explains: "The barley loaves are broken by the disciples when,

---

[138] Op. cit. (PL 122:348a).

in the mysteries of either Law, they separate the historical facts from their spiritual meanings. The carnal are fed by the simple history, while the spiritual gather together the divine meanings of that history, as they would fragments... The simple Christian, still seated on the grass of temporal and carnal things, feeds only on the history... But the intelligence of the letter itself he cannot apprehend, and this is why it is gathered by those who know the savor of spiritual realities, in order that it not be lost but of profit to valiant intellects."[139] We therefore see something like an inversion: the surplus of fragments, far from being lost, is not only saved by the spiritual intellect but is also that which saves us. On the contrary, the history fed upon by the simple believer is actually irrelevant and is not in itself saving. "For the mystery, composed of letter and spirit, partly dies and partly subsists eternally: dies in what is seen, because sensible and temporal; subsists in what is not seen, because spiritual and eternal."[140]

As for the fish — the symbols — their essential characteristic is that they leave no remainder. If there is no remainder, it is because they cannot be broken. And if they cannot be broken, it is because they are simple, one, indivisible. Offered to all Christians, they must be received by them: "Whole and undivided by carnal men, whole and in their unity by spiritual men."[141] But then what good are these symbols which only the spiritual can understand? John Scottus's response is very clear: "Since they are indivisible, the symbol is committed entirely to the memory of the carnal faithful, *that they may believe a spiritual meaning resides in these words*, even if they don't understand them."

In other words, only the existence of the symbol can awaken our awareness that Scripture contains a hidden meaning; it alone can reveal to us that the bread of the mysteries must be broken so that we can reach what is eternal within them. Were there only mysteries, only words referring to historical facts, there would not even be any possible *allegoria*. We would never understand that history itself, sacred history, harbors a spiritual and divine meaning that is alone salvific because alone imperishable. But by receiving the symbols — simple and undecomposable, yet

---

[139] Ibid. (PL 122:346b–c).
[140] Ibid. (PL 122:348a).
[141] Ibid. (PL 122:347a). Note that these fish (symbols) have historical existence.

unintelligible to the carnal mind—and receiving them *in faith*, we understand that these symbols speak of another world and another reality, that in them we must hear the very word of invisible and eternal Beauty. By symbols, we penetrate the mysteries in the Temple of Scripture: if they correspond to the holy things, "the realities of which they are the symbols are the holy of holies,"[142] Jesus Christ, "the truth of the symbols of the law" and "the end of prophetic vision."[143]

The Twelfth Century and After

We are now approaching a period that inherited a well-established lexical tradition: there can be no question of even a summary listing of the particularly numerous authors known to this golden age of theology and Christian thought. We must be content with gleaning here and there from attestations of *symbolum* to prove the term's wide usage, notwithstanding the importance of its employment in designating the Creed. Certainly, this usage is due to the influence of the Dionysian writings, "full of the doctrine of the monk-bishop Dionysius, held for more than a thousand years to be the first Father of the Church."[144] But the word or its derivatives seem to come from the pen of these writers spontaneously, at least where usage does not impose *allegoria* or its derivatives, as in the case of scriptural symbolism, where because of St Paul it is almost an imperative. This is an astonishing observation, insofar as the word "symbol" seems to sometimes imply a sort of unreality in what is symbolized, as we saw in the Eriugenian distinction. (However, we emphasize that this "unreality" of what is symbolized is the manifest indication of a higher reality.) Yet this unreality that the word "symbol" seems to carry with it, encountered for example in Fulbert's (†1028) condemnation of the Berengarian heresy,[145] does not prevent it from being used also in a very realistic sense: it is applied to the beings of nature themselves, the world being a book written by God.

---

[142] *Super Hier. Caelest* § 2.5 (PL 112:170a); Rorem, 196.
[143] *Homily on the Prologue to the Gospel of St John* XXIII (PL 112:296d); Baumford, 114.
[144] We take these words from the beautiful dedication that Dom Chevalier placed at the beginning of his *Dionysiaca*, 1937, I.1.
[145] "In the Eucharist, there is not the symbol of an empty mystery (*inanis mysterii symbolum*) but the true body of Christ, which under the visible form of a created element invisibly produces a hidden virtue" (PL 161:199).

It should be noted first that the medieval vocabulary includes a great terminological richness with often varied and sometimes precise nuances: *imago, similitudo, forma, effigies signum, parabola, symbolum*, and more.[146] The careful study of all these terms indeed constitutes a veritable treatise on sacred symbolism, in which a fundamental Platonism emerges at every moment and which can be considered one of the latter's major metaphysical expressions. Indeed, Plato declares in the *Parmenides*: "Let these [intelligible] forms be permanently in reality, as paradigms; let things resemble them and be their copies, and this participation of things in forms consists solely in the fact that they are images of them... This is the best solution."[147] Yet for the medievals, the image is first of all the Son, the primary Image of the Father and Place of the divine paradigms. The expression in Genesis ("Let us make man in our image, after our likeness," *ad imaginem et similitudinum nostrum*) is interpreted in this sense, emphasizing the importance of the preposition *ad* and its implied dynamism. It is as if the verse were to be understood as "*conforming to* our image and likeness," which is then identified as the Son (image of the divine nature) and the Spirit (Who realizes and is the likeness).

This theological dimension of the primordial Image is reflected more or less in all other images (or symbols). Thus for Bruno di Segni, "Electrum is a metal of silver and gold, symbol of the Redeemer who is of human and divine nature."[148] All created things, sacramental signs, parables and images of Scripture that must be interpreted "*spiritualiter*"—which Abbé Javelet calls "the esoterism of spirituals"[149]—forms an immense *symbolic demonstration (demonstratio symbolica)*, as Hugh of Saint Victor says.[150] This idea of demonstration, of revelation, properly constitutes

---

[146] We draw most of our information from the very erudite study of Abbé Robert Javelet, *Image et Ressemblance au XIIe siècle, de saint Anselme à Alain de Lille* (Strasbourg: Université de Strasbourg, 1967).

[147] *Parmenides* 132d.

[148] *Sent* IV.12 (PL 155:1013a). Electrum is a metal composed of four parts gold and one part silver (Gaffiot, *Dictionary Latin-Français*, s.v., referring to Pliny). The word *elektron*, "electrum," is found in Ezekiel 1:4 and translates a Hebrew word (*hamsal*) of poorly-understood meaning. For Bruno di Segni, this also shows the relationship of Christ to the four Evangelists.

[149] *Image et Ressemblance*, t. II, 32.

[150] *In Hier.* I.1 (PL 175:941). "By forms, signs, resemblances, what is hidden is made manifest, or else what has become manifest, what is described, constitutes a symbolic demonstration."

The Symbol from Antiquity to the Middle Ages　　　　　　　　　　　　　　47

the Victorine concept of the symbol. The symbol as such is essentially a means of knowledge, therefore a sign of recognition. This teaching is summarized in the celebrated definition of *symbolum* given by Hugh of Saint Victor: "*symbolum*—that is, gathering (*collatio*)—designates that harmony by which visible forms are able to clearly manifest that their meaning belongs to the invisible world."[151]

The same understanding, associated with other, sometimes curious ones, is found in Alain de Lille (†1202–1203). He writes in his "Theological Dictionary":

> *Symbolum* signifies "sign." Hence Dionysius, in the *Hierarchy*, calls *symbolic* the resemblances transposed from earthly to heavenly things. It also signifies "sacrament," hence Augustine—in connection with the verse, "Except a man be born of water and of the Spirit"—speaks of *symbol*. Also, "gathering" (*collatio*), when several portions of food are gathered together for a banquet. *Symbolum* derives from *syn*, meaning "together"; and *bolus*, meaning "portion of food," "morsel," since each Apostle brought his own morsel to it. It thus designates the speech containing the diverse articles of the faith.[152]

In another text, he provides a different etymology that clearly lends a distinctly cognitive meaning to *symbolum*: "an expression is said symbolically [in St Dionysius] when it *signifies* a hidden reality, and the word is formed from *syn*, meaning "together"; and *olon*, meaning "all." This is because such expressions include "all together," such that the superficial understanding of the letter is one thing, and its interior understanding is another."[153]

The thirteenth century is dominated by the presence of St Thomas Aquinas, who almost always uses *signum*, following the example of Augustine rather than Dionysius, and reserves *symbolum* to designate the Creed.[154] But the term is found in St Bonaventure

---

[151] *In Hier.* III (960d).
[152] *Distinctiones dictionum theologicarum* (PL 210:964c). The same curious etymology can be observed in Jocelin of Soissons (†1152), where Alain de Lille might have encountered it.
[153] *Expositio super symbolum apostolicum Nicenum*; in Marie-Thérèse d'Alverny, *Alain de Lille, Textes inédits* (Paris: Vrin, 1967), 84.
[154] Perhaps excepting the case of Scriptural commentaries, in which we encounter *symbolice* in the ordinary sense of the word. St Thomas also admits

with a Dionysian valence, and the Seraphic Doctor takes great care to define it: "He [the Word] has taught the knowledge of truth according to the threefold mode of theology: symbolic, literal and mystical, so that through the symbolic we may rightly use sensible things, through the literal we may rightly use intelligible things, and through the mystical we may be lifted above to ecstasy."[155]

In this respect, must we accept the exegesis of P.V.M. Breton, who distinguishes *symbolism*, in which the sensible reality is only a figure without value in itself; and *exemplarism*, in which the sensible reality, though a sign, retains its full consistency?[156] In fact, "symbolism concerns the divine vestiges and there is no question of depriving them of all consistency; they exist and are already sacramental matter. It is a recurring idea that the sensible world is an immense sacrament of God."[157]

We thus find a ternary structuring the universe of the symbol—the World, the Sacred Book, the Rites—in which each of the terms can exchange names. For if creation is a book and a sacrament, the Book is also a world and a rite, and rite is itself a sacramental universe where the Word of God is realized.

The Latin history of *symbolum* has nothing further to teach us, at least in its religious form. In conclusion, we will only mention a few uses attesting in exemplary fashion to the meanings encountered in this survey: the texts dedicated to the Eucharist and its rite at the Council of Trent (13th section, 11 October 1551). Three times this sacrament is described as a symbol, in accordance with a traditional use[158] implying no attenuation of the real presence of Christ in the bread and wine of the sacrifice of the Mass.

In the *Preamble*, the Council speaks of the "*symbol* of that unity and charity, with which He would have all Christians be mentally joined and united together." It is therefore a symbol

---

the use of a "symbolic mode" of expression in theology, since reason is there not proportionate to its object (*In I Sent.* prol. a. 5, ad. 3).

[155] *Itinerarium mentis in Deum* I.7; in *Bonaventure: The Soul's Journey into God, The Tree of Life, The Life of Saint Francis*, trans. Ewert Cousins (Ramsey, NJ: Paulist, 1978), 62–63.

[156] *Saint Bonaventure* (Paris: Aubier, 1943), 79.

[157] Robert Javelet, "Réflexions sur l'exemplarisme bonaventurien," *San Bonaventura*, IV, *Theologica* (Rome: Collegio S. Bonaventura Grottaferrata, 1974), 361.

[158] Witnesses to this include Theodoret of Cyrus, St Basil of Caesarea, St Dionsyius the Areopagite, St John Chrysostom, etc.

in the literal sense of "gathering" (*collatio*). More precisely, it is an "operative *sign* of gathering," that which, across distance and dispersion, constitutes a reminder of lost unity and a pledge of future unity. This is declared in Chapter II: "He would have it be a pledge of our glory to come, and everlasting happiness, and thus be a *symbol* of that one body of which He is the head, and to which He would have us as members be united." Finally, in Chapter III finally appears its meaning as real and effective sign, which moreover defines sacrament generally: "The most holy Eucharist has indeed this in common with the rest of the sacraments, that it is a *symbol* of a sacred thing, and is a visible form of an invisible grace."

These uses are all the more remarkable in that they date from the very time when Zwingli and his disciples denied the real presence by rightly describing it as "symbolic," and further that they are found in texts devoted to the reaffirmation of this presence.

By this the strength and persistence of the "realism" pregnant in the word "symbol" can be measured, despite semantic drift often giving it the sense of a non-real substitute. It is as much the sign that indicates as it is the sign that "makes present," or as we will put it later, "presentifies."

This presentifying power of the symbol, this symbolic realism, now comes under threat, and Goethe and Schelling will have to reaffirm it by opposing it to allegory. The history of the symbol will now develop outside the religious sphere and have to do primarily with literature, philosophy, and art.

CHAPTER II
Symbol and Allegory in Modernity

THEIR INITIAL EQUIVALENCE

IN THE PRECEDING CHAPTER, WE SAW that there was no defined specialization in the use of the words *symbolum* and *allegoria*, and that John Scottus himself, who did develop a precise distinction, nevertheless did not strictly adhere to it. Before returning to the relatively recent origin of their widely held opposition, then, it is necessary to first consider Jean Pépin's thesis, according to which "the ancient and medieval definition of allegory is so broad that it is suitable for nearly any variety of figurative expression, and certainly for symbolic expression."[1]

Should we therefore conclude that "the notion of *symbolum* not only is not isolated from that of *allegoria* but is most often included within it"? Doubtful. The cited texts do not always confirm the subordination of the former term to the latter. Particularly in Clement of Alexandria, the reverse seems rather to be the case. Clearly, in reading ancient texts — Greek or Latin, pagan or Christian — we must keep in mind that *allegoria* does not necessarily involve the representation of abstract concepts, as it does in modernity, but that it often has the same connotations as "symbol."

However, some clarification is required. The first, and most indisputable, is that "allegory" for the Ancients is always discursive, whereas "symbol" designates speech as well as a concrete sign or object. The distinction between *allegoria in verbis* and *allegoria in factis* should not mislead — it is situated entirely within the world of discourse. Moreover, the etymology itself implies as much: it is always a saying [*agoreuo*] of one thing that *another* [*allos*] may be understood. It therefore designates, if you will, the symbolism used in speech.

Second, it follows that the term's grammatical origin should not be lost from view. St Jerome states, "Allegory is properly part

---

[1] *Dante et la Tradition de l'Allégorie* (Paris: Vrin, 1970), 15–16.

of the art of grammar,"² and this is reiterated in the Middle Ages.³ The term retains from its rhetorical origins not only a narrower meaning than *symbolum*, but also carries a tinge of unreality, first serving the pagans in "saving" the implausibility of the mythological narratives by discarding their historicity. Christian authors thus distinguished two kinds of allegory, "in word" and "in fact," maintaining that Christian allegory belongs essentially to the second. Augustine teaches this: "where the Apostle speaks of the allegory, he finds it not in the words but in the deed."⁴

According to Fr Henri de Lubac, this distinction was Christian allegory's greatest novelty. Pagan antiquity knew nothing of it, such that St Paul was expressing something altogether different in his use of this pagan term. In his monumental *Medieval Exegesis*, the learned historian attempts to prove this assertion, devoting entire chapters to it. "The Christian exegetes have practiced 'allegory'—if one wants to look deeply into the matter—only in a sense quite remote from that of the ancient philosophers. They saw in it, as they do not cease to assure us, a requirement of their faith in Christ."⁵

The medieval writers were doubtless aware of the specifically Christian character of their hermeneutics. But was there indeed no *allegoria in facto* among the pagans? Particularly if the term is given the broader sense of "symbol," it is not at all difficult to find events in Antiquity that were at once completely historical and yet seen as truly symbolic. For example, Plato was born of a mother impregnated by Apollo on the 7th of the month Thargelion (May), the anniversary of the god's birth, and lived 81 years—nine times nine, nine traditionally being the number that "measures" a cyclical duration. And this was not an isolated case.

On the other hand, the story of *allegoria* in Christian culture is not a uniformly happy one. There is an ancient resistance to

---

² *In Gal.* II (PL 26:389); in *Commentary on Galatians*, trans. Andrew Cain (Washington, DC: Catholic University of America, 2010), 186.
³ For example, Aimo of Auxerre: "Blessed Paul has the custom of calling the spiritual understanding allegory. Allegory, however, pertains properly to the grammarians; for it is a figure of speech by which something other than what is said is signified" (*In Gal.* [PL 117:687c]; in Henri de Lubac, *Medieval Exegesis*, v. 2, 232, n. 90).
⁴ *De Trinitate* XV.9.15; in *The Trinity*, trans. Stephen McKenna (Washington, DC: Catholic University of America, 1963), 471–72.
⁵ *Medieval Exegesis*, v. II, 106.

allegory going back to Tertullian, who sometimes uses the term pejoratively to imply the fictitious character of a text, while at other times using it in a positive sense, when he sees in the letter of the Old Testament the prophetic figure of the New.[6] Such resistance to allegory persists through the Middle Ages, often in the form of a reaction to excesses that transformed symbolism into rhetoric. Not that each part of Scripture does not have a meaning, but rather that the meaning given can sink into the discursive and abstract. Allegorical excess is in the interpretation, not the figure itself; the allegorical text can become a pretext for didactic construction.

As Pépin has noted, this is because *allegoria* is both a method of interpretation and a mode of expression.[7] The danger of the method was not only in treating "symbolic actions originally designed to make the mysteries palpable ... as so many 'explanations' ... finely analyzed and intellectualized" or even of falling into "the analytical exploration of an *idea* which made use of details dissected and abstracted from an image, with each detail having specific meaning."[8] The danger lay also—and let us not forget that all of this occurred in the twelfth century—in making dictionaries or lists of allegorical meanings. This tradition had been pioneered by St Isidore of Seville a few centuries earlier,[9] continuing through the *De Universo* of Rabanus Maurus and, above all, in *The Key* of Melito of Sardis, a mysterious compilation of dubious authenticity appearing at the beginning of the tenth century.[10] Clearly, producing such compendia of allegorical meanings favored the appearance of a systematic procedure for the manufacture

---

[6] Cf. the texts collected by Henri de Lubac, *Exégèse médiévale*, 2e pt. (Paris: Aubier, 1964), t. II, 131ff.
[7] *Dante et la Tradition de l'Allegorie*, 12.
[8] Marie-Dominique Chenu, *Nature, Man, and Society: Essays on New Theological Perspectives in the Latin West*, trans. Jerome Taylor and Lester K. Little (Chicago, IL: University of Chicago Press, 1968), 142.
[9] *Allegoriae quadedam sacrae scripturae* (PL 83:99–130).
[10] Cardinal Pitra—born near Autun in 1812, a man of prodigious erudition, reformer of the science of hymnography—passionately argued for the attribution of the *Key* to Melito, second-century bishop of Sardis, though he did not win scholarly consensus. J.P. Laurant republished Pitra's dissertation through Trédaniel in 1979, under the title *La clef du symbolism de Méliton de Sardes*, with a preface by Émile Poulet. A long introduction provides unpublished details concerning the Christian esoterism of certain antimodernist ecclesiastical circles around 1850.

of allegories. From allegory as mode of expression to allegory as method of interpretation, an inversion took place. The symbol no longer "gave rise to thought," but it was rather the concept, taken as the starting point, giving rise to allegory. Hence the success of sacred writings, but also of secular works populated by personified abstractions: "biblical commentary, homily, liturgical texts, formularies of dogma, poetry, and even legal texts" trafficked in "personified natural forces, virtues, ideas, or sciences" with "complacent satisfaction." Examples of this tendency include Bernard Silvestris, Alain de Lille, and Chrétien de Troyes.[11]

The considerations leading the German Romantics to the now-commonplace opposition between symbol and allegory are thus gradually clarified. There are others, however, relating to iconography, that have not received sufficient attention. True, through the end of the Middle Ages, the word *allegoria* was applied only to speech and never to its graphic or figurative representation. Yet, despite this restriction of the word, the thing itself was widespread. From the twelfth through the fifteenth centuries, there was a proliferation of figurines, illuminations, and pictorial representations in philosophical, logical, dialectical, grammatical, and even moral treatises. These illustrations were truly allegorical—which is to say, figurative abstractions—but they were still linked to the text rather than independent of it, as in the Renaissance. They are not referred to as *allegoria*, yet they show a deterioration of the symbol's presentifying function, in that the graphical or figurative representation of a written allegory necessarily intensifies and reveals its nature as a "trope" within a rhetorical method. A basic example demonstrates this: ordinary language contains many figurative expressions which vary from one language to another, the speaker barely recognizing their figurative nature. Yet their translation into graphic images creates comic and absurd effects, for we thereby "reify" them, introducing into the order of sensible reality what has meaning only for thought and language, and this insofar as we retain from the image only a guiding *schema*. Indeed, the interest in such schemata is the *possibility* of representation rather than its realization. This allows for great diversity, in that the simple

---

[11] Chenu, 141. It appears that these symbolic repertories increased both in number and popularity over the centuries. The printing press certainly had much to do with this.

rhetorical allegorization of an abstract idea leaves indeterminate all that is not captured by the figurative schema. We can say that time is the "reaper" of human lives, but the shape of the scythe, its color, the reaper himself, what he is reaping (wheat, oats, grass), the place of the reaping (a field, a mountain)—all this is left to the illustrator's imagination. This is why painted allegories can truly be works of art, and yet their aesthetic value is itself non-allegorical, superadded to the allegory itself.[12] On this trajectory, allegory disappears or becomes merely a pretext, but before reaching that point, the passage from rhetoric to painting clearly "reifies" less the image itself than the schema, the process by which rhetoric illustrates an idea. This is obviously very far from the symbol, in which everything is necessarily symbolic.[13]

The transition from rhetorical to painted or drawn allegory and its generalization as a determinate pictorial genre, which "realizes" the allegory's guiding schema and thereby reifies the trope as such, seems to lead progressively to the Goethean opposition between allegory and symbol. Yet the fact remains that, during the fifteenth and sixteenth centuries, *allegoria* continued to be used in a way hardly different from "symbol," and the famous distinction between allegory "in word" and "in fact" continued in the form of a distinction between *allegoria rhetorica, grammaticalis, litteralis* and *allegoria theologica* or *spiritualis*, as in Dom Hieronymus Lauretus's *Sylva allegoriarum totius sacrae Scripturae* (1583).[14] Indeed, this use never disappeared, at least not among Catholic exegetes. They could have endorsed the following remark from the fifteenth-century *Dream of the Orchard*, which attempts to demonstrate the relative temporal independence of King Charles V from the Pope, writing with respect to the "two swords," "this comment does not concern the historical or literal sense, but only the mystical or spiritual, that is to say allegorical sense."[15] The same

---

[12] This feature, while still relatively unmarked in Piero di Cosimo (cf. "Allegory," Samuel H. Kress collection, *National Gallery of Art*, Washington, DC), appears clearly in Titian (cf. "Three Ages of Man," Collection of the Duke of Sutherland, *National Gallery of Scotland*, Edinburgh).

[13] To understand this point, compare a Byzantine icon to the paintings just mentioned. There may yet be intermediate cases, such as Nicolas Froment, whose painting is allegorical in form while nevertheless remaining symbolic in substance.

[14] We see that Baudelaire's "forest of symbols" has distant origins. References taken from Lubac, *Exégèse médiévale*, 2e pt., t.2, 131.

[15] Ibid., 383.

distinction can be seen in the eighteenth-century *Institutiones ad Verbi Dei scripti intelligentiam* of the Dominican Joseph Marie de Turre;[16] or, closer to our own times, in the quite classical *Abrégé de Théologie dogmatique et morale* of Abbé J. Berthier.[17]

To tell the truth, even for figural representations in the iconography of more recent (seventeenth and eighteenth) centuries, it is by no means easy to separate the allegorical from the symbolic, because if the general idea governing the representations clearly derives from a rhetoric of the image, the individual elements are often symbolic. In Daniel Poirion's excellent phrase, allegory can be defined as "the logical, systematic, and detailed development" of the symbol.[18] This definition is universally valid, as the aforementioned example of Titian (and many other modern paintings)[19] proves, and could describe numerous engravings, paintings, and even sculptures, particularly those relating to alchemy. Allegorical by reason of their didactic intention, discursive and rhetorical insofar as they must be *read* and deciphered like an alphabet, such works are nevertheless symbolic in most of their individual elements. Indeed, these are true sensible presentifications of intelligible realities, superior principles they are charged with making known. The alchemical Mercury represented by Hermes' staff is not an idea or an abstraction, neither is it discursive — it is a permanent cosmological reality.[20]

Works began to appear at this time enumerating not biblical allegories, such as those we have already discussed, but what could be called figures of universal symbolism. On the basis of a "slim treatise" by the fifth-century Alexandrian grammarian Horus Apollo, the Italian humanist Pietro Valeriano published "the first dictionary of allegories and symbols" under the title *Hierogliphica*, which he took from Horus Apollo and which sufficiently indicates his derivation of symbolic science from Egyptian sources. Following Valeriano, there appeared "numerous collections of emblems [and] treatises on iconology, used by all painters and sculptors from the sixteenth through the eighteenth centuries." "Emblems" and

---

[16] Ibid., 131.
[17] (Paris: Emmanuel Vitte, 1927), § 217.
[18] "Allegory," *Encyclopedia Universalis*.
[19] What is symbolic in a painting like Prud'hon's *Justice and Divine Vengeance Pursuing Crime*?
[20] Cf. Titus Burckhardt, *Alchemy: Science of the Cosmos, Science of the Soul* (Louisville, KY: Fons Vitae, 1997).

"Iconology" moreover serve as titles for two of the most important such works: the first, from Andrea Alciati (French edition, 1574), containing many engravings; and the second, from César Ripa (only illustrated in the 1603 edition) and translated into many languages, read by all artists and reprinted for several centuries.[21]

Finally, and to conclude this brief history of the equivalence between allegory and symbol, we turn to the article that the "Abbé" Alphonse-Louis Constant (Éliphas Lévi) devotes to "allegory" in his *Dictionnaire de Littérature chrétienne*.[22] The witness of Abbé Constant is all the more interesting in that we know how influenced he was by German Romantic philosophy, and that he disseminated the major themes of occult philosophy through all the literary salons of the nineteenth century by his tireless authorial activity.[23] After recalling Quintilian's definition of allegory as "extended metaphor" and observing that all religions "have had allegory as the basis of their symbolism," the author explains, "In religious literature, allegory touches very closely on symbolism, with which it must nevertheless not be confused."[24] That said, and without explaining the distinction,[25] Abbé Constant uses *allegory* and *symbol* synonymously in a long poem included within the article:

> Formed from visible speech,
> Our world is dreamt by God;
> His Word selects its symbols,
> His Spirit fills them with His fire.

Later, commenting on his poem, he states that "this natural symbolism of all created beings appears to have been the dominant way of thinking for the Egyptians and other ancient civilizations." He also suggests the study of "allegories or symbolism

---

[21] André Masson, *L'Allégorie* (Paris: Presses Universitaires de France, 1974), 12, 14.
[22] *Nouvelle Encyclopédie Théologique*, (Paris: Migne, 1861), v. VII.
[23] It may have been he who suggested the title of Baudelaire's "Correspondences." If the idea unquestionably comes from Swedenborg, Claud Pichois has pointed out that the word was already used by Abbé Constant as the title of one of his poems in the 1845 *Trois Harmonies: Chansons et Poesies*: "Baudelaire en 1847," *Revue des Sciences humaines* 89, Jan–March 1958, 133.
[24] *Dictionnaire de Littérature chrétienne*, col. 56.
[25] It is necessary to have recourse to the article on "Palingenesis" in the same *Dictionnaire* to discover that (to turn a phrase) symbolism "is the science of spiritualizing form" (col. 928).

in the Bible" as examples.²⁶ In the end, if there is a distinction to be made between symbolism and allegory, it is that between nature and culture: allegory is a method of explanation or interpretation applied to the natural symbolism of things, beings, and ideas. This distinction is certainly not unrelated to that of Goethe, but in no way exhausts it. We therefore come to the opposition of the allegorical to the symbolic sign, now so pervasive that tilting at this particular windmill has become necessary for any reflection on symbolism.

THE GOETHEAN OPPOSITION BETWEEN SYMBOL & ALLEGORY

The preceding considerations may be somewhat surprising, as the opposition between symbol and allegory seems self-evident, even necessary as a preliminary for any discourse on symbolism. Yet the opposition was introduced quite recently, only entering European thought with Goethe. Its history is too complex and involves too many actors to retrace here,²⁷ so we will give but a few signposts.

It is widely believed that Kant suggested the idea of such an opposition to Goethe, not directly but rather through the influence of Schiller's theory of the symbol. Kant's very subtle theory must be passed over in silence, as it would lead into the weeds of a particularly difficult philosophical structure.²⁸ It is necessary to know only that Kant returns to "symbol" the sense of a "concrete" and figurative representation, thereby indirectly bringing into play sensible intuition (perception). He rejects the terminology of the new logicians, in this case Leibniz, who instead opposed "intuitive" to "symbolic" knowledge,²⁹ insofar as mathematical and algebraic "symbols" are only the written and generally

---

[26] Ibid., col. 60, 61, 67. This article coherently presents a complete and precise theory of symbolism.
[27] A good summary can be found in Tzvetan Todorov, *Theories of the Symbol*, trans. Catherine Porter (Ithaca, NY: Cornell University Press, 1982), 147–221. The most complete study of Goethe is Marache, *Le symbole dans la pensée et l'œuvre de Gœthe* (Paris: Nizet, 1960). On Kant and Schelling, consult the articles by Marty and Tilliette in *Le mythe et le symbole: De la connaissance figurative de Dieu* (Paris: Beauchesne, 1977).
[28] Developed by Kant in § 59 of *The Critique of Judgment*.
[29] Leibniz, "Meditations on Knowledge, Truth, and Ideas," in *Philosophical Papers and Letters*, ed. & trans. Leroy E. Loemker, 2nd ed. (Dordrecht: Kluwer Academic Publishers, 1989), 291.

arbitrary signs of objects or operations for which there is no possible sensory knowledge.

But Goethe's understanding is completely opposed to Kant's: for the latter, the sensible or "concrete" aspect of the symbol, its pictorial quality, is truly *indirect*. The symbol is indeed a figurative representation of an invisible reality, but there is no ontological relation between them, no *presence* of the figured in the figure. The relation is entirely mental, such that Kant's "symbol" in fact corresponds exactly to what Goethe means by "allegory."[30] Kantian philosophy moreover completely rejects the possibility of presentifying (not representing) the intelligible in the sensible: as he asserts contemptuously, "to claim ... that the real appearances of the world present to the senses are merely a *symbol* of an intelligible world hidden in reserve is *enthusiasm*."[31]

For Goethe, by contrast, the symbol is distinguished from allegory in that, while both are "signs," the symbol is one in which the signifier has a certain identity with what it signifies. This is why the symbol is (1) natural, whereas allegory is artificial; (2) intransitive, its meaning being found only *within itself*, in its immediate presence, not elsewhere; (3) inexhaustible and finally indescribable, whereas allegory disappears in explanation. Goethe puts it this way in one of his last works: "Allegory transforms an object of perception into a concept, the concept into an image, but in such a way that the concept continues to remain circumscribed and completely available and expressible within the image. Symbolism transforms an object of perception into an idea, the idea into an image, and does it in such a way that the idea always remains infinitely operative and unattainable so that even if it is put into words in all languages, it still remains inexpressible." "True symbolism" is therefore that in which "the particular represents the general, not as dream and shadow, but as a live and immediate revelation of the unfathomable."[32]

---

[30] Schelling's definition of allegory takes up exactly the same terms that Kant uses to define the symbol (cf. Todorov, 207–12). No philosopher gave more importance to symbolism than Schelling, but by radicalizing the allegory/symbol opposition and by making the symbol the very thing symbolized itself, he forgets its nature as a *sign*. Such was his error: the truth is that the symbol both is and is not what it symbolizes.

[31] *Anthropology from a Pragmatic Point of View* I.38; ed. & trans. Robert B. Louden (Cambridge: Cambridge University Press, 2006), 85.

[32] *Maxims and Reflections* § 1112, § 1113, § 314; ed. Peter Hutchinson, trans. Elizabeth Stopp (New York: Penguin, 1998), 138, 47.

Goethe's theory enjoyed considerable success. It was timely and addressed a need, at least insofar as the Renaissance had witnessed a general weakening of the Symbolist mentality, allowing rhetoric to take primacy in the domain of plastic forms. Certainly, allegory in the modern sense has always existed, but it was neutralized by the immanent power of universal symbolism. And certainly, there is no symbol that cannot be considered allegorical from a certain angle. It had become urgent, however, if one wanted to avoid its complete disappearance, to vigorously assert the purity of the symbol in its full and irreducible reality against a general allegorism, and this by means of a meditation on art, which had replaced religion as the meeting place of the spiritual and the physical. And yet this rediscovery of true symbolism could only be theoretical or philosophical, linked to the contingency of artistic genius and without any significant effect on society, being unable to take root in the only field that could answer to its needs—sacred and ritual forms.

CONTEMPORARY EXPRESSIONS OF THE SYMBOL/ALLEGORY OPPOSITION

It would be impossible to review here all the modern authors who have presented a necessary distinction between symbol and allegory. What we find most interesting is that most authors seem to believe the distinction to be grounded in the very nature of things, that it is self-evident and without a history. As we have seen, this is not the case: its articulation is modern, and it is valid only insofar as allegory has been twisted from its original meaning, as a scholarly (and abstract) synonym for symbol, and applied to didactic and rhetorical representations. It is no less remarkable that this distinction—real, but altogether banal—is often presented as an innovation putting an end to centuries of confusion.[33] This is obviously not the case for the authors discussed briefly below.

---

[33] For example, Dr. Jolande Jacobi, in his *Complex/Archetype/Symbol in the Psychology of C. G. Jung*, trans. Ralph Manheim (New York, NY: Princeton University Press, 1959), 74–124: "To this day a certain confusion prevails in the use of the terms symbol, allegory, and sign. Each author uses them from his own subjective point of view, often different from that of others" (81). This is not at all the impression given by our study. Quite the opposite: we are struck by the extraordinary semantic consistency of *symbolon* across its history.

René Guénon made constant use of it, yet without falling into the error we have observed. Indeed, he clearly affirms that the distinction results from a distortion of allegory's original meaning: "In myth, then, what is said is something other than what is meant; and let us note in passing that this is also the etymological meaning of allegory (from *allo agoreuein*, literally 'to say something else'), which provides us another example of the deviations of meaning in current usage, for at present this word in fact designates only a conventional and literary representation with a merely moral or psychological intention, one that most often falls under the category of what is commonly called 'personified abstractions.'"[34]

Henri Corbin, who not only discovered the mystical world of Shi'ism in the West but also developed important theories of spiritual cosmology, has strongly insisted on the distinction, in line with German romanticism: "Allegory is a more or less artificial representation of generalities and abstractions which can be perfectly well grasped and expressed in other ways. Symbol is the only possible expression of that which is symbolized, that is to say of the thing signified *with which* it symbolizes. It can never be deciphered once for all."[35] Many features of the Goethean definition can be recognized here.

A vigorous, even somewhat schematic formulation is found in Jean Baruzi.[36] Considering the experience of the mystical Night, he observes that it "is at once the *most intimate translation of the experience and the experience itself*... The Night realizes a permanent impotence in our imagination through its complete negation. *It is therefore incommensurable with its meanings and deserves to be called, in the technical sense of the word, a symbol*." Taking this privileged example as his point of departure, he constructs the opposition between allegory and symbol as between the translatable and the untranslatable. There is "allegory wherever there is a parallelism between a system of images and abstract thoughts, whether expressed or not," whereas the clarity inherent in the symbol

---

[34] *Perspectives on Initiation*, ed. Samuel D. Fohr, trans. Henry D. Fohr (Hillsdale, NY: Sophia Perennis, 2001), 120.
[35] *History of Islamic Philosophy*, trans. Liadain and Philip Sherrard (New York: Routledge, 2014) 12–13. See also *Creative Imagination in the Ṣūfism of Ibn ʿArabī*, trans. Ralph Manheim (Princeton, NJ: Princeton University Press, 1969), 14.
[36] *Saint Jean de la Croix et le problème de l'expérience mystique* (Paris: Alcan, 1924), 323–29. Bear in mind that he approaches St John of the Cross from a neo-Kantian perspective.

"hides within the images themselves, captured and held before us as an absolute, as an object of pure aesthetic contemplation." And if the symbol is untranslatable, this is essentially because it is not itself a translation.[37]

Can such symbolism, strictly speaking, be found anywhere other than in poetry, where the image is given directly to contemplation without any underlying abstraction? Mystical symbolism that translates dogma is "practically allegory." But if it is the mystical experience of a Beyond radically transcending the world, it would then need a language "that would equally have nothing in common with the world," expressing itself in a symbolic form constitutive of that very experience. In this truly "symbolic experience," the symbol "directly embraces experience. It is not a representation of experience."[38]

The Baruzian conception reaches a limit at which it becomes somewhat contradictory. The signifying function has completely disappeared, leaving only the function of presentification—yet the symbol is *always* a sign, even when it signifies what is not signifiable. Of course, it can only do so by a certain immanence of (even the highest) Transcendence. We therefore do not reject such a symbolic embrace in mystical experience—far from it. But there must still be a difference between this experience and That which is experienced. The mystical subject himself becomes the symbol: in him the Untranslatable and Inexpressible is translated and expressed, has Itself been imprinted upon him.

This erasure of the signifying function leads to the transformation of the symbol/allegory opposition into one between symbol and sign. This can be seen in many philosophers, Karl Jaspers in particular. In the first volume of his *Philosophical Logic: On Truth*,[39] he explains very clearly: "There is a radical difference between symbol and sign. The sign allows for an explanation of its meaning by another object, since the signified is itself equally an object. The symbol can only be deepened within itself, become expressive. In the sign, something is thought that is also *there* in the sign's absence. In the symbol, something is present that absolutely could not express itself to us without the symbol."[40]

---

[37] Ibid., 325.
[38] Ibid.
[39] *Philosophische Logik: Von der Wahrheit* (Munich: R. Piper & Co, 1947).
[40] Op. cit., 256.

Jaspers's distinction between sign and cipher (symbol) is highly relevant, showing once more the symbol's semantic persistence and corresponding in a philosophical key to what Baruzi expressed mystically. Yet it nevertheless risks obscuring the fact that *symbol* is a species of the genus *sign*, not the reverse. It is precisely from this perspective that we approach the symbol in the second part of the present work. Before proceeding, however, there remains to bring together the symbol's primary meaning as it has been revealed over this long history. Its essence — sometimes obscure, yet ever present — must be recaptured, drawing from all the examples in the assembled evidence. The foregoing was a massive investigation, certainly, but a necessary one, in that it allowed us to *see* the symbol before attempting to *think* it. It was required first to make contact with this unique entity, to know it historically as an impenetrable treasure passed from generation to generation, bearer of hope and truth, subject neither to rejection nor reduction to reasonable banality, often hidden, ever reborn, ready to reveal its luminous heart to the mind's attentive gaze.

CHAPTER III
The Essence of the Symbol

THAT THE SYMBOL HAS AN ESSENCE should not be doubted. Though it has many uses, this does not entail the symbol's complete dissipation into its various meanings. It clearly operates from a unique and more-or-less apparent semantic core and with unmistakable cohesive power.

But can the nature of this semantic core be determined, and how can a survey of its historical development assist us? Would a comparative distillation of shared features produce a positive definition? This is unlikely, first, because it would end only in an artificial and hypothetical reconstruction; second, because such an operation may not even be possible. In reality, and I have often stressed this, I am less interested in what theologians and philosophers have said about the symbol, in the set ideas that they attempt to construct, than in *what they cannot help but think and say about it*. What seems most remarkable is the symbol's *resistance* to the many uses to which it has been subjected, for only here will its essence be recognized. And this is a methodological point of great importance. Uses of the term have been collected across more than two millennia, not to give way before the contingency or artificiality of definitions, but rather to yield to the supraformal truth expressed within and despite these definitions. Plato, after all, proceeded in just this way, for our questioning is yet maieutic, however historical it may be. By no means are we retracing an evolution of the term, which seems problematic. Quite the opposite: we are stressing its semantic permanence, a permanence that finds different expressions according to circumstance.

THE TWO POLES OF THE SYMBOLIC FUNCTION

The supraformal truth of the symbol, the symbol as such, thus does not lend itself to contemplation. It can be grasped only indirectly through its function in human culture, since human culture is its principle and enabling condition.

Now the entire history of the symbolic function seems to represent a tension between two apparently antagonistic but really indivisible poles: the signifying and the "presentifying" functions. These two poles realize their dialectical unity, their raison d'être, precisely in the symbol.

One problem, though, needs to be dispelled from the very start. The signifying function proper to the sign and the representing function proper to the symbol are often irreducibly opposed: "Signifying is always something other than representing."[1] Thus the word "table" signifies the thing so named while in no way representing it, whereas a portrait represents its model without signifying it. It is not "read," it is seen. Conversely, it serves no purpose to merely look at written signs or to consider them pictorially:[2] they must be deciphered, interpreted, which demands a knowledge of their meaning. This is why Husserl could say that the apprehension of a sign stems from the *intellectio*, that of a symbol from the *imaginatio*.[3]

Yet this division of functions and faculties seems groundless: the symbol is always a sign, but not always a representation. It is always a sign because, like every sign, its function is to make known by means of a visible form an invisible reality, either essentially invisible (God, an essence, or a thought) or accidentally so (Socrates, sacred realities, or the Body of Christ). It is also a sign in that its meaning should be deciphered and therefore learned, initially within a hermeneutic tradition. It is not enough to *see*; we must also *know*. Of course, the symbol is not a sign in the manner of an algorithm, but neither is it merely a simple image. It is certainly correct to contrast a sign with a representation, but wrong to identify the latter with a symbol. Indeed, to "represent" is to "present a second time": the second presentation can only be distinguished from the first, the only real one, by its figurative or unreal character. Hence the relationship joining the second presentation to the first can only be one of formal resemblance, imitation.[4] In this case, its contrast with the sign is obvious: precisely because the sign "table" does not resemble the thing

---

[1] The phrase comes from Paul Ricœur, summarizing Husserl; in *The Rule of Metaphor*, trans. Robert Czerny et al. (London: Routledge, 2003), 356.
[2] This is the error of the "Whole Language" method, which applies the laws of perception to reading instruction.
[3] *Logical Investigations*, vol. 1, trans. J.N. Findlay (New York, NY: Routledge, 2001), 206–7.
[4] It could be purely conventional, though this would return us to the sign.

so named, it signifies it, requiring us to "read" it, to intellectually grasp its significance. Conversely, the picture of a table has no significance—it represents. It is a substitute, a replacement.

Some, like Gadamer,[5] see in this substituting function the very definition of a symbol, but this is impossible. Is it really just a representative substitute? Insofar as it substitutes, it necessarily enjoys independence and self-sufficiency with respect to the substituted; otherwise, it could not fulfill its function as a second presentation. It has to be itself in order to be another. And insofar as it represents, it must bear the image of its model, just as a valet bears the livery of his master; otherwise, it would be an unidentified substitute, which is a contradiction in terms. By definition, such a mimetic relationship can only be external—the being of the substitute is not involved, only its appearance. The portrait of a famous individual represents him; it is not his symbol. This is true for every allegory (in the Goethean sense). A representation is inevitably, then, if not a lie, at least a fiction: a face is not a painted canvas, death is not a skeleton. This is the source of idolatry and therefore of iconoclasm.

The symbol answers to neither of these descriptions. It is not a substitute, for it is nothing apart from what it symbolizes; nor is it a representative, for it maintains *an inner relationship with the thing symbolized, and this makes it a symbol*. This is why a symbol truly *signifies*: like the sign, it beckons and *draws us toward* something other than itself, whereas the representation approaches us, casting us back on ourselves.[6]

But what is the mode of this signification? As demonstrated in the preceding historical survey, all those who have dealt with the symbol have felt themselves confronted by a mystery. If a single conclusion is to be drawn from these examples, it is that there is a "strangeness" to the symbol. There is something about it that baffles, disquiets, and ceaselessly exercises the mind, something in it at once conceptually irreducible and nourishing, refreshing, a hopeful enchantment, a promise or festive anticipation of being.

This is because the symbol realizes not so much a (second) presentation as a *presence*. A portrait is not a face, but a tree "is" the axis

---

[5] *Truth and Method*, 65–66. Gadamer does speak of the symbol as a non-figurative substitute, but then it is unclear what distinguishes it from the sign, for example, from the mathematical sign only improperly called "symbol."

[6] This is not unrelated to the inverse perspective of traditional painting.

of the world, water "is" Universal Possibility, the rock "is" Christ. This means that, in order to be present in our corporeal world, the axis mundi "becomes" tree, All-Possibility "becomes" water, Christ "becomes" rock. The symbol is not then a representative substitute, but a mode of presence: it has what we call a "presentifying function." Just as the soul is the "form" of the body, such that the body is the soul made visible and present to corporeal beings, so a true symbol is that through which the symbolized Invisible is made present. It is not present a second time in this mode, not substituted by a figurative entity (which leads to idolatry and therefore iconoclasm). It is simply made present *for us*. There are not then two presences, one real but elsewhere, the other unreal, here but figurative; for there can only be one, and one that is truly *always present*. It is we who are absent, we who are made present to it through the radiation of the symbol, which is itself a "vision" (Hindus would say a *darshan*) of archetypal reality. But mediation (or *darshan*, perspective) also implies "modality." The symbol presentifies, but necessarily according to certain determinations and figures. No more than the body is the soul in its totality (or any part of it), the symbol is not a total presentification—that would be nonsensical. Hence it is always a sign before being deciphered, read, and examined in its determinate intelligible structure.

The symbol therefore never lies. In that it is only an extension of the symbolized on our plane of its manifestation, it depends upon it entirely. It does not imitate through a relation of formal similarity, but signifies through an internal relation, conforming to the laws and needs of its own plane of manifestation and by virtue of an ontological correspondence expressing the essential unity of all the degrees of universal existence. Conversely, in presentifying its archetype, it makes us present to it and thereby transforms us.

What the symbol truly demands, always, is a conversion of the spiritual gaze: breaking with ordinary consciousness, which sees only the separative exteriority of physical beings, we enter the inner relation binding them together and leading toward their archetype. In short, a symbol is always both anamnesis and summons. This is why, like leaven, it "works" human thought. Signifying by presentifying, it allows us to glimpse the unity of the intelligible (signification) and being (presentification). But this is also the source of its corruption. Lacking conversion, we lose sight of the internal relation of correspondence between symbol and archetype. It then decomposes, sometimes being transformed into a pure sign, as in mathematical algorithms; sometimes into a pure representation, as in "allegories" or even (the ultimate degradation) psychoanalytic symbolism.[7] This is why we speak of a tension which makes the history of the symbol oscillate between two poles: signification and presentification. I could explain this dialectic abstractly, but better now to approach the essence of that of which the symbolic function is only the cultural manifestation. And because only the symbol knows how to speak of the symbol, we will do so by meditating on the symbol in which this essence is presentified in exemplary fashion.

THE SYMBOL OF SYMBOLS

Whichever symbol is used to express the essence of all symbols will also be the symbol par excellence, the prime and founding symbol from which all others derive. Is such a thing possible? Would it not raise more difficulties than it resolves? *Is there* such a primary symbol? This last question demands two different answers, according to whether it is considered primary in itself or for us. In itself, metaphysically, the primary symbol is the one with which all symbolism begins, the one that symbolizes what lies beyond every symbol. In this sense, the symbol of symbols is the Non-Symbol. Metaphysically, this could only be Being itself as a symbol of "Beyond-Being," as a principial self-affirmation of absolute and infinite Reality, defining itself as the creative ontological source, and appearing to creatures as Uncreated Being.

On the other hand, everything emanating from this ontological Source, everything produced, is necessarily linked to the Principle granting it existence—otherwise it would soon cease to exist—whether the various degrees of universal existence (all of the hierarchically ordered worlds) or the conditions that respectively determine and therefore distinguish them. The trace of this relationship is indicated by an "umbilical point" playing the role of origin-center or (secondary) principle for a particular world or condition, for itself as well as all beings found there. And so the image of the cosmogonic process is to be seen everywhere, reflecting the same exemplarist continuity and ontological discontinuity. There are then many (secondary) "primary symbols," since each

---

[7] Jung, that demonic spiritualist, perverted the meaning of symbols differently from (but also as radically as) Freud.

analogically exercises in its own domain the function that the (primordial) ontological Symbol exercises for Creation as whole.

Now insofar as what is primary for man is what is given to him first and most immediately, stemming from the most elementary order, the primary symbol necessarily belongs "for him" to the lowest realm of existence, that condition beyond which there is only nonexistence. The primary symbol, that with which symbolism begins, is found here because it founds the very possibility of symbolism. Thus, the Symbol which is primary in itself finds its inverse analogy in the symbol which is primary for us: the one defines the upper limit of symbolism, because That which is symbolized is, in reality, no longer symbolizable, there being no longer any *thing* to symbolize. The other defines the lower limit, that which symbolizes being minimally distinguished from nothingness, beyond which there is no longer any symbolism.

Man, the image of God, is himself the primary symbol for the terrestrial world and its order of existence; he is the synthesis and microcosm in whom the universal macrocosm is symbolized. But, as for those conditions defining our world—form, life, quantified matter, time, space—space is obviously its minimal condition of existence, below which there is nothing. We find in space the primary elemental symbol, image of the creative Principle, center-origin of spatial extension: the point. However, the geometrical point can be defined in two distinct and irreducible ways: either as the principle generating all possible space by its radiating, omnidirectional expansion, or as the limit of its dissipating concentration. Again: the point generates the perpendicular, which generates the plane, which generates volume; or else the plane could be the result of two intersecting volumes, the perpendicular from two intersecting planes, and the point from two intersecting perpendiculars. These different approaches to the principle of space express its nature as limit (it is and is not *in* space) and thus reflect the continuity and discontinuity of the creative principle with respect to Creation. This necessitates a twofold representation: a sphere or circle (image of the point) and a cross transecting it. To my mind, this is the fundamental symbol, the symbol of symbols.

The resulting figure is a circle divided in fourths by two perpendicular lines, corresponding to the earthly paradise with its four cardinal rivers, as described in the Bible, and therefore to the primary image of this world. It is also a *symbolon* in the original sense: a *tessera*, token, a broken ring, which, by the fitting together of its parts, enables its owner to recognize the bearer of the complementary half (or quarters), attesting to the preexistent pact that joined them and makes restoration possible.[8] If this is the correct meaning of *symbolon*, it expresses well its figurative meaning, that of symbol. By meditating on this *symbolon*—sign of recognition in the form of a broken ring—we see the basic character of the symbol's essence unfold.

THE SYMBOL WITHIN THE SYMBOL

We have returned to our beginning, that material object the Greeks called a *symbolon*, something that, "losing its own meaning," becomes the metaphor for a mysterious class of signs: the symbol. If followed attentively, the lessons learned in observing the *symbolon* (which "gives rise to thought") will also give us a complete outline of the symbol's essence. From *symbolon* to symbol: to speak of one is to know the other. Indeed, the *symbolon* was ever a symbol, never having any proper or root meaning. Its meaning is always already symbolic.

Think of a *symbolon*, an earthenware or metallic object—a broken ring, for example. The remaining, visible part of this ring, which might be called its "vestigial being," is to be seen as the present part of an absent whole. Not simply as itself, like an ordinary physical object, but as a witness to, a fragment of, something else. It is therefore precisely a sign, as the sign has its being in standing for something else. However, this vestigial and fragmentary being—this broken ring—is not a sign by virtue of an extrinsic character bestowed from without; it is a sign in its very nature. Its incomplete form invisibly extends itself by outlining the absent image which is alone able to restore the fragment's lost totality. The vestigial and fragmentary being of the broken ring is thus a portion of that to which it witnesses. But, if we reverse perspective and start with the invisible side, the vestigial half of

---

[8] This practice of the *symbolon* has persisted through the ages. In his bizarre and monumental *Iconographie chrétienne: Histoire de Dieu*, Adolphe Didron reproduced a circular seal in silver from Mount Athos, which was cut into four equal parts belonging to the four monks who each governed the monastery for one year ([Paris: Imprimerie Royale, 1843], 291). The reunification of the four pieces of the seal was required to authenticate the minutes of the proceedings. Didron witnessed this in 1839.

the ring can be seen as the visible part of an invisible circle, the extension in the perceptual world of something surpassing it. It is moreover quite appropriate that we are dealing here with a segment of a circle, since the circle's arc is the only curve that necessarily determines the complete geometric figure, in such a way that the circle is entirely defined by the merest fragment of circumference, provided of course that we know it to be the fragment of a circle.

Neither pure presence nor pure absence, such is the *symbolon* in its sensible reality. If pure absence, it would not exist and so could signify nothing. But if pure presence, it would be the very reality itself and everything would be already given. The two aspects of the *symbolon* are therefore dialectical: in its present reality, it is indwelt by an absence which it in some way makes present. The purpose of the *symbolon* is to make us see something unseen, or to make us first see that there *is* something unseen, something of which we would be otherwise unaware. But conversely, this absence is not purely and simply the negation of presence. Quite the opposite: absence establishes and actualizes presence, endows it with meaning and reality, since the vestigial and fragmentary presence reveals its true nature only in being completed, totalized, and integrated into the perfection of the invisible figure.

As we can see, the most elementary description of the *symbolon* in its vestigial nature already conveys a wealth of insight about the symbol as sacred sign. This is precisely why the etymological thesis is at once irrefutable and incomplete: it forgets the essential. For the two halves of the *symbolon* to fulfill their assigned role, the complete and original ring must first be seen as a symbol uniting two or more people. *Symbolon* presupposes symbol. The material ring is itself symbolic of a prior invisible pact which is in essence "intentional."[9] And it can symbolize this because of its form, and therefore because the object is itself ultimately identical to the pact — it *is* the pact become gold or silver. But that is not all: however intentional, a pact is also the symbol of that lost unity that persons are seeking to reestablish, no matter how incomplete and separated. Does not Plato teach that each of us is the symbol of a man seeking his symbol?[10] And so we are at last led back to archetypal unity.

---

[9] This is a Scholastic term qualifying the action by which the mind *inclines toward* an object, that is, thinks and knows.
[10] Cf. *supra*, 9.

The Essence of the Symbol

In short, it is as if there were two invisible "complements" of the *symbolon*, one material, the other spiritual or intentional. The former first shows us that we are dealing with a symbol, with a vestigial being. Only on the basis of this knowledge can we cross over to its complement, which is no longer its physical "half," but its metaphysical completion and perfection. This "dual articulation," one mediating the other, is distinctive of the symbol. The symbol is not a closed unity, shut in upon itself, but manifold, vibrant, resonant; in other words, every true symbol achieves a kind of self-resonance, symbolizing itself in a certain way and exhibiting a harmonious structure. Thus, for Plato, the three parts of the human body (stomach, chest, and head) clearly symbolize the three parts of the soul (desiring, incensive, and rational). But the last of these, the head (mouth, nose, and forehead) itself symbolizes the whole person: body within body, man within man, symbol within symbol. The symbol is always fractal, analogical and rhythmic in structure. It always contains a lack, something requiring completion; there is also always a surplus, something inviting us beyond, like those irrational divisions (such as the relationship of the side of a square to its diagonal) in which the unit of measure is never commensurable with the measured quantity: it is always larger or smaller. For the symbol is measured by the archetype presentified within it, and ultimately by the One itself, the Supreme Archetype. What is more, it *is* this measure as such,[11] the One-in-the-many, at once lacking all multiplicity and wholly encompassing it.

The *symbolon* therefore adequately symbolizes the symbol, since, by its visible incompleteness and physical lack, it shows the essential incompleteness and metaphysical deficiency of all manifested reality. It both signifies and awakens us to this unfinished state. In some instances, a symbol might appear as an integral whole: a rose, a star, a triangle, or a circle. But in its symbolic being, it is open and crying out to the Invisible as what completes, unifies, and realizes it. Before our very eyes, the ring of the physical world is always tending to close in upon itself, and us within it. Each sacred symbol is a place where this ring reopens, revealing its brokenness, and offering us deliverance from the threat of finitude.

Is this all that the *symbolon* teaches? Surely not. To this point, we have considered it chiefly in its physical nature, which accounts for the presentifying function (just as it implies an ontology that

---

[11] This is why "number" is symbolic.

cannot be treated here). But now we need to account for its intentional nature, according to which it signifies a pact. And this clearly takes the signifying function into account (just as it refers to a "noetics," a theory of symbolic knowledge, which we are also unable to treat here).

As for its intentionality, the *symbolon* attests to and makes known the prior existence of a pact, which conferred on the ring the value of a sign, each half giving proof that the pact was sealed and remains in force. As such, the *symbolon* can be called a "memorial" sign, even a "traditional" sign: it is turned toward the past and preserves its origin. Of course, its memorial value cannot be revealed merely by examining the perceptible form. A simple observation of the ring might inform its owner that it is indeed the sign of something, but he turns it about in his hand in vain, unable to guess what this half-ring memorializes, unless tradition instructs him or explains the significance of any decorations adorning it. Even the most attentive examination of the ring will moreover not reveal why this ring is in *his* hands specifically, why he is its rightful owner. But this too should be something meaningful, since the sign of a pact essentially concerns persons. The ring not only has meaning *in itself* but also and necessarily *for someone*. Now the only means of knowing this personal meaning is to *trust* the tradition (the word of the ancients) transmitting it. Ultimately, then, the ground of this meaning is the authority of the person conferring it on the ring, thereby establishing the agreement of which it is the evidence.

To be clear: the ability of the *symbolon* to signify a covenant is not in question. The broken ring by its very nature symbolizes this covenant—indeed, it is by virtue of this nature that someone in authority has chosen it, and not arbitrarily. But if the legitimate authority had not decided to confer on it the *meaning* of a memorial sign for its owner, there is a sense in which this covenant would be a covenant for no one. Traditional authority does not create the symbolic significance of the ring. It does not invent it—it realizes it, reconnecting it to the actuality of a human existence, for such a relationship can only be the result of an action. In other words, the intervention of a legitimate authority *establishing* the sign's significance is necessary whenever we pass from the order of things to that of persons and introduce a relation between them. This institutional significance can only be transmitted orally, eventually with the aid of writing. Along with the broken ring, the owner will hand down to his descendants the teaching that makes its meaning explicit, that they in turn might pass it on to their own heirs. But, if oral transmission is interrupted, the meaning of the *symbolon* will be irrevocably lost. Such is the *symbolon* as a memorial sign.

There is still a third characteristic revealed by our meditation on the *symbolon*. The vestigial symbol led to the memorial symbol and now to the *symbolon* as sign of recognition, which we will call the "directing" symbol. Here, the symbol realizes the union of its presentifying and signifying functions—and this refers us to a "ritualics" of the symbol, a theory of the symbol as rite (again, not to be treated here).[12]

This third aspect of the symbol's essence is the most misunderstood, as well as the most important, insofar as ritual activity joins being and knowing in the symbol, thereby fulfilling the injunction and promise implanted in its very nature. Not only does the *symbolon* reveal the "invisible" existence of the previous pact which it presentifies and memorializes; insofar as it directs, it also invites and summons us to rediscover the other half of the ring, *orienting us toward* its future reconstitution. A concrete form (the *symbolon*'s vestigial being) and its traditional significance (its memorial value) are both at work in directing us toward the work of recognition. Tradition teaches us about the pact, what unity it signifies; but like a touchstone, the concrete form discriminates between true and false reunions, confirming as false or illusory all halves that claim to restore the lost unity without being able to align themselves with the remaining half. It is the vestigial being, the concrete form, then, which proves and confirms tradition, while tradition reveals and gives meaning to the vestigial being. Insofar as we remain in the simple knowledge taught by the memorial sign, we should be content with an anticipatory assurance, with *faith*. Traditional knowledge may well provide us with the meaning of the *symbolon*'s vestigial being, but a proposed hermeneutic will only be confirmed on the day when it meets the other half which perfectly matches it, which it has been anticipating *in hope*. As master of our spiritual destiny, the directing symbol leads us to the fulfillment of all human history: the Eternal Marriage Supper, when the One himself will slip the ring

---

[12] Ontology, noetics, ritualics—these are the three components of the metaphysics of symbolism, which we will perhaps explore in the future.

of His *love* onto the finger of His elect. Having become identified with those rites accomplished under the symbol's direction, it is finally man himself who becomes symbolic and who is thereby integrated into the gathering (*symbolon*) of all creation in the One's embrace.

CONCLUSION: THE SIGN OF THE COVENANT

We thus see the symbol's essence in all its breadth. It is that "half" of reality, that broken ring which the Invisible has left in our hands as a sign of recognition, as the pledge of our election, the promise of our salvation, at once memorial and prophecy, awakening us to original knowledge and guiding us toward ultimate reality.

In this all the world's religions speak the same language and give the same teaching. The Gospel reveals that "Mary kept all these things, and pondered (*sumballousa*, "gathering") them in her heart." After the multiplication of the loaves, Christ orders the Apostles to "gather up the fragments that remain" (with John Scottus seeing here the esoteric sense of the Scriptures), and He himself "shall gather together his elect from the four winds," restoring in each one the true Adam — the symbol of God in man, mutilated and scattered by original sin.[13] But God had already declared to Noah, "I do set my bow in the cloud, and it shall be for a token of a covenant between me and the earth." Likewise the *Bhāgavata Purāna* reveals that the Veda, that "ambrosia come down from Heaven," has been brought to men by Dhavantari, that is to say "the one who stands amidst the rainbow."[14] This is echoed in the *Iliad*, which informs us that the bow of Iris is a "a sign to mortal men . . . arched

---

[13] Matt. 24:31. There is a tradition taken up and developed by St Augustine that relates the four letters of ADAM to the first letter of each cardinal direction in Greek: *Anatole*, East; *Dusis*, West; *Arktos*, North, and *Mesembria*, South (Homily 9.14; *Homilies on the Gospel of John 1–40*, ed. Allan D. Fitzgerald OSA, trans. Edmund Hill OP [Hyde Park, NY: New City Press, 2009], 194). Taken in this order, the four cardinal directions trace the number 4, which in turn, according to the ancients, corresponds with the four elements: East with air, West with earth, North with water, and South with fire. Fr Dominique Cerbelaud OP argues that this tradition, neither in the Hebrew nor the Septuagint, originates with Alexandrian Judaism (*Les cahiers de l'Abbaye de Sylvanes* 3 [1982]). It is common in the Middle Ages.

[14] Georges Lanoë-Villène, *Le Livre des Symboles: Études de Symboliques et de Mythologie Comparée* (Paris: Librarie Générale, 1935), 1.130.

The Essence of the Symbol

on the clouds by Cronus's son."[15] The rainbow, that ring of light encircling the *Merkavah* in Ezekiel, is also the mandorla encircling the throne of Christ on the church's tympanum. But this celestial *symbolon*, revelatory sign of the primordial pact at the foundation of every religion, is also the one that signs and seals the restoration of the divine nature in creatures: nimbus of the Roman gods and Buddhist wisdom, halo of the Christian saints, noble turban of Islam, radiant headdress of the Native American warrior.

The symbol's corona truly envelops all things: it is the radiance of the Divine Glory.

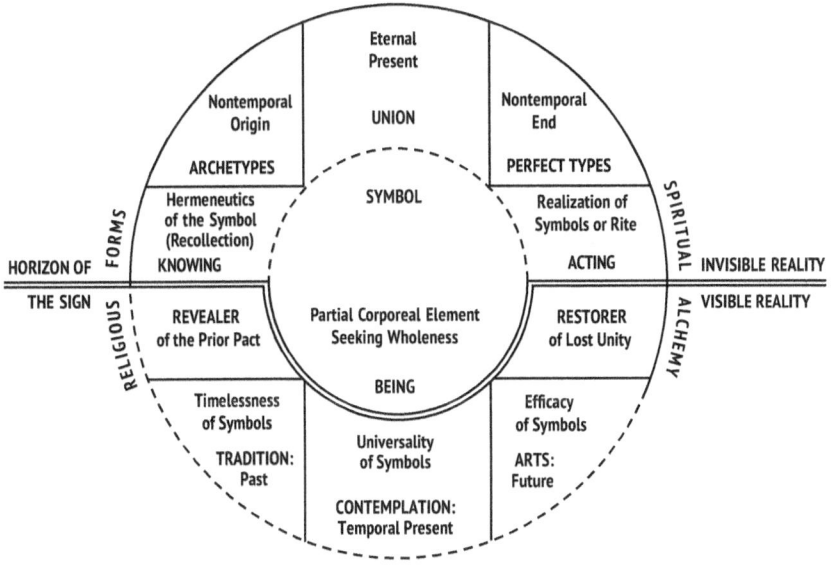

The Cross-Circle of the Symbol

The symbol is represented by the lower half of the small circle (double line). Its horizon separates the two regions of reality. The upper half, which is invisible (dotted line), seems to complete the lower half. But the opposite is true. Hence the large circle that surrounds the symbol on all sides. Its upper half represents the order of intelligible realities (solid line). And yet it is somehow incomplete without the lower half, which expresses the necessary but invisible immanence of the One in the many. The key to this schema is the principle of inverse analogy.

---

[15] *The Iliad* XI.29–30; trans. Robert Fagles (New York, NY: Penguin, 1991), 297.

PART II
STRUCTURAL ANALYTIC OF THE SYMBOL

INTRODUCTION

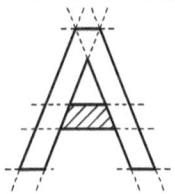AS PREVIOUSLY NOTED, A SINGLE object can be defined from two different perspectives, viewing it either in its metaphysical essence or in the functional structure necessary for its concrete realization within a determinate order of existence. In itself, the essence is independent of all existential conditions: it is free. But its realization entails the formation of a structure adapted to its conditions of existence, lacking which it cannot fulfill its charge, perform the action implied by its nature, or even "be itself"—*become* what it *is*.

It is important to note that we spoke of *functional* structure, not simply "structure"; structural perspective cannot be dissociated from function, for one cannot exist without the other. Structure is function considered under its static and "spatial" aspect; function is structure considered under its dynamic and "temporal" aspect. However, analytical and mechanistic reason tends to dissociate them, seeing in function only a secondary effect of structure, a "functioning." It takes the machine as its explanatory model, perceiving primarily an easily describable physical system or device whose operations are easily accounted for by its organization and articulation: explanation then entails the decomposition of the whole into its parts. In so doing, reason evidently forgets that the machine was built in view of its function, and this accounts for its structure: it is both the formal and the final cause.

This inseparability of structure and function is true in every domain. In physics, the wave-particle duality is presented as two sides of a single phenomenon, functional (the wave) and structural (the particle). In biology, the scholarly distinction between anatomy and physiology blinds us to the fact that, for example, the ocular apparatus is only the bodily mode of the visual function: the eye's anatomical structure is not only unintelligible apart from this end, but is in fact simply vision actualizing itself in the body, as embryology demonstrates irrefutably.[1] The same goes for linguistics: the structure of the sign cannot be separated from the signifying function, no more than can the symbolic apparatus be separated from the symbolic function. Yet this is what structuralism attempts in the name of scientific rigor.

One could object that the foregoing is interesting, perhaps, but rather philosophical, merely a speculative game completely untethered from reality and so having nothing to say about it. It would be impossible to countenance such a division of roles: philosophy is nothing if not knowledge of reality. But its knowledge differs from that of science according to how concepts relate to reality in either case.

It is therefore impossible to undertake a study of the symbolic apparatus from the requirements of our perspective without first addressing this conflict between science and the "pretensions" of philosophy. This project may seem outrageously presumptuous, but we are not concerned here with the conflict between science and philosophy generally, rather a comparison of the philosophical "concept" with that of science in terms of their relation to reality. This will give us a criterion of the scientific (understanding this in the modern, "Galilean" sense) which, in defining the domain of science, clears a space in which philosophy is not only possible but necessary. Treatment of the symbolic apparatus within the framework of its regulating function thereby becomes possible, without the risk of censure for mixing "metaphysical" and positive considerations. Science may content itself with the analytical exploration of observable structures, since this is indeed *one* dimension of the object, and a real one. Yet true knowledge of reality—and such knowledge is the privilege of philosophy—demands much more.

---

[1] This is obviously a reference to the results of Ruyer's work, particularly those set forth in *The Genesis of Living Forms*, trans. Jon Roffe and Nicholas B. de Weydenthal (London: Rowman & Littlefield, 2020).

CHAPTER IV
The Sign According to Linguistics

EPISTEMIC CLOSURE OF THE CONCEPT

"**S**CIENCE IS ONLY A WELL-FORMED LANguage." This thesis of Condillac's—often repeated, variously discussed—is largely undisputed, at least in what it affirms. Science cannot be *only* a well-formed language, but it certainly is one. This can be considered the criterion of the scientific: the possibility of expressing knowledge relative to a given order of reality in a well-made language defines the threshold of admission onto the scientific stage, in the modern sense of the term. (There are other senses, but these derive from a different understanding of knowledge.)

Coherence of Language and Coherence of Thought

We should inquire into the nature of this possibility. In general, a language expresses the thought of the speaker in order to communicate it to an addressee. There is "benefaction" in a language when there is a perfect (one-to-one) correspondence between expression and communication, what is communicated and what is expressed being identical. A speaker of this language would know exactly what is meant and what is said: the concept expressed by the speaker and that understood by the addressee would have the same content.

How is such a correspondence obtained? The influence of linguistics has tended to reduce the concept to discourse, though we will show later that this is impossible. Roughly, though, we can observe that thought is an activity of the mind, whereas there is speech only in the articulation of phonemes. We think "in our head," but we speak "with our mouth." It is obviously possible to think with one's mouth and speak in one's head, but this does not change the strictly mental nature of the thinking activity. True, it maintains a privileged relation with language, which expresses thought, subjecting it to the limiting and defining rules of its own structure. Language arrests and crystalizes thought by objectification, transforming it into an object. It bestows upon it the *realization* of which it is capable. Any linguistic expression is therefore a test for the cognitive act, and consequently an aid and criterion of its precision and coherence.[1] The linguistic order is indeed made up of discrete units at different levels—for example, books, parts, chapters, articles, sections, paragraphs, sentences, words, morphemes, and phonemes. These are mutually organized according to determinate laws that vary among different languages. These unities and articulations impose themselves on thought, which agrees to express itself within them as a relatively permanent and invariable order. It cannot do with language what it wishes, though its own dynamism naturally desires this; the art by which it uses language allows it to retroactively verify its own permanence and invariability, its non-contradiction. Here, everything is a matter of possibility: the coherence of thought is confirmed only if it can sustain a discourse.

Obviously, but against a great deal of modern reflection on language, discourse is not itself the coherence of thought; it only potentially verifies it. Thought's need to express itself is a function of an awareness of its own coherence and certainty, its objectivity, even its *openness* to the object. The need for expression is all the stronger when this certainty is weaker.[2] But the coherence of the verifying instrument is of a different nature than conceptual coherence. Linguistic coherence results from the quasi-contractual stability of the elements of discourse. Words cannot constantly change their meaning: speaker and addressee must agree on their stability, else there is no language. But the non-contradiction of thought cannot be defined solely as an internal agreement; rather, this agreement itself depends necessarily on that between thought and what it thinks, the object

---

[1] Written expression is a more decisive test than oral, but against a certain "grammatology," they do not differ in nature (at least, not from the point of view that interests us here). In certain oral literatures, moreover, speech is as fixed and canonical as writing. This is the case not only for the "word of mouth" transmission of massive works like the *Mahabharata* or the *Ramayana* which were "composed" orally, but also for free and spontaneous teachings that flow directly into the mold of fixed forms, like those of Rabbi Yeshua—what Fr Jousse, in his magisterial work, has called the oral *style*, rhythmo-melodism.

[2] Thus, for example, we resort to logical formalization where the complexity of the domain under investigation exceeds our conceptual grasp. Elsewhere, intuition leads, followed by logical exposition for the benefit of the reader.

of the concept. The principle of non-contradiction may well be a requirement for thought, but only insofar as thought is essentially the action by which an object is known; it is the thought of *what is* and is ordered toward being. From this point of view, the principle of non-contradiction would be a requirement of being itself. When a thing is truly known and grasped in its essence, thought understands that the thing cannot be other than it is, and therefore that the concept of the thing (the mental act by which it is grasped) cannot be identical to that of its opposite. Obviously, something poorly understood can be transformed into its opposite without contradiction — thought, as a merely psychological act, is not averse to contradiction, perhaps even finding it pleasant. Thousands contradict themselves without realizing it, and even the greatest philosopher is not immune to such misfortune. Thought indeed only feels constrained not to contradict itself insofar as it attempts to think being, is *attentive to reality*. The requirement for the mutual non-contradiction of concepts results from the relation that each has with reality — the principle lacks necessity outside of this ontological orientation. We cannot speak of a purely formal coherence of thought.[3]

The coherence imposed upon thought by language therefore differs greatly from that imposed by its openness to being: the former is formal and external, the second ontological and internal. And while the former is more or less verified and verifiable, depending on the "perfection" of the language, the latter is not. It eludes all criteria, depending entirely on the knowledge imparted by reality, and so ultimately on spiritual intuition. As Spinoza said, *verum index sui*. Yet such intuition — not strictly thought, in that thought is motion, whereas intuition is immediate, contemplative vision — does not necessarily occur. The work of thought is only not to be an obstruction, persevering in expectation of the real, of the concept's opening out toward being. This openness is the acceptance of something beyond the concept, that *what* it thinks by means of the concept does not exhaust reality. There is *for it* a hidden face of being, constantly issuing forth in a cognitive outpouring that flows into the concept and imbues it with content. This hidden face is not unknowable, but it is a knowledge

---

[3] This is precisely why the coherence or non-contradiction of (purely formal) logical discourse is not demonstrable, as proved by Gödel's theorem (1931). It therefore comes down to the order of intuition.

requiring the transformation of the subject, a radical conversion of his speculative intention, as Plato describes in the Symbol of the Cave — transcending the ordinary plane of philosophy to reach true "gnosis."

Whatever the case, conceptual *objectivity* clearly must not be confused with linguistic *objectification*. The concept is not the psychological "face" of a semiotic unity, which language carves out of the intellectual mists according to the requirements of its own structure. The inner content of the concept is not a word, but a thing, an object, and this object defines its objectivity.[4] There is thus an inverse relation between the coherence of language and of thought: the more thought is open to being, the less certain it can be of the soundness of its discourse and the more it finds itself inadequate. Think of the words of St Thomas Aquinas a few days before his death, when he emerged from an illumination received after celebrating the Sacrifice of the Mass: "All I have written appears to be as so much straw (*mihi ut paleae vedetur*) after the things that have been revealed to me." Conversely, the formal coherence of language can be illusory or false — a rigorous syllogism is false if its premises are. Ultimately, the most rigorous language would be one without the slightest connection to being. A perfectly verifiable coherence is after all one dependent only on pure relations that entirely define the elements of discourse. If instead these relations derive from the nature of the concepts they signify — from the relations of concepts to the essences of things — then they would elude all formalization. Mathematics and (even more so) modern logic endeavor to create such a "verifiable" language.

---

[4] The thesis claiming that the objects of the world are themselves distinguished by language — so often repeated today, radicalized by Benjamin Lee Whorf — is in fact untenable. On the one hand, a lack of different words to specify different things (e.g., the vocabulary of colors) does not prove that these are indistinct for us, any more than the presence of different words for the same object proves that we ignore their identity (e.g., the forest and the trees). On the other hand, we should speak rather of culture than language: true, there is for man no nature without culture, but culture cannot order the world as it pleases. It can only realize certain aspects of it, in accordance with its type. A curious example is provided by the so-called seven colors of the solar spectrum, whereas there are actually only six: three primary and three secondary (indigo being only a shade between violet and blue). Even Newton made this mistake. The cultural archetype "seven" obviously shaped the "distinction" of the color indigo. Yet this nuance does exist, as do an indefinite number of others (René Guénon, *Symbols of Sacred Science*, trans. Henry D. Fohr [Hillsdale, NY: Sophia Perennis, 2004], 335–36).

Science Completes the Concept from the Side of Action

The question posed above can now be answered: how is the perfect correspondence between expression and understanding achieved? Or, at the very least, how can it be sought? Insofar as science is knowledge, it clearly cannot be reduced to a pure language, even if one agrees with the Vienna School that the criterion of coherence is the *possibility* of formalized translation. The concept must be involved, since science aims to speak about an object; it is therefore at this level that the concept must be carved out from the indeterminacy (for thought) implied by its openness to being. We speak of the concept's "epistemic closure" with respect to precisely this operation: closure, in that it separates anything preventing exhaustive definition from the concept; and epistemic,[5] in that this closure is peculiar to scientific knowledge.

Science is therefore not defined as the reduction of the concept to a well-formed language, but is rather the act by which the scientist decides to renounce the concept's ontological openness. This entails renouncing the possibility of knowing things in their essence, for this openness, characteristic of philosophical knowledge, implies a different renunciation—that of knowledge as conceptual totality. Philosophy awaits a revelation of the essence, and it can only be satisfied by the illumining encounter with the very being of the object. This choice makes it what it is, entailing an incompleteness accepted in speculative humility. It remains on the side of the supra-conceptual, persisting in incompleteness even during its most rigorous efforts at definition, as this is the sign and condition of an absolute speculative imperative. Philosophy is love of the *Divine Sophia*, the self-revelation of the Principle. It is the desire for the Absolute's self-knowledge.

The consummation of knowledge requires either that conceptual understanding, as noetic starting point, disappears through a transformative incorporation within its own transcendent content, and this is the telos of philosophy; or else that the concept find a way to define itself, allowing the mental act that produced it to reach its terminus, and this is only possible as a theoretical moment within a technical activity. For the former, the concept indeed belongs to the order of knowledge, but disappears in

---

[5] We mean by "epistemic" what is relative to the general form of science, whereas "scientific" denotes what is relative to science considered in its actual realization.

its consummation. For the latter, the concept remains, even attaining the consistency of exhaustive definition implied by instrumentalization ("ideas" virtually becoming objects for the mind) while leaving the order of knowledge for that of technical activity. Essentially, the philosopher has never finished thinking so long as thought has not discovered its Master in the very thing it thinks; the scientist, on the other hand, brings thought to an end by a technical decision, because practical activity is the very "beyond" of thought from which it becomes possible to close the concept as precisely the concept *of* this activity. There are only two ends for thought in a living being: contemplation and action.[6]

Galileo and Saussure – Two Illustrations of the Epistemic Closure of the Concept

The history of modern and contemporary science testifies clearly to the above principle, which could certainly be demonstrated in other forms. Scientific knowledge is said to appear when it manages to solve the following problem: how can the phenomenon under examination be conceptually reduced such that it can be considered only in terms of pure relations, independent of related beings? Insofar as the relations between phenomena are considered to result from their nature or essence, science remains pervaded by philosophy. The day when a man, more "brilliant" or "philosophical" than the rest, manages to discover a legitimate means of reducing beings to networks of relations, modern science comes to exist in its own right.

The case of Galilean physics is exemplary in this respect.[7] The transformation facilitating the passage from Aristotelianism to science was conceptual: empirical investigation did not compel the

---

[6] The proper end of science is therefore technique and not pure knowledge. Auguste Comte said as much long ago. This is an observation, not a criticism. This technical orientation constitutes the modern scientific project: this is the choice it has made. Interests of a purely speculative nature fall under philosophy. Obviously, speculative and technical interests can coexist within a single individual, and we may not even be aware of the distinction. But as soon as we leave the order of intentions for that of effects, their confusion is no longer possible, even if, in practice, science is led to open itself to aspects of reality which concern knowledge rather than technique.
[7] We refer here to Alexandre Koyré, *Galileo Studies*, trans. John Mepham (Atlantic Highlands, NJ: Humanities Press, 1978); and Maurice Clavelin, *The Natural Philosophy of Galileo: Essays on the Origins and Formation of Classical Mechanics*, trans. A.J. Pomerans (Cambridge, MA: MIT Press, 1974).

renunciation of Aristotelian physics, but rather our abandoning a philosophy of motion seeking causation in the nature of bodies.[8] For Aristotle, movement is intelligible, meaningful; by its means, the being undergoing motion is realized.[9] In this respect, the purpose of physics is to account for sensible appearances by knowing the essences of things, and this is why it is subordinated to mathematical sciences such as astronomy, which accounts for movement simply through geometrical relations. Geminus, a Greek astronomer of the first century AD, explains that "to physical theory belongs the study of all that concerns the essence of the heavens and the stars, their power, their quality, their generation and destruction. And, by Zeus, physics also has the power of providing demonstrations concerning the size, shape, and arrangement of these bodies. Astronomy, on the other hand, is not prepared to say anything about the former." This is why only physics can rule out the hypothesis of Heraclides Ponticus, for whom "the sun stays fixed" and "the earth moves in a certain way."[10]

By contrast, Galileo gave up seeking the meaning of movement and instead considered it as a *state*, such that it no longer required explanation, employing it in an abstract system of spatiotemporal coordinates deprived of hierarchical organization. The epistemic closure of the concept of "body" (reduced to its center of gravity and hence defined by the concept of "material point") functions, not through a process of abstraction retaining only certain aspects of the empirical object and rejecting others, but rather through a process of construction, through which Galileo defines an "ideal body."[11] There is thus an identity of nature between the concept and its object, since the latter is itself also a concept, whereas in philosophical knowledge the concept is only a means for knowledge of the object: it is essentially transitive and thus remains ontologically open. The Galilean universe is therefore one of conceptual

---

[8] Koyré, 1–3.
[9] Ibid., 6–7; Clavelin, 7: for Aristotle, "every concrete being is constantly impelled, from the inside as it were, to make all sorts of changes."
[10] Germinus's text is cited by Simplicius, *In Aristotelis physicorum libros quattuor priores commentaria*, trans. Hermann Diels (Berlin: Berolini, 1882), 291–92. We cite here from Pierre Duhem, *To Save the Phenomena: An Essay on the Idea of Physical Theory from Plato to Galileo*, trans. Edmund Doland and Chaninah Maschler (Chicago: University of Chicago Press, 1969), 10. This question receives full treatment in *The Crisis of Religious Symbolism*.
[11] Koyré, 37–38.

objects moving within a conceptualized space-time. Rendering space geometrical entails the forfeiture of all qualitative distinction. Galileo wrote, "for my own part, never having read the pedigrees and patents of nobility of shapes, I do not know which are more and which are less noble, nor do I know their rank in perfection. I believe that in a way all shapes are ancient and noble, or ignoble and imperfect, except insofar as for building walls a square shape is more perfect than a circular, and for wagon wheels, the circle is more perfect than the triangle."[12] A statement like this, completely unintelligible for the symbolist mind, demonstrates clearly that activity and technical utility *determine* qualitative differences within an otherwise-indistinct corporeal world, confirming what was said above. The world as the site of technical activity is the only ontological reference for the epistemological concept. This implies closure, however, rather than openness: the concept must be *complete* to serve as a means of action.[13] On the other hand, it must be *open* if it would be a means of knowledge.

We conclude with these words from Clavelin: "Eschewing a prior speculation no less than pure description, Galileo set himself the task of elaborating a conceptual system in which rational necessity took the place of physical causality... The reason, therefore, why no question was ever the same again as it had been before Galileo tackled it[14] lay largely in his redefinition of scientific intelligibility and in the means by which he achieved it... As we read his works, we are struck above all by the remarkable way in which he impressed the features of classical science upon a 2000-year-old picture of scientific rationality."[15]

We are not purporting here to have developed a theory of science. For one thing, the history of science is necessarily contingent, and for another, the epistemic closure of the concept is a descriptive rather than explanatory theory. Science does

---

[12] *Saggiatore* VI; cited by Clavelin, 212.
[13] Koyré dismisses the technical concern as a possible cause of the birth of science (12). In the ordinary sense of the word, he is certainly correct: it does not pre-exist the scientific method that caused it. Moreover, the Middle Ages saw extraordinary technical progress without the appearance of the scientific per se (Jean Gimpel, *The Medieval Machine: The Industrial Revolution of the Middle Ages* [New York, NY: Penguin, 1977]). But it is indisputable that the "technical" (mechanistic) concern is current and constitutes the scientific viewpoint as such.
[14] We would add, "in the field of science."
[15] Op. cit., 383.

not inevitably result from conceptual closure, which is found among the possibilities of any system of thought. This includes even philosophy when it degenerates into a system. Were this not so, the theory of science could itself create science, or else provide a recipe by which all thought could become scientific. This is obviously delusional. A body of knowledge has a scientific nature only when the right perspective is found, within which it becomes possible to perform conceptual closure. *The scientific*, not science: it is not even necessarily a matter of approaching exact knowledge, as the first step in approaching the scientific may yet include many errors and approximations. Galileo is again a good example: if he definitively bestowed a scientific nature on physics, his own results were often far from indisputable. And besides, humanity had exact knowledge long before science, as ancient astronomy demonstrates. All of this is well established.[16]

But we were granted to witness the birth of a new science, or more exactly, the entry of a new field of knowledge—linguistics—into the realm of Galilean scientificity, which likewise occurred through the epistemic closure of a previously open concept, language in this case. It has special interest because we are its contemporaries and so can observe the process and its effects.

Linguistic science obviously did not come into being with Saussure, neither in the West, nor (especially) in the East, as Hindu grammar had already reached a high degree of perfection by the time Panini's *Aṣṭādhyāyī* appeared in 500 BC, which likely summarizes much older works.[17] Knowledge not only of Sanskrit but also of Hindu grammar upended the study of language in the West at the end of the eighteenth century, giving birth to historical and comparative linguistics. Yet linguistics still did not have a closed concept of its object that would lead to the scientific. Indeed, the concept of language is open to the real inexhaustibility of an object that gives itself in the most diverse forms: divine revelation,

---

[16] Nor is it certain that Galilean science will not give way to another sort of intelligibility: such could be precisely the case with contemporary physics. It is striking that Einstein, for example, begins his presentation of Relativity by wondering about the *Truth* of concepts in physics (their relation to physical reality) and how much his "naively realist and physicalist" reasoning would surprise someone like Laplace. Cf. *Relativity: The Special and General Theory*, trans. Robert W. Lawson (Mineola, NY: Dover, 2001), 1–5.

[17] R.H. Robins, *A Short History of Linguistics* (London: Longman, 1967), 133–49.

creation of nature, work of history, expression of human nature, psychological mechanism, biological determinism, philological evolution, and so on. Saussure's genius was to have found the conditions of possibility for a science of linguistics, in which the laws governing language are conceived no longer as properties flowing from its mysterious depths, but purely positional relations deprived of substance. These conditions effected an epistemic closure of language through the closure of its concept, which now excludes any elements extraneous to itself. "The true and unique object of linguistics is language studied in and for itself."[18] Even if this famous definition that concludes the *Course in General Linguistics* is not Saussure's, it perfectly expresses the closure of the epistemic field of linguistics, a necessary condition for its scientific treatment. It merely formulates explicitly what had been established at the beginning, when Saussure distinguished speech from language and characterized the latter as a "self-contained whole."[19] There is no real difference between Galileo's epistemological "reduction" of body to the material point and Saussure's epistemological "reduction" of language and speech to a *system* of language. Criticizing this idea as exclusivist amounts to implying that there is no difference between philosophical and epistemic concepts, attributing to the Saussurean theory a "realism" which would exclude any other considerations in the philosophy of language, such as the role of society. Given its intention, however, it is not a theory *of language* at all, not really, since it affirms nothing in principle about its nature or metaphysical essence.[20]

Suffice it to reread the pages Saussure dedicates to the search for the *linguistic object* to recognize that, for him, the problem boils down to the following choice: either linguistics can include the whole of speech, in which case "the object of linguistics appears to us as a confused mass of heterogeneous and unrelated things." Or it can situate itself on "the ground of language" and so use it "as the norm of all other manifestations of speech,"[21] in which

---

[18] Ferdinand de Saussure, *Course in General Linguistics*, trans. Wade Baskin (New York, NY: Philosophical Library, 1959), 232.
[19] Ibid., 9.
[20] Indeed, the philosophical neutrality of epistemic concepts is more apparent than real—Saussurean linguistics gave birth to structuralism. And besides, one can legitimately reject one epistemic closure of the concept in the name of another.
[21] Ibid., 9.

case linguistics would have a specific object—language as a "system of signs that express ideas."[22] Thus "we can dispense with the other elements of speech; indeed, the science of language is possible only if the other elements are excluded."[23]

Obedient to this epistemic requirement, Saussure is led to a purely structural conception of language. Admittedly, though he speaks often of "system" and "mechanism,"[24] the term "structure" cannot be found in the *Course*. Yet it clearly expresses the understanding of the sign entailed by the Saussurean perspective, whose philosophical validity will be examined after formulating the general conclusions emerging from the foregoing.

Speculative Openness of the Philosophical Concept

The previous two examples are striking illustrations of the concept's epistemic closure, each corresponding to an inaugural event in the history of science: the birth of "the scientific," first in physics and later in linguistics. The following article will give further treatment to the latter in terms of the theory of the sign. But first to draw the major conclusion of the present analysis: the concept's epistemic closure presupposes its philosophical openness.

Obviously, there is no claim here to having discovered a sure way to found science. There is no discounting the role of genius for all who have managed to raise human knowledge to a truly scientific level.[25] In each case, a real speculative creation was necessary to find the means of *legitimate* epistemological closure for the object studied, pinning down and thereby narrowly defining it. Galileo's reduction of body to the material point and his geometricization of reality, along with Saussure's understanding of language as a system of differentiated units structuring speech, were discoveries of such means, delimiting the epistemic field within which physics and linguistics could subsequently develop as sciences. Such "means" in each case meant tearing oneself away from fascination with the givenness of the object and substituting a construct. Unquestionably, thought now has full possession of

---

[22] Ibid., 16.
[23] Ibid., 15.
[24] Ibid., 120 and *passim*.
[25] Yet Francis Bacon maintains differently: "For my way of discovering sciences goes far to level man's wit and leaves but little to individual excellence"; in *The New Organon and Related Writings*, ed. Fulton H. Anderson (Indianapolis/New York: The Bobbs-Merrill Company, 1960), 112.

the object, since understanding has become one with construction and therefore closure, yet it also renounces the most fundamental act of the intellect—openness to reality. The intellect exists in perfect expectation and hope for the real, submits itself to it primarily and inherently. Yet the epistemic act is initiated precisely by the inversion of this fundamental attitude, doing violence to the intellect's natural inclination, the spontaneous direction of its gaze. Reaching the scientific concept requires forsaking the source of its own life, the light arising from the object, thereby committing true speculative suicide. It is at least felt as such by all those who refuse this shift, perhaps failing to see what can be obtained from it. While not necessarily in bad faith, then, Aristotelian reactions to the Galilean theses express the jolt of awakening for an intellect that instinctively understands itself as an openness to reality and feels itself losing its footing in the face of the new physics. The conceptual construction of the very object we must study, which would seem rather to demand our humble attention, is a highly paradoxical task for human thought.

Such anti-Galilean reactions may provoke a condescending grin, yet many criticisms of Saussure are not so different. To fault him for separating language from society, history, economics, and psychology[26]—the real dimensions of language—is to ignore that he defines the linguistic object precisely by means of this separation, which is therefore not an omission but the very act by which this object comes into being. We may as well fault geometry for ignoring the thickness of its figures. It is well known that mathematical progress has been made possible by a seeming exclusion of any "realist" preoccupation: the Greeks had difficulty considering powers greater than the third degree because these lacked any geometrical correspondence.[27] If the first power corresponds to the line, the second to the surface, and the

---

[26] Lous-Jean Calvet gives an example: "Structuralism in linguistics therefore originated in a denial of what lies outside language, in a desire to abstract it from all social practices in which it manifests" (*Pour et contre Saussure* [Paris: Petite Bibliothèque Payot, 1975], 61).

[27] Descartes initiated this break with the intuitive realism of the Ancients, who confined themselves to "the theory of functions in the three dimensions of Euclidean space and prohibited the strictly analytical study of curves" (Jules Vuillemin, *Mathématiques et métaphysique chez Descartes* [Paris: Presses Universitaires de France, 1961], 92; cf. Descartes, *Rules for the Direction of the Natural Intelligence*, XVI).

third to volume, the fourth corresponds to nothing and therefore has no (realist) meaning. Its meaning is entirely operational: it is identified with the very act by which the mathematical object (a^4) is produced. This clearly illustrates the epistemic closure of the concept of mathematical being, and how, by becoming purely operational, it closes upon itself and so is reduced to its own constructions. But is "operational" meaning truly *meaning*? Does not this imply a relation and openness to reality? Must we not agree with Russell that it is necessary in mathematics to know what we are speaking *about*?[28]

A *scientific* critique of structural linguistics therefore cannot base itself on the ground of linguistics *qua* science, which is the epistemic closure of the concept of language. It can dispute the concept itself, seek to show its insufficiency, incompleteness, irrelevance, ineffectiveness, or internal contradiction, but it will necessarily be just as closed, isolated, and confined. If not, it would be not a scientific but a *philosophical* critique, which presupposes that the scientific perspective falls potentially under that of philosophy. We explicitly affirm this, as well as its necessary foundation: that there is philosophical knowledge. Yet this is not a belief shared by many other critics of structural linguistics. Quite the opposite: it is now assumed that science is the only form of true knowledge, and that the role of philosophy is merely to note this and to describe the different scientific procedures as exactly as possible. This is indeed true of science properly speaking, and philosophy has nothing to say about particular sciences. That water can be analyzed as two units of hydrogen to one of oxygen, that language can be parsed into morphemes and phonemes—these are facts which one can only observe. But this is not true of *the scientific*. Science is mistress of its own domain only through the circle enclosing the epistemic field, and yet this circle, the foundation of scientific intelligibility, does not, and by definition cannot, itself have any scientific support. Science therefore cannot test its validity, only observe its potential fecundity. It is moreover only from

---

[28] This is to know the real objects designated by mathematical "symbols," in which case the (logical) relations depend on knowing those between objects. To liberate "symbolic" relations from this dependency in order for them to obey a purely logical necessity is to deprive the "symbolic" of all meaning (p and q, for example).

the philosophical perspective that the circle appears *as a circle*, that the epistemic closure appears *as closure*. For Galileo and (perhaps) Saussure, their respective conceptual constructions are purely and simply expressions of objective reality. It will take the entire crisis of modern physics (which is enormous and has no end in sight) to somehow loosen Galileo's mechanistic "lock," requiring physics to open itself again, forsaking its own closure — forsaking narrow and perfect definition and, therefore, exact knowledge of what its concept intends. This ignorance is not that of Russell's deliberate indeterminacy of mathematical objects, but is rather a philosophical ignorance of overdetermination, of openness to reality. If philosophical concepts are "perforated," transpierced by reality, this means that, from the side of conceiving thought, they contain the unconceived, the unthought, the "unintelligized" — a *beyond* of all present knowledge. The speculative field of the philosophical intelligence is therefore essentially and definitionally open. Philosophy is alone aware that all conceptual knowledge effects a certain speculative closure: vulgar thought simply ignores its own limits, while science consciously ignores them, confining itself to the epistemic circle delimiting the unique space of rigorous thought, or so it believes. Yet philosophy knows that this circle can only be traced within a much vaster speculative field: we can only limit the unlimited, can know the limits of the concept only in the awareness that something lies beyond it. This awareness is a *permanent condition* of our knowledge: the epistemic circle cannot be so perfectly traced as to completely exclude it, and the philosopher perceives this. In other words, philosophy does not consist in claiming unduly to surpass science, but rather exists wherever human thought becomes aware of its own finitude and yet decides to go beyond it by following its *own rigorous effort* despite — yet with and by means of — this very finitude.

Philosophy must therefore be understood as (metaphysically) primary, in that it defines the most general speculative field possible. The various sciences are often said to have been originally encompassed by philosophy, having now detached themselves from it and seemingly won their autonomy. But this story is entirely false. On the one hand, Plato and Aristotle distinguished clearly between philosophy and science. On the other, the sciences are not islands broken off from the philosophical continent: they are delineated *within* philosophy's general speculative terrain. The difference between pre- and post-Galilean science (the latter characterized by "the scientific") is that such boundaries between the various sciences traced within the general philosophical domain were, for the Ancients, not entirely settled. Particular sciences remained open to and governed by the general science of philosophy. By contrast, epistemic closure in post-Galilean science seeks to carve out its own completely self-contained intellectual space, yet this construction is permeable and obviously occurs only within the larger speculative field, that ordered whole called "philosophy," the principles of which still apply to all its parts. Despite its hopes, the scientific has created no new speculative field, no new intelligibility or "new rationalism," as Bachelard falsely believed. He described, perhaps, the (ideological) discourse of an ideal scientific project concerning itself, but not that of actual scientific practice. If the notions of substance and physical identity were only imaginative residues of a poorly psychoanalyzed rationality, the crisis of contemporary physics would have been resolved long ago.

Like it or not, human thought cannot avoid philosophical requirements any more than science can slip from under its authority. This will be established in what follows, not through attacking the positive conclusions of linguistics, which would be outside our competence, but rather by subjecting its epistemic principles to philosophical critique, particularly its concept of the linguistic sign. This has two aspects: first, assessing its potential logical coherence; and second, and above all, confronting its closed concept with the openness given by philosophical intuition and the demands it imposes upon us.

THE LINGUISTIC CONCEPT OF THE SIGN

Language is defined as a totality underlying every manifestation of speech, such that our discourse about it need not depart from the linguistic order and refer to anything "external" (psychological, social, physiological, physical). If language is simply a system of signs, then no extra-linguistic considerations need be brought to bear in accounting for signs themselves. These constraints of the rigorous Saussurean position seem problematic, and so are perhaps open to question.

The Sign is Primarily a Sign of the Sign

Indeed, this should be suspected from the outset. The sign is not like any other system or apparatus; it can only with difficulty be separated from its function, even by a provisional abstraction. It is challenging enough to do so in the biological or even physical orders, where this is made possible only by subscribing to a materialist fiction that inverts the world and views it "upside down," as Ruyer says. But within semiotics, it becomes truly paradoxical. One could possibly understand the ocular apparatus as the *instrument* of vision and thus endow it with its own (corporeal) consistency; its separate treatment would be justified insofar as the eye performs its function only in being physically what it is. But the sign is never just there in its own right—its *dasein* is always for another. It is an essentially relative being. Its structure *is* its function.

These two aspects can therefore be isolated only abstractly and provisionally. A sign without significance is not a semiotic apparatus lacking its function, but nothing at all. The sign is a sign through and through: it not only signifies something other, but signifies also the signifying function itself. In fact, the latter is primary. The sign is first recognized *as a sign* before it can signify anything, whereas the eye does not necessarily imply vision—some animals have eyes yet cannot see. The natural order often presents such a divorce of structure and function (essentially that of essence and existence) which could perhaps be seen as constituting the "external" reality of the world. The purpose of the sign is to create an order of reality in which this divorce is abolished *a priori*, where essence and existence are unified, even if it is clear *a posteriori* that the sign "symbolizes" rather than perfectly realizes that unity.

The Saussurean Sign

We turn now to Saussurean linguistics. It cannot be said to ignore function, yet it reduces this to an absolute minimum below which there is no longer any sign to speak of. This could be called the "requirement of recognition": a sign is meant to indicate, to make known, and the only condition it must fulfill to exercise this function is to be recognizable and identifiable. It must be distinct from every other sign. We are led to understand that the sign's meaning, its intelligibility, is *difference*. The sign is differential, but this property cannot exist on its own; it is relative to others, and particularly others for whom this difference would be relevant. These relevant relations of difference therefore bring signs together and make them what they are. Language is indeed a self-contained whole, a stable system of differentially related signs: "in language there are only differences *without positive terms*. Whether we take the signified or the signifier, language has neither ideas nor sounds that existed before the linguistic system, but only conceptual and phonetic differences that have issued from the system."[29]

It follows that the sign would have a "two-sided unity," signifier and signified, as inseparable as the front and back of a piece of paper. One cannot cut the front without also cutting the back, and neither can the signifier's "cut" in the phonetic field be isolated from that of the signified in the mental order.[30] Moreover, since the signifier is an entirely linguistic reality, the signified too is purely linguistic, being only the counterpart of the former. The signifier plays the critical role: it holds the scissors. And so signs are not linked to a particular meaning—meaning is only an effect, the *value* the sign receives within the system: "Instead of pre-existing ideas then, we find . . . *values* emanating from the system. When they are said to correspond to concepts, it is understood that the concepts are purely differential and defined not by their positive content but negatively by their relations with the other terms of the system . . . it is quite clear that initially the concept is nothing, that is only a value determined by its relations with other similar values, and that without them the signification would not exist."[31]

There are few examples of the epistemic closure of a concept in the history of science that are so clear. And epistemic closure entails the denial of ontological openness. There is a fear constantly conjured by Saussure and haunting every sentence of the *Course in General Linguistics*—the mortal sin of linguistics, the unforgivable crime—which is to understand language as a glossary, "a list of words, each corresponding to the thing that it names."[32] The concept of the sign seems naturally to imply a relation to reality, linking each sign to a *res*, but this must be either eliminated or

---

[29] Saussure, 120.
[30] Ibid., 113.
[31] Ibid., 117.
[32] Ibid., 97. It is doubtful that such a view has ever been held.

reduced to a bare minimum in favor of the horizontal relations between signs within the linguistic structure. Saussure very clearly demonstrates this by means of figurative diagrams: the "glossary" relation is represented by a vertical arrow linking name and thing, which is overlaid, whereas the structural relations forming the chain of signifiers are represented by horizontal arrows. Saussure then applies himself to reducing the vertical arrow until it can be identified with the horizontal line separating the "two sides" of the sign. "It seems impossible to liken the relations represented here by horizontal arrows to those represented above by vertical arrows."[33] Yet this is precisely what must be done to express "the linguistic fact in its essence and fullness."[34] One need only recognize the purely differential nature of the signified concepts: "Their most precise characteristic is in being what the others are not."[35]

Consequently, language cannot be understood to reflect concepts that would themselves reflect reality. "Language is not a copy of reality. This notion . . . is based on the naïve idea that the whole world is ordered, prior to its perception by man, into perfectly distinct categories of objects."[36] In fact, however, the structure of language lends order to the undifferentiated mass which is the world.

Refutation and Rejection of the Structural Concept of the Sign

To question the descriptions of linguists would be outside our competence, and that is not our intention. Among the greatest of these — Saussure, Benveniste, Martinet, and Mounin, to cite only those writing in French — it must be emphasized that linguistics is based on an extensive and meticulous collection of the *data* of language prior to its becoming a system. (A trivial observation, but worth keeping in mind: one could otherwise get the strong impression that linguistics no longer studies *speech* at all, only *language*.) But this ceases to be the case once linguists set out to define their analytical terminology. Here philosophy reasserts itself, since discourse at this level implies philosophical theses bearing on the present discussion.

---

[33] Ibid., 115.
[34] Ibid., 117.
[35] Ibid.
[36] André Martinet, *Elements of General Linguistics*, trans. Elisabeth Palmer (Chicago, IL: University of Chicago Press, 1964), 20.

The Sign According to Linguistics

Such is indeed the purpose of *general* linguistics, which is at bottom nothing other than a metalanguage concerning the science of language,[37] at least in its essentials, and as such cannot elude the constraints placed on any other metalanguage. Anglophone linguists are more aware than the French of this metalinguistic nature in their search to define the principal elements of linguistic science. We see this in G.L. Bursill-Hall, for example: in both his edition of Thomas of Erfurt's *Grammatica Speculativa* and in his general study of the medieval Modistae, he makes a point of exhibiting the "metalanguage" used, since this reveals "the structure of their descriptive system and also much of the system of thought which created it."[38]

The impossibility of constructing a metalanguage using terms other than those of the language concerned has long been known,[39] but with Gödel this intuitive knowledge became a principle, which we will formulate with Jean Ladrière as follows: "to demonstrate that a formal system is not contradictory, we must appeal to methods of proof which are foreign to the system and so, in a sense, more powerful."[40] In other words, a metalanguage cannot possibly be drawn entirely from the discourse it would describe, and in the case of linguistics, it follows that this metalanguage is necessarily metalinguistic and not intralinguistic. It cannot be the simple record of processes employed by language in its operation. The epistemological closure of the concept therefore finds its limit at the metalinguistic level.

Yet the Saussurean project violates this rule, attempting to define the sign on a purely linguistic basis, and it is praised for this by its partisans and by structuralists in general. Yet while

---

[37] "Metalanguage" is a language used to speak about another language. In the sentence, "Peter is a proper name," *Peter* pertains to the language and *proper name* to the metalanguage (to the grammar). Cf. Saussure, 98–100.

[38] *Speculative Grammars of the Middle Ages: The Doctrine of Partes Orationes of the Modistae* (The Hague/Paris: Mouton, 1971), 66. See also Thomas of Erfurt, *Grammatica Speculativa*, ed. & trans. G.L. Bursill-Hall (London: Longman, 1972).

[39] Plato, Aristotle, and St Thomas Aquinas have all taught that any science requires first principles which are not themselves demonstrable from within the science itself, but rather are self-evident: *principia non sunt demonstranda sed per se nota*. St Thomas Aquinas, *Commentary on the Posterior analytics of Aristotle*, trans. F.R. Larcher (Albany, NY: Magi Books, 1970), lib. 1, l. 5, nos. 6–7.

[40] This is the corollary of Gödel's theorem; cf. *Les limites de la formalization*, in *Logique et connaissance scientifique*, Encyclopédie de la Pleiade, 1967, 317.

purporting to remain at the level of linguistics, it is necessarily metalinguistic. It appears to rigorously define linguistic unity by "closing" the sign: it makes of it a two-sided whole composed of sign and signified, the one correlative to the other alone, both situated entirely within language. This comes at the price of a contradiction which goes unnoticed only by deliberate misrepresentation: in reality, the Saussurean definition of the sign does incorporate nonlinguistic elements, or it could have no degree of operational validity, yet this validity only obtains through a principle to which it can have no appeal. This principle is the *signifying function*, the property by which signs signify, are related to an extralinguistic object. It falls within the philosophy of language insofar as it relates the order of signs to that of things. Benveniste pointed out this sleight of hand: "It is clear that the argument is falsified by an unconscious and surreptitious recourse to a third term which was not included in the initial definition. This third term is the thing itself, the reality. Even though Saussure said that the idea of 'sœur' [sister] is not connected to the signifier *s-ö-r*, he was not thinking any the less of the *reality* of the notion."[41]

This is the most general formulation of the contradiction within the Saussurean perspective. Yet it is possible, and enlightening, to examine the more particular consequences entailed by this initial contradiction for the object of definition itself.

As we know, one of the major theses of the *Course* is the purely differential nature of the linguistic sign. Since the sign can no longer be defined by its relationship to the referent—which would lead to the false conception of language as glossary—it has no possible description other than its difference from all other signs within the same linguistic system. After the linguistic reduction, the necessity of difference is all that remains of the sign's signifying function. The sign is no more than a mark which, to be identifiable and so guarantee successful communication, has no purpose other than to not be other marks. Otherwise, it could not be identified, and communication would be impossible. The upshot, as Saussure says, is that "in language there are only differences."[42] This principle of functional differentiation is thus the only criteria allowing identification of a sign. In other words,

---

[41] *Problems in General Linguistics*, trans. Mary Elizabeth Meek (Miami, FL: University of Miami Press), 44.
[42] Saussure, 120.

when the linguist analyzes language by decomposing it into its constituent units, this is the sole principle applied. With signs no longer defined by their relation to a referent, as we have observed, there remain only the lateral relations structurally distinguishing one from another within the linguistic system.

Applying the principle of differentiation leads to the definition of two types of linguistic units: significant (morphemes, monemes) and non-significant (phonemes). Martinet pointed out this double articulation, which reveals the essential characteristic of human language.[43] As Mounin said, "Whether we consider road signs, maritime flags, all the old or modern insignia, the international symbols of the Michelin Guide, and so on, we always find that the minimum stable units constituting the message in these systems of communication are significant units . . . endowed with form and semantic content, which are therefore units of primary articulation. These are never (as in language) decomposable into smaller units forming a system of their own."[44]

It is quite strange to find that no one has, to our knowledge, ever wondered how it could be possible to obtain two levels of

---

[43] André Martinet, *Langue et Fonction* (Paris: Denoël, 1969), 35–43; Georges Mounin, *Clefs pour la linguistique* (Paris: Seghers, 1968), 45–60. Let us briefly recall the nature of this double articulation: as Martinet writes, "Monemes are the smallest units of discourse that have meaning" (38). It is not always the word—as the segment *-ons* in *dé-barqu-ons* signifies the first-person plural—it is the *mark*. This word therefore has three morphemes (or monemes). But the principle of differentiation allows us to push the analysis further and identify other segments that, like monemes, are articulated between them: phonetic marks, or phonemes. Phonemes are not sounds, as one may think, but relevant phonetic traits within the phonetic system specific to a language: for example, the phoneme *r* in French can correspond to many different *sounds* (rolled, guttural, and so on), but these are nonetheless designated by the same sign in the language itself. It is therefore a *linguistic* reality. However, the difficulty comes in identifying these units. Any substitutable segment qualifies: *-ons* is a unit because it can be substituted by *-ez* or *-ent*. The speaker identifies *-ons* as a mark of the first person plural because he is unconsciously comparing it with all the units in the French language that could be substituted for it and from which he differentiates it. The axis of these differentiations is called "paradigmatic." Yet there are other substitutable units that are larger than the word: for example, "father" in "here is my father," for which one could substitute "great aunt." It could even be an entire sentence. Conversely for phonemic analysis: should "ice" by decomposed into two (*aï-ss*) or three (*a-i-ss*) phonemes?

[44] Mounin, 59. Prieto, however, tried to find the double articulation in certain codes: cf. *Messages et signaux* (Paris: Presses Universitaires de France, 1966), 101ff.

articulation so different from each other *starting from one and the same principle*. There is an obvious contradiction here. In no way are we contesting the (linguistic) existence of this double articulation, which, despite some divergences among specialists, seems to correspond to an observable fact.[45] But the claim that one could *define significant linguistic units starting solely from a principal of definition allowing us also to objectively define non-significant units*—this must be formally rejected. One or the other: on the one hand, it could be that the founding principle of linguistics (that language is a system of communication, entailing the purely differential nature of the message's constituents) leads to the true definition of the sign as a two-sided unity. Yet why then do phonemes not display this two-sidedness? On the other, it could really lead to defining the constitutive units of the linguistic system as purely differential, as phonology clearly confirms, but then there would be no explanation for the existence of units which have significance. There is no doubt that the latter horn of this dilemma represents the truth of structuralism: it fails to define the linguistic *sign*, defining only *marks* or signals, some of which are significant and some not, being entirely unable to account for the former.

There is therefore no true definition of the sign in Saussure. It is doubtless possible to admit that in a fully constituted signifying system, the signified indeed appears among linguistic *data* as a pure correlate of, and relating only to, the signifier. But the (linguistic) sign is not being defined here, only linguistic units, "morphemes" and "monemes." We know that these signify, given that they are located and identified within a signifying system, but this is a property in which they *participate*—they cannot account for it. From the linguistic point of view, it can be more *expedient* to consider the signifieds *sister, tree,* or *ox* as pure correlates of the signifiers "sister," "tree," or "ox," so as to eliminate all sorts of problems, but we could not then claim to have given to semiotics a satisfactory definition of the sign. Again, perhaps this is unimportant from the perspective of the science of linguistics. After all, the Galilean reduction of a body to a material point through its identification with the center of gravity has as little "reality" as Saussure's reduction of the sign. It is a major element in modern science: what matters in a basic definition is not that it be true,

---

[45] With the reservation that phonetic units should be regarded as not "originally" meaningless.

but that it work — in this case, that it allow for linguistic analysis. It hardly matters whether such a reduction is actually possible. But we must be careful not to transpose a concept developed in view of a particular application beyond its field of validity: no doctor thinks of their patient's body as a material point. Yet this is what the structuralist of any stripe intends, having in a half-century founded all their constructions on the dichotomy of signifier and signified, as if they could not escape from the enchantment in which Saussure has imprisoned semiotic thought. It is also rather strange to find ourselves reintroducing, by a consequence paradoxical only in appearance, the glossary paradigm and "thingism" which were originally cast aside as the original sin of linguistics. Granted, the relation uniting words and things has been broken, but now words themselves have become things: signifiers and signifieds are now beings entering into relation with one another, which do things — powerful enough to order the world — and which become, by an epistemological construction, true *objects* of study and observation. It is doubtful that we have profited by this exchange.

The Function of Communication

Our critique of the Saussurean sign would be incomplete if we did not at last consider what secures it and serves as its real foundation, that is, the function of communication defining the essence of language. If the function of language were to speak the world, we could not take account of it without including the order of things and our knowledge of it. Language, responsible for *expressing* this knowledge, would thereby find its direct explanatory principle. On the other hand, if language is only the instrument proper to realizing communication between a speaker and an addressee, it need only obey the rule of differentiation: the units composing the message must be distinct from one another, else the transmission of information is impossible. But the content of the message is of no importance. This is proved by digital technology and the problems of composing a language usable by computers: the messages transmitted may have meaning, but as Shannon and Weaver write, "the semantic aspects of communication are irrelevant to the engineering aspects."[46] This counterexample shows that it is unnecessary to take the meaning

---

[46] *The Mathematical Theory of Communication* (Urbana: University of Illinois Press, 1964), 8.

of language into account in its analysis as an instrument of communication.

It is surprising to note that this communicative function, which plays such an essential role, "appears only implicitly in the *Course in General Linguistics*,"[47] and is seemingly never examined in itself. And if this is the case, could a true analysis reveal its insufficiency in defining the essentials of the linguistic function? Communication is here only a *minimal convention,* as soon forgotten as mentioned, included only insofar as it is obligatory to any consideration of language.

In the name of the communicative function of language, some linguists have revolted against the structuralist's *a priori* formalism, positing instead a linguistic realism which, rather than opposing the Saussurean project on this point, would in fact complete it. Martinet's important work obviously comes to mind, particularly the space devoted to this question in his aptly titled *Langage et Fonction* [Language and Function]. However, Martinet does not actually distinguish between function and functioning: as he writes, "In a language, structure only manifests, as it were, as an aspect of functioning... Function is the criterion of linguistic reality."[48] But he explains as follows: "What is decisive in language is to achieve communication, and this is ensured if, at every point in the utterance, the chosen unit is kept distinct from those which could have been used in exactly the same context to transmit a different message."[49] We see that what is at stake is not communication per se but its success, that is to say, the conditions ensuring it, as Martinet has said repeatedly.

It could certainly be objected that linguistics does not have to concern itself with knowing what communication is in itself, or that there is no communication beyond the transmission of a message. This is also affirmed by certain specialists, implicitly or not, when elaborating a general model of communication.[50] However, such radical positivism is untenable insofar as the function of communication is responsible for ensuring the intelligibility

---

[47] Oswald Ducrot and Tzvetan Todorov, *Encyclopedic Dictionary of the Sciences of Language*, trans. Catherine Porter (Baltimore/London: The Johns Hopkins University Press, 1979), 15.
[48] Op. cit., 15.
[49] Ibid., 22.
[50] For example, Léo Apostel, *Épistemologie de la linguistique*, in *Logique et connaissance scientifique* (Paris: Encyclopédie de la Pléiade, 1967), 1058.

of linguistic phenomena. If it is not itself intelligible, or if its intelligibility is not considered in itself, it clearly explains nothing, and nothing is said by invoking it. We are therefore justified in concluding that the function of communication is the major blind spot of linguistic science.

Speaking is Not Communicating

Martinet's work, to which we have earlier alluded, bears in its subtitle a phrase that would summarize the essential thesis of modern linguistics: "Speaking is Communicating." We will show that this is not the case, and that the illusory character of this equivalence would not have gone unnoticed if, instead of considering the function of communication as a self-evident principle, it had been studied in its own right and taken for what it is: an obstacle to the signifying function, which epitomizes the conditions of possibility for speech. In taking this up, we rely in part on Ruyer's analysis,[51] to which we attach a particular importance because it concerns a major locus for philosophy.

When Mounin wondered if there were non-linguistic systems of communication functioning according to double articulation, he was considering only systems of signs: road signs, cartography, and the like. But if he had considered other systems with communicative functioning, particularly in biology, he would have realized that, on the one hand, such systems are incredibly numerous; and on the other, they do not involve the use of signs at all but rather what Ruyer calls "signal stimuli." And yet these really are communications, to such an extent that the use of cybernetic modeling and analysis of biological systems in terms of *information* has become quite common in the life sciences.[52] From the functioning of genetic code to amorous displays, biological processes are governed by feedback "systems" maintaining vital

---

[51] *L'animal, l'homme, la fonction symbolique* (Paris: Gallimard, 1964), 87–103. We prefer, however, to speak of "signifying function" rather than "symbolic function."

[52] François Meyer, "Épistemologie de la biologie," in *Logique et connaissance scientifique* (Paris: Nouvelle Revue Française), 804–5; Raymond Ruyer, *Cybernetics and the Origin of Information*, trans. Amélie Berger-Soraruff et al. (London/New York: Rowman & Littlefield, 2023), 73–80; Jack Baillet, "Homéostasie," in *Encyclopedia universalis*, s.v.; Theodosius Dobzhansky and Ernest Boesiger, *Essais sur l'évolution* (Paris: Masson et Cie, 1968) (concerning genetic homeostasis).

equilibrium and responding to information communicated in ways that are highly diverse and sometimes poorly understood: nerve impulses, inductive chemical substances, variations in pressure levels, etc. All confirm the principle of differential distinction that seems so fundamental in linguistics, and even illnesses could doubtless be described as disturbances in the transmission of information. There is therefore continuity between social and biological communication: "This signal-based pattern of behavior follows the natural course for that of all living organization, as embryological development and vegetal development take place through a chain of responses to interagency stimulus signals. There is no essential difference between the formation of an embryo and the constitution of a territory, of a domain, in the sense of Hédiger or Bourlière."[53]

But the same is true when considering certain manifestations that seem to use language, in higher animals and in man. The signal-response pair remains unchanged. Such "linguistic" behavior comes from the same explanatory model of communication. The dog reacts to the sound of its name, the Kellogg chimpanzees respond better to human words than small children[54]—and so long as the training is competent, we ourselves respond immediately and with the appropriate behavior to the fire alarm, to the ringing of the telephone, to words like *Stop!* or *Attention!* Conversely, higher mammals (and *a fortiori*, man) can use signals to provoke a response: a particular monkey can be taught to say "Daddy" to call its master, or to emit a defined articulation and obtain a banana.[55] All these communicative behaviors take place in a relation of need, demand, utility—yet none constitutes a true manifestation of language.

Nothing better illustrates this little-known fact than the story of Helen Keller, a little girl who was born deaf, blind, and mute, who nevertheless became a polyglot. All those who speak so complacently about animal language—who peremptorily assert that this dolphin or that chimpanzee has finally attained language and that the thing is now assured—should meditate carefully on the exceptional experience undergone by this disabled woman. This

---

[53] Ruyer, *L'animal*, 93.
[54] W. N. Kellogg and L. A. Kellogg, *The Ape and the Child* (New York/London: Whittlesey House, 1933), 289.
[55] Ruyer, 94.

is crucial evidence indeed, inasmuch as she was able to recount her own discovery of language, whereas for most of us, this event is buried in the most secret layers of our memory. It is precisely here, following Ruyer, that we will ground our doctrine of the linguistic sign.

Sharing in the error of many theorists of language, who consider only its functioning, Helen Keller's teacher, Ann Sullivan, endeavored to teach her student to communicate using signs — then confused with signals — by tapping in specific ways in the child's palm. She wanted thereby to associate the perception of a signal with the sensation of an object. For example, she placed Helen's right hand under a stream of cool water while tapping the given signal on the other. In this unwittingly behaviorist technique, the sign is conceived as the index of its referent, which it would evoke as its essential function. We prove that we understand a sign if we can use this index to designate the referent when necessary. Any being capable of such behavior could be said to know how to "speak." However, Ann Sullivan encountered the surprising difficulty that the six-year-old Helen, though able to communicate some of her needs using the signals given by her teacher, seemed nevertheless to be floundering on the threshold of a world she could not enter. All the elements of communication were present: transmitter, receiver, medium of transmission, code. What's more, the system worked. Yet little Helen still did not know how to *speak*.

The miracle happened on April 5, 1887. Ann Sullivan tirelessly tried to spell the word "cup" in Helen's hand, then gave her one to hold. "Then she would pour a little water into the cup, dip Helen's fingers into it, and wait hopefully for Helen to spell back, W-A-T-E-R."[56] In vain. Having gone down to the garden to distract the child, she led them toward a well from which the gardener was drawing water. One last time, she put the cup in her hand, poured a little water into it, and spelled "water" in the other, more and more quickly, this water that Helen enjoyed flowing over her hand. Suddenly, the child dropped the cup and, petrified, allowed a thought to invade and illuminate her mind: w-a-t-e-r! w-a-t-e-r! This wonderfully fresh thing, this friend, it was w-a-t-e-r![57] She had just understood that everything has a

---

[56] Lorena A. Hickok, *The Story of Helen Keller* (New York: Tempo Books, 1964), 40.
[57] Ibid., 42.

name, that everything can be spoken or signified, that the sign announces the thing, even *expresses* it: the relation between the thing and its index is not that of an *association* between two sense perceptions (the perception of this "wonderful something" and that of w-a-t-e-r) but rather one of *representation*, such that the sign w-a-t-e-r is identified with the wonderful something while remaining distinct from it. It "stands for" the thing. In such a relationship of signification, the two elements placed in relation are no longer of the same order. They are both clearly perceived as two equally sensible realities, and so from this perspective are indistinguishable. However, in the relationship of signification, the sensible presence of one ceases to refer to itself, ceases to signify its own (as if obscured) existence, and finds itself referring to the existence of something other, standing for it. This is the fundamental experience of signification. The two sensible elements are no longer united by a horizontal relation of juxtaposition but by one that is vertical and purely intellectual, one of placeholding. Such a relation is simply not materially achievable; it cannot be compared to any material sequence of sounds or the elements of any code. Observers can study all the perceptible elements of the process of communication as long as they want—they will never be able to identify the property constituting them as signs, for this property is radically and necessarily *invisible*: nothing sensible, nothing physical distinguishes the order of signs absolutely from all other sensible forms in our experience. Even if such a mark existed, it would still be necessary to know that it itself has the value of a "sign of signs," and we would thus be drawn into an indefinite *regressus*.

This is exactly the error committed by the behaviorists, who see in all psychic life only the pattern of the reflex arc formed by the stimulus-response pair to which they would reduce any purely communicative process: this signal, that response, and communication is assured. But this is precisely why Helen Keller could not begin to understand language, though her teacher had already taught her twenty-one words by associating signal and response. Entirely absorbed by the communicative process and the reception of sensible signals, her consciousness lacked the broader perspective necessary to grasp the invisible, purely mental dimension, through which these signals could become signs. As Ruyer explains, "the illumination took place, not when she associated a signal and a result, but when *she associated a name and a being*—water, the "wonderful something" — *in its expressiveness or timeless meaning*, in a state of mind not without analogy with that of a poet or nature lover when he wants to write a poem about water." But this requires that "the signal function not block the symbolic function." For her, the defining moment in the understanding of the sign was that "w-a-t-e-r was not necessarily a sign that water was wanted or expected, but 'was the name of this substance, by which it could be mentioned, conceived, remembered.'[58] So long as Helen Keller was being obstinately conditioned with a *word*, she was in fact being prevented from understanding *language*. She had to be suddenly struck with the discovery that the word had a signification, and further that all things had a name, and that all names had a signification."[59]

We could only find this original experience of signification by starting from what could be called the "zero degree" of significance. This is because, for one who lives and moves within its world, this relation of signification becomes so natural and essential to the mental life that it goes completely unnoticed. When we would make it the object of the scholastic "secondary intention,"[60] it seems to be presupposed: it is itself the basis of any intellectual act, lacking the background against which it could take shape in the mind's eye. It is therefore only in terms of non-significance that the relation of signification can be seen in its truth, as the transformation—invisible, lacking any identifiable material mark—of signal into sign.

To summarize: there is true language whenever the sign "is understood no longer as announcing or indicating a nearby object or situation, but as capable of being used *to conceive of the object even in its absence*... The word indicates or requests [the object it designates]; but on the other hand, it also evokes the *idea* [of this object]. It fixes the idea, is an instrument of thought and not only of immediate action."[61] In fine, there is language, not when a being expresses or communicates a need, a request, pain,

---

[58] Suzanne Langer, *Philosophy in a New Key: A Study in the Symbolism of Reason, Rite, and Art* (New York: New American Library, 1954), 51.
[59] Ruyer, 98.
[60] The first intention is the act by which the mind *tends toward* the object it grasps; the second intention is the act by which it knows the first intention by turning back upon it.
[61] Ruyer, 94.

pleasure, refusal; but rather when it speaks *about* something, when it uses the sign as the sensible representation of the thought of a being. This conclusion will obviously seem banal, but it had to be recovered in the face of contemporary semiotics.

* * *

We have just discovered a truly philosophical concept of the sign, which renounces epistemic closure, renounces being able to completely define it, but thereby opens it to the reality of semiotic *being*. What is it? From the philosophical perspective, which is to say from the perspective of a knowledge fundamentally open to the being of what it thinks, what are the constitutive elements of the sign emerging from the foregoing analysis? Does such a concept correspond to other definitions in the history of thought? And what is its relation to the definition of the symbol? Does this provide a model on which we can rely in its construction? Or, on the contrary, should they be carefully distinguished? Such questions demand answers. No doubt, scientific linguistics sometimes poses these questions, or rather happens to encounter them. But it cannot solve them. We cannot win on all fronts. With the epistemic closure of the concept of language, linguistics has indeed created a scientific object susceptible to a closed and perfectly measurable definition, but at the same time, linguists are seen condemning the aporetic nature of everything that refers to what is "outside" of language, which their definition denies. But is language not a quintessential "crossing point," where what is within exists only to be exchanged for its own beyond? What fowler would take words for themselves alone and so clip their wings? "Honor of men, holy language!" Only the philosopher has ears for the "language of the birds."

CHAPTER V
The Sign According to Philosophy

THE SEMIOTIC FIELD

Semantic Extraction and the Discovery of Meaning

HOW IS THE SEMIOTIC FIELD OPENED? How is signification achieved?[1]

If we refer to the paradigmatic experience of Helen Keller, we notice the following: access to signification is governed by awareness of a rupture in the sensible order. A sensory event, which as such cannot be distinguished from the sequence of all other events of which we can become conscious, is suddenly lifted out from this sequence by an invisible, utterly non-sensible extraction and converted into a sign, a sensible entity standing for something else. While the sensible is perceived directly as a being manifesting its presence ("giving itself to be seen") through its action on the senses, the linguistic sign is primarily a sensible entity making known something other than itself. This is perhaps the minimal observation provided by the experience of signification when described from the most external perspective.

We cannot remain here, however, insofar as this extraction is invisible to the senses, unless we fall back into the pattern of communication, within which speech is *never* encountered. We should consider how this extraction by the invisible, this wresting of a sensible entity from its natural order, is possible. Again, we can learn from the experience of Helen Keller. What the child discovered in a single act is that the signifying entity is the place where a signifying intention, a "meaning," and a signified object are joined together inseparably yet distinctly. She intuitively grasped that w-a-t-e-r is not a sensory sequence associated with the perception of water, but is rather the sensible

---

[1] *Semiology* is the general science of signs: linguistic, symbolic, pictorial, musical, social, etc. *Significance:* meaning seen as a general property of signs. *Semiotics:* what concerns the signifier as such. *Semantics:* what concerns meaning, in particular (the meaning of a sign) or in general.

expression of a signifying intention, which has a mental or non-sensory nature, and which *concerns the "wonderfully fresh thing."* Ruyer observes this quite well when he speaks of the association, not between a signal and a result, but between a sign and a *being*, grasped in its "expressiveness or its timeless meaning"—literally, its essence. It could not be otherwise: if everything has a name, if everything can be named, if everything can be spoken, this is because there is something to be said about everything. It is not enough to speak here of the signifying intention, especially if reduced to a psychological act. It must be asked, under what primary condition is a signifying intention possible? When there is something to signify. The designative or denotative function does not necessarily require the use of language: a dog knows perfectly well how to indicate what it wants, so long as it is near, just as when a child or an adult points a finger. The situation in which Helen Keller found herself was in this respect a sort of privilege, perhaps, in allowing her to understand the nature of the sign, for, in her case, everything was sensibly absent, or nearly so. Designation, then, had by necessity to give way to signification.

What now of "something to signify"? What does this indicate, if not a meaning to be expressed? There would never be anything to say if reality were not already "meaning," "intelligible speech" for us, if it did not "say something" to us, if the awareness we have of a thing's existence were not at the same time and intrinsically the awareness of a meaning, an essence, a "truth" in the thing. But it is not enough to speak of meaning: this meaning must be spoken, that is, we must (intellectually) perceive it as a silent word demanding to be revealed, calling for its own manifestation.

These are the conditions of any signifying intention. We therefore propose to define as *semantic extraction* the operation by which a sensible entity is captured by a signifying intention. This semantic extraction converts signal into sign and introduces it into the sphere of signification. This principle is secure: there would be no speech if there were not a "meaning," a desire to express something within the world to another. From this point of view, all speech is an act, however assertive or indicative it may be, and it is a semantic act, the communication of a meaning. We can summarize this in the following proposition: *to speak is to say something about something to someone* (including oneself).

We thus have a solid foundation for constructing a complete theory of the sign. Only certain consequences will be developed — the most important, we think — and will be restricted to those concerning the primary purpose of our reflection: the symbolic sign. An exhaustive explication would lead to an entire philosophy of language. However, before constructing this theory, we can already reap from our teaching its most important philosophical lesson, which we will have the opportunity to mention many times, and which concerns human existence in the broadest sense.

The semiotic experience lived by Helen Keller did not originate only in relation to the discovery of signification and a theory of the sign, but also in the correlative discovery of the objective world and of the mental world. By understanding what a sign is, Helen did not only learn to speak; this awareness was born at the same time and in conjunction with that of the external *and* the internal world. As soon as semantic extraction invisibly captures some sensible entity, it cuts the tissue of non-signifying reality in two, setting out the beings of the world in their objectivity and revealing to consciousness, under the form of the invisible activity of thought, the existence of its own reality. Insofar as thought thinks the world's meaning, the semiotic experience reveals also a third dimension of reality: an intelligible, semantic universe, in which external and internal worlds would find their original unity, just as they found in the sign their *discrimen* or realized separation. This is why the discovery of signification is accomplished in wonder and joy: reality suddenly unfolds and expands "infinitely" at the same time as it is ordered and differentiated into distinct worlds, intercommunicating through the mediation of the sign — just as, in the newborn's first cry, when the pulmonary alveoli unfold and swell in contact with the oxygen of the outside air, the arterial and veinous circulation are distinguished and ordered in relation to one another by the mediation of the heart. Significance truly introduces *play* or, if you prefer, *freedom* into reality, which is no longer a system of rigorously interlocked articulations governed by an implacable necessity. There is no longer just functioning; there is also signification, which opens the field of the "possible"[2] and prevents the world from closing in upon itself. Helen Keller's

---

[2] The possible is not only relative to human existence, but also and above all the world of archetypes and essences. It is because there are "eternal" possibilities that there can be temporal ones, a history, "things to be done" and not simply a functioning.

suffering, her irritation and anguish, was in the first place the protest of a suffocating freedom that found itself always "locked" in the chains of behavioral processes. But when the net of mechanical relations is suddenly torn by semantic capture, she suddenly finds herself free, master of the world and of herself, since she can name them both, setting them in their own objective order. If there is no world (as autonomous order of existents) for the animal, this is because there is no signification for it either. Man realizes his true mastery[3] only in this act of naming, not in an act of technical appropriation, which requires rather our submission to the nature of things. Thus Adam named the beings of the Earthly Paradise.

To the extent that the linguistic sign *per se* realizes a true speculative openness, it leads us necessarily to a renunciation of the Saussurean closure of the concept of language. And this allows once more for a refinement of our position. We are in no respect denying the right of science (in the modern sense) to perform the closure of the concept with which it deals. The idea of epistemological closure, we believe, shows as clearly as possible that this is in fact the preliminary condition of the scientific (again, in the modern sense). It is no different for linguistics. Indeed, Saussure's first act was to precisely distinguish language and speech and so to construct a proper and perfectly discrete object for linguistic science. Everything else that he says follows from this more or less by necessity, and if there are divergences among the experts, they are situated within this epistemological closure. We have nothing to say on this score, if only for lack of competence. But it is otherwise when it comes to philosophy, and we know that

---

[3] We would point out, without being able to dwell on it here, that the same correlation is made in Eastern tradition. The same process is encountered in all the degrees of reality, though obviously under different forms, from the Principle down to the human being: the manifestation of the "word" corresponds, on the one hand, to the appearance of reflective consciousness (or, at the principial level, of the supreme "I"); and on the other, to the cosmological production of different beings. This is the constant theme of this "theology of the word," or "theological linguistics," as André Padoux phrases it in his *Recherches sur la symbolique et l'énergie de la parole dans certains textes tantriques* (53). This correlation is found particularly on pages 12; 21 (the original christening, *namádheya*, is equivalent to "giving existence"); 50 (each *mantra*, or formula of invocation, being a phonetic aspect of the universal energy, corresponds to a level of consciousness, and therefore also to a level of the cosmic process); 69; 74 ("The birth of each phoneme is understood to result from a synthetic awareness [*parámarsha*] of Shiva"); 83, 126ff; etc. See below, 169–78.

the Saussurean definition of the sign has reigned nearly unchallenged over all contemporary semiotic thought. In what follows, we are therefore referring not to Saussure himself, but rather to the philosophical use of his ideas.

Unity of the Semiotic Field – Linguistic and Non-Linguistic Signs

The vast majority of linguists consider the linguistic sign to be the sign par excellence. They differ only in their identification of the source of this superiority. Some, of a more psychological tendency, see this as resulting from its widespread use by virtually all human beings. Others, to the contrary, attribute this use itself to a property of the linguistic sign, which must be specified in accounting for its supremacy. In that case, the semiotic field is found divided into at least two heterogeneous regions: one includes only language, and the other, all non-linguistic systems. Yet it is impossible to ground a general theory of the sign on the sole example of the linguistic sign. An examination of this thesis is therefore unavoidable.

We have already encountered a first attempted explanation of the semiotic primacy of language: the doctrine of double articulation (as phonemic and as morphemic unities) highlighted by André Martinet and which many specialists regard as specific to the linguistic sign. But we know that this analysis raises difficulties. On the one hand, the definition of morphemic and phonemic unities is not always simple, no more than their respective distinction. On the other hand, it considers the linguistic system only from the point of view of its functioning and attributes its universal use only to convenience. In other words, a non-linguistic system should involve more cumbersome and more numerous means. Finally, this is a superiority merely of degree rather than nature, the linguistic sign simply achieving more easily what other semiotic systems could themselves also manage. This statement would need serious nuancing: in the first place, because there are many cases where a brief sketch is more eloquent than a long discourse;[4] and second, because in the face of the extraordinary

---

[4] Not counting the messages that no linguistic code can transmit. For example, it is impossible to explain to someone ignorant of it and with whom we had no other contact than pulse codes (e.g., a telephone or radio transmitter) the signification given to the words "right" and "left." This very simple mathematical problem — which to a certain extent returns us

profusion of meaningful non-linguistic forms (customs, dress, hairstyles, gestures, dances, rites, forms of life, arts, and the like), the fecundity of language appears less impressive.

More convincing is the attribution of language's superiority to its "secondariness": the linguistic system's capacity for speaking about itself and therefore being its own metalanguage.

In *De Doctrina Christiana*—which, along with the first three chapters of Book IV of Origen's *On First Principles*, is one of the first hermeneutic treatises of the West—St Augustine remarks concerning the diversity of signs, "I have been able to express in words all the various kinds of sign that I have briefly mentioned, but in no way could I have expressed all my words in terms of signs."[5] This highlights the non-reciprocity between language and other semiotic systems and therefore specifies the linguistic sign as against all others. If it is true that this property of language divides the semiotic field into two heterogenous regions, it is worth investigating its origin, for which the double articulation theory obviously cannot account: what explains the superiority of language as the only semiotic system capable of referring to other systems?

On this point, we will consider the answer offered by the great linguist Émile Benveniste in his famous article, "The Semiotics of Language,"[6] which rests on the fundamental distinction between the semiotic and the semantic. Let us say at once that, even if Benveniste's brilliantly simple distinction has brought to light one of the fundamental aspects of language's functioning, less convincing are the consequences he draws from it concerning the semiotic

---

to Kant—should elicit, if not surprise, at least the interest of our linguists fond of the scientific. The case of two interlocutors invisible to one another, and with no real possibility of referring to common asymmetrical forms, puts us in an "ultra-Kellerian" situation. We should assess the "semantic capacity" of a language in view of this limit case, which the American mathematician Martin Gardner proposed to call this the "Ozma problem" (*The Ambidextrous Universe: Left, Right, and the Fall of Parity* [New York, Toronto: New American Library, 1969], 158–65). We see that language without reference cannot entirely speak about itself: it is impossible to indicate only by means of language what language calls right and left.

[5] II.vi.7; in *De Doctrina Christiana*, trans. R.P.H. Green (Oxford: Oxford University Press, 1996), 60–61.

[6] Trans. Genette Ashby and Adelaide Russo, *Semiotica*, supp. (1981), 5–23. Among contemporary linguists, Benveniste seems to us—along with Noam Chomsky, though from a different perspective—to have posed the most interesting philosophical questions.

The Sign According to Philosophy

superiority of language. For our part, we would first maintain that the metalinguistic capacity is not one of the essential characteristics of language but is rather only a particular aspect of its very general property of always *speaking about* something: language cannot not "speak about," cannot speak without introducing a distance and distinction between itself and its object. Language is therefore always indirect: it never says things directly—as a cry "says" suffering, or a smile joy—but only *speaks about* them. It establishes simultaneously what it is speaking about as its object and itself as a universal authority: it cannot function except as the semiotic system that "says something *about* something." Yet, and this is the second part of our argument, this "mediatory" or "designative" nature of language is not the effect of the structure of language *per se*, but rather that of the conceptual thought of which language is the instrument of expression, and therefore also of operation. The reflexivity of thought grounds language's mediatory role and so also its secondariness—the only question that arises is why language is so tightly linked to cognitive activity. We will attempt an answer, but first, we yield the floor to Benveniste, because no theory has distinguished so strongly between the linguistic and other systems or more seriously called into question the unity of the semiotic field.

He begins by proposing that, in principle, no sign system duplicates another system: this he terms *non-redundancy*. There are no synonyms between systems. What is said musically cannot be repeated in painting, in sculpture, or in speech. This is rigorously true: every system is unique, and there is no trans-semiotic system. Does it follow then that each system is completely closed upon itself and so has no relation to any other? Within a single culture, there are necessarily external relations between them; as for internal relations, they are all equally semiotic, given that every such system necessarily represents something. In this respect, language alone maintains a semiotic relation with all other systems and with itself, since it can designate them, refer to them, which they themselves cannot do. Every system therefore either interprets or is interpreted, and all systems are interpreted by language, which maintains with them a *relation of universal interpretance*.

Inquiring into the nature of the interpreted systems, we find that the very idea of the sign, the unit of signification, causes difficulty. In music, for example, there are indeed units—sounds—but these are deprived of signification: they are not signifying elements in themselves, whose meaning could be recognized and identified by a community of listeners, as are linguistic signs. There are therefore systems of signifying units, such as language, and others of non-signifying units, such as music. But there are also systems where the simple idea of "unit" becomes a source of debate, as in figurative arts such as painting, drawing, and sculpture. In any case, in none of these arts, including music, is meaning "inherent in the signs themselves," and so it "may never be reduced to a convention accepted by two partners." It results from the combination and arrangement of elements, is "imparted by the author to the composition,"[7] whereas language possesses meaning in and of itself, which is to say that it can indicate its own meaning and so is proven capable of revealing that of all other systems. It follows that language reveals the semiotic nature of other systems, the distinct and differentiated units that make them up, transforming them into signs by "*semiotic modeling.*"[8]

The question concerning the source of this property yet remains. It has been seen that language is different from other systems in being made up of signifying units, but this is not its only mode of signification. In fact, it "combines two distinct modes of signification," the semiotic and the semantic—such is Benveniste's fundamental distinction. The semiotic mode is that of the signifying element linked to the lexical code, *recognized* identically by everyone within a given language. But the "sign" is not the whole of language, and its importance in Saussurean linguistics represents an obstacle for thought, for there is also discourse, which arises from the semantic mode. For the latter, meaning is not the result of the successive identification of the signifying units it comprises, for it can elude us even when we know each of these units. It is therefore necessary to understand what we are speaking about (the soon to be broached question of reference) and what we are saying about it. The semantic mode cannot be *recognized* but must be *understood*.

Here is his conclusion: "Language is the only system whose meaning is articulated this way in two dimensions. The other systems have a unidimensional meaning: either semiotics (gestures of politeness, *mudrās*) without semantics; or semantics (artistic

---

[7] Ibid., 16.
[8] Ibid., 19.

expressions) without semiotics."⁹ Language has both, and this accounts for its metalinguistic capacity, its power of universal interpretance.¹⁰

We are therefore faced with a new double articulation theory, situated on a level different from that of Martinet: no longer of signifying and non-signifying units, but of the semiotic and the semantic orders, or rather of signifying units and discourse, or enunciation.

There is no question of challenging the existence of this double articulation—far from it. As Paul Ricœur has said, "The distinction between the semiotic and the semantic is of considerable philosophical importance": it effectively allows for the opening of the concept of language onto reality itself.¹¹ However, and without delving into a question concerning the very foundation of the entire linguistic field, it can be challenged on two points: first, it is not at all obvious that language alone functions according to the principle of double significance, appearing rather to be characteristic of all modes of expression to one degree or another; and second, it does not seem that the linguistic mode of signification is a property of language itself but derives instead from the signifying intention and so from cognitive activity.

On the first point, as we have seen, Benveniste's theory implies that every system except language functions either semiotically or semantically, never both at once. But why do these two modes exclude each other?

With respect to the purely semiotic mode, Benveniste cites the example of manners and of *mudrās*, the placement of fingers and hands in the sacred iconography and dance of Hinduism and Buddhism. These are certainly signifying units, and such signs are indeed recognized and identified within a given culture, and others can even respond in kind. And yet it seems impossible to consider them as having no semantics, as would be the case if their constituent elements bore meaning only within a *code*, meaning nothing but themselves, as with pure semiotic units.¹² But they also

---

[9] Ibid., 20.
[10] Ibid., 18.
[11] Émile Benveniste, *Problèmes de linguistique générale II* (Paris: Gallimard, 1980), 236.
[12] Benveniste clarifies the semiotic/semantic distinction in the following passage: "The semantics of a language can be transposed into that of another, *salva veritate* (the truth being preserved); such is the possibility of

express a signifying intention, are utilized as means of expression, and every signifying intention aims at an *intended*, to use Benveniste's terms. They say, "friendship," "the joy of meeting again," "mutual respect," "class community," or "initiatory recognition," and there is no need for language to signify this semantics.[13] In the case of *mudrās*, these symbolic gestures also designate *a fortiori* an intended reality, an often very specific and complex metaphysical or spiritual reality.[14] More generally, they express the compassion of the divine for the human, or anger and chastisement, or grace and adoration, supplication, prayer, concentration, detachment, and so on, according to a "discourse" mobilizing the entire iconographic work which is inseparable from the *mudrās*. They carry out the semantics of divine-human relations, of great religious truth. To ignore this is once again to reduce a huge part of the life of human societies to inexplicable semiotic processes, to a meaningless exchange of signifying elements.

Conversely, it is difficult to accept that artistic expression realizes a semantics deprived of signifying units. This is doubtless the way things seem, at least as a first approximation and with respect to classical art. In painting, for example, pictorial elements such as colors, forms, and organization, to the extent that they are identifiable, have signification not inherently but only by imposition, according to the will of the artist and depending on the general meaning of the work, on its signifying intention. The same is true in music and sculpture. Benveniste, however, mentions

---

translation. But the semiotics of one language cannot be transposed into that of another; such is the impossibility of translation. Here we touch on the difference between semiotics and semantics" (ibid., 228). For example, only in French is there the morpheme -*ons*, which signifies the first-person plural, and to want to translate this into German would obviously be nonsensical.

[13] This semantics can even attain a high degree of refinement: consider the etiquette of a royal court. The master of ceremonies who establishes this etiquette sets himself a problem not very different from that of the poet: one finds himself before his signifying elements (gestures, bodily postures, gaits, deferential movements, articles of clothing, etc.) just as the other finds himself before his words. In fact, and this perhaps justifies Benveniste's position, these signs of *politesse* act as *performative enunciations* (effecting what they express) and therefore function in a purely semiotic manner. But they are also enunciations and so are also part of "discourse."

[14] See in particular Lama Anagarika Govinda, *Foundations of Tibetan Mysticism* (New Delhi: B.I. Publications, 1960), 115–22. Here, however, language is necessary for understanding, yet it must be admitted that, in the last analysis, the *mudrās* rely on a natural symbolism.

The Sign According to Philosophy

the objection that there was a certain lexicality in medieval iconography: "Certainly, in medieval sculpture, a definite iconic repertory can be recognized, corresponding to given religious themes, to given moral or theological teachings. But these are conventional messages... In addition, the scenes depicted are the iconic transposition of stories or parables, reproducing an initial verbalization."[15] Such downplaying is very far from the truth.

Most historians of religious art emphasize, to the contrary, the striking semiotics of iconic elements. It is striking because, if at first they seemed to follow only a private semantics of the artist, they are progressively revealed to form a true grammar and vocabulary. Acceptance of this fact does not follow from examining dozens, or even hundreds, of cases, but when presented with thousands, it becomes irresistible. In the foreword to his study of *Le langage de l'image au Moyen Âge* [The Language of the Image in the Middle Ages], referring to the fruit of his experience, François Garnier writes, "Contact with a larger number of documents gradually gave rise to the conviction that this language exists, that the illuminators consciously or unconsciously use a common syntax to express themselves, and that this syntax is irreducible to the transmission of copies, models, the reproduction of stereotypes."[16] A similar conviction can be found among most experts,[17] and also, more importantly, among artists themselves whenever they have revealed the process of their art and we have had access to it.[18] It

---

[15] Benveniste, op. cit., 59.

[16] (Paris: Le Léopard d'Or, 1982), 10. The author explains, "The syntax is linked neither to defined morphological types, nor to determined subjects. The structures that make it up have a capacity for expression independent of the contents to which they are applied and to which they give a coherent significance." They are truly semiotic.

[17] Among others, we cite here Gérard de Champeaux and Dom Sébastian Sterckx, *Le monde des symboles* (Saint-Léger-Vauban, Yonne: Zodiaque, 1976); Olivier Beigbeder, *Lexique des symboles* (Saint-Léger-Vauban, Yonne: Zodiaque, 1979); Alphonse Kirchgassner, *La puissance des signes*, trans. Sr Pierre-Marie, OP (Paris: Mame, 1962); M. Madeleine Davy, *La symbolique romane* (Paris: Flammarion, 1964); Régine et Madeleine Pernoud and M.M. Davy, *Sources et clefs de l'art roman* (Paris: Berg International, 1973); Jean Hani, *The Symbolism of the Christian Temple*, trans. Robert Proctor (Kettering, OH: Angelico, 2016); *Divine Craftsmanship: Preliminaries to a Spirituality of Work*, trans. Robert Proctor (Kettering, OH: Angelico, 2016); Jean Canteins, *Phonèmes et Archétypes* (Paris: Maisonneuve Et Larose, 1972); *La Voie des Lettres* (Paris: Maisonneuve Et Larose, 1981); *Le Potier demiurge* (Paris: Maisonneuve Et Larose, 1986); *Les Baratteurs divins* (Paris: Maisonneuve Et Larose, 1987); etc.

[18] We are thinking in particular of the Compagnonnage.

would have seriously scandalized medieval stonemasons or painters to suggest that only the religious theme they were depicting, but not the figures themselves, had significance. To take this a step further: here we see the real difference between truly sacred art and post-Renaissance religious art. This point is not a minor one, for "religious" art is often only profane art on a religious theme: the idea is religious, but the manner in which it is treated, and the means employed, are often profane and at best reflect the religious sensibility of the artist. In the painting of an icon, on the other hand, everything is significant—from the wood and its preparation, to the colors, their nature, their disposition, to the style of clothing, the postures of the subjects, and so on.

What is true of the figurative arts is also true of sacred music, whether it be Gregorian chant or Eastern music, Hindu or Arabic. The extreme complexity of the elements and of their organization is always related to a definite signification, such that it is rigorously legitimate to speak here of a grammar and a vocabulary.[19] Furthermore, and above all in the sacred music of the East, it is unclear how it could be otherwise, since these are at once purely traditional and yet *improvised:* they therefore use sound elements, particularly modes and styles of interpretation, that have been absolutely fixed in their meaning by tradition, but do so in an "enunciation" that is new and unique every time. Comparing musical to articulated sounds according to Indian teaching, Alain Daniélou writes, "their meaning is more general, less particularized than that of articulated sounds and represent general laws of sonic expression, of which articulated language is a special application. In this sense, music is much like the language of the angels or that of the sages of old, closer to the Creative Principle, a luminous language of few words, where each sound has a fundamental meaning capable of multiple applications."[20]

---

[19] Cf. the work of Marina Scriabine, *Le langage musical* (Paris: Éditions de Minuit, 1963), which distinguishes three categories of elements: rhythm, melody, and polyphony. Refer also to the work of Norma McLeod and Charles Boilès in ethnomusicology, research proceeding not only from the signified to the signifier but also *from the signifier to the signified* (J.J. Nattiez, *Sémiologie musicale*, in *Organon*. Encyclopedia Universalis, 1977, 562). Also, Marc Loopuyt, "Aspects musicaux du Moyen-Atlas," *Études Traditionelles*, n. 481 (1983), 119–26.

[20] "La théorie métaphysique du Verbe et son application dans le langage et la musique," *Approches de l'Inde* (Paris: Cahiers du Sud, 1949), 164. The divine origin of music is affirmed by Hindu tradition: "The Lord drew

It therefore cannot be denied of any sacred art that it uses inherently significant elements (the semiotic mode) to express a general meaning, a "speech" about the divine world, nature, or man. This is much less evident in classical art, from the Renaissance to the beginning of the twentieth century. These four centuries witnessed a "de-semiotization" of aesthetic elements correlative to their progressive naturalization, to such a degree that these elements become to a certain extent enemies of the "idea," the semantics of the work. The artist had to "fight" *against* a rebellious sensible matter, force it to be expressive. This fundamentally angelist and anti-metaphysical understanding finds its limit "from below" in the non-figurative art of our era, where the semantism of the work disappears completely to allow for the free existence of the aesthetic elements, which thereby recover a sort of direct and basic semiotics: sounds, colors, forms are significant in themselves and also caught up as little as possible in the semantics of discourse.[21]

It seems impossible to maintain the principle of universal interpretance, or at least make it specific to linguistic signification: if there is indeed something universal in language, it is likely not its hermeneutic capacity.

We have already mentioned the limit case of impossible messages, information which absolutely cannot be transmitted by code of any type but which is yet not imprecise: a point is to the right or to the left of a given location, and information about this placement plays a considerable role in mathematics and physics (for example, the concept of counterclockwise rotation, or the deviation of light in crystallography). But there are other cases in fields which are nonscientific but no less important. Benveniste argues that iconography only "reproduces an initial verbalization." This is doubtless true and inevitable for anything related to Holy Scripture. However, this initial verbalization does not only depict, "illustrate" in the modern sense, but offers a theological and spiritual interpretation that is not adventitious or incidental but rather entirely essential and necessary.[22] In reality, there is

---

music from the *Samaveda*," cited by C.R. Shrinivasa Aiyangar, "Les aspects culturels de la musique et de la danse hindoues" (ibid., 263).

[21] These brief remarks condense a more ample reflection concerning art generally and its Western evolution.

[22] It can even add meanings not given explicitly by the scriptural text. Thus "the meal of bread and fish which Jesus gave to the seven disciples (an obvious

not *a single medieval image* that is only the figurative reproduction of a text: each offers us important keys to Christian hermeneutics, a typological "reading" of Scripture. It does so not only by relating, for example, Eve's birth from Adam's side to that of the Church from the opened side of the crucified Christ, or the Tower of Babel to Pentecost; but also through the colors of clothing, postures of subjects, their reciprocal positions, and so on. Are these images only the sensible translation of patristic commentaries? This may be true of many, but not all. Particularly concerning the sacramental and liturgical life, iconography often precedes text and even speech, and always has done, for in this domain there are things that can only be shown, not explained. The most incontestable example is the sacrificial liturgy of the Mass.[23] It is a "gestural" and formal commentary (quite surprising to those who limit themselves to the text alone) on New Testament narratives of the eucharistic institution. However, as shown in numerous historical studies,[24] the Last Supper on Maundy Thursday, taking place as part of the Jewish ritual of the Passover meal, is much closer to the (Tridentine[25]) Mass — with its own sacred language, its ceremonial, its benedictions, its hymns, the temple and its architecture — than a meal shared with family or friends. It is sufficient to study a little of the history of sacramental liturgy to realize that there are innumerable *gestural practices* that do not rely on any text (neither biblical nor patristic) but which are normative for the faith and the first Christian sources, since their antiquity and their universality attest to their apostolic

---

parallel to the feeding of the multitude upon the like fare) is treated in early Christian art as an alternative expression of the eucharistic idea; but the text of the gospel gives no hint of this" (C.H. Dodd, *The Interpretation of the Fourth Gospel* (Cambridge: Cambridge University Press, 1965), 431.

[23] But there are others. The baptismal liturgy, at least for the first four centuries, is known to us as much through iconography as through texts. And in any case, the two do not say exactly the same thing. Thus the majority of texts speak of baptism as an immersion (the *Didache* VII.1-3, however, already admits the possibility of infusion) while no representation of baptism between the first and fourth centuries depicts a complete immersion.

[24] Cf. in particular, Louis Bouyer, *Eucharist: Theology and Spirituality of the Eucharistic Prayer*, trans. Charles Underhill Quinn (Notre Dame, IN: University of Notre Dame Press, 1968), especially Chapter XI.

[25] This specification is required today because the liturgical revolution has made possible the celebration of Masses without *rituality*. As for liturgical "style," it is so degraded that even Fr Bouyer speaks of its "decomposed cadaver" (*Le métier de théologien* [Paris: Éditions France-Empire, 1979], 50).

character.²⁶ Think only of the Sign of the Cross! *Lex orandi* thus determines *lex credendi*. In many of these instances, gesture and depiction come first, the eventual verbalization second.²⁷ Yet it must be added that concerning Revelation, the verbalization itself is *never* an act of speech in the exclusively linguistic sense of the word but is *always* taken up in gesture and song, as Fr Jousse has shown irrefutably (calling this "rhythmo-melodism").²⁸ We are not speaking here of an adventitious accompaniment, but of a mode of synthetic communication indissociable from its elements, since it is a living *and* vivifying speech. Still more generally, a given sacred message is never communicated by means of a single mode of expression; there is no sacred painting as such, no sacred music, sacred architecture, sacred speech, sacred dance or theater. To consider an icon as an aesthetic work is both a perfect misinterpretation and a sacrilege. There is only the liturgy as a whole: it alone truly expresses the message. The non-redundancy of semiotic systems is only an aspect of their functional synergy: they have neither more nor less independence than our five senses.

Finally, we must also account for what Ruyer calls "expressiveness,"²⁹ opposing this to signification: the latter determines the meaning and object of discourse, while the former concerns what things "seem to be saying." Yet as Ruyer shows, this is a reality much more fundamental than signification, more basic and global, which we could identify as a radiance from the essence of things. This radiance, hardly expressible in speech, is experienced in the real presence of sensible forms, and while not discursive or conceptual, communicates to the mind a distinct knowledge, a clear *idea* of the essence from which it emanates. This is denied only by those who cannot think beyond concepts and language³⁰

---

²⁶ This is particularly clear in the rites of ordination (sacerdotal or episcopal), confession, penitence, extreme unction, etc.
²⁷ Christ Himself said, "Come and see." At the Transfiguration, the fount of all Christian iconography, He teaches directly by revelation of His glorious form, later teaching by exposition at the Crucifixion; the Buddha reduced a sermon to the showing of a rose; and so on.
²⁸ Cf. in particular, *L'anthropologie du geste* (Paris: Gallimard, 1974).
²⁹ "L'expressivité," in *Revue de Métaphysique et de Morale*, 1955, n. 1-2, 69-100.
³⁰ In a 1958 article entitled "Categories of Thought and Language" (*Problems in General Linguistics*, 55-64), Benveniste contends that intellectual categories are reducible to linguistic categories, and that apart from formulation, thought collapses, if not to nothing, at least to something so vague and undifferentiated that we have no way to apprehend it as a "content" distinct from the

and so remain ignorant of the obvious noetic potency of art in general, and above all of sacred art. Even beyond the semantics and symbolism of its semiotic elements, to the extent that we allow its sensible presence to shine forth within us, we perceive in a Byzantine icon a characteristic spiritual interiority, profound and hieratic, which is as if the secret of Orthodoxy. In the same way, through the freshness of the monodic *planus cantus*, its long, serene modulations and leaps, a Gregorian sequence reveals more to us about Latin contemplation than many treatises on spirituality. True, expressiveness is not absent from linguistic communication—it can be seen in style, tone, in poetic color—but this has nothing to do with the specifically linguistic mode of signification.

We can now return to this mode. The undisputed universality of language is not of a hermeneutic nature; it is essentially "mediatory," it designates or "de-marks." Language speaks about everything because it speaks *about:* it signifies by "de-marking." The act by which language speaks about something is also the act by which it is distinguished from that thing, placing it at a distance, and is therefore de-coupled from any whole it formed with it. In this resides its "universality." In other words, it is not based on the observation that language shows the unique capacity to express the meaning of all other semiotic systems, as our investigation has shown, but is rather part of its essence, making it to be what it is. To speak about one thing is potentially to speak about everything, since to speak is not to express but to "de-mark." And so, to "designate," in the sense intended here (say something *about* something) is to form into a distinct object whatever is thus "de-marked."

---

form given it by language. He takes as an example the Aristotelian doctrine of categories. Besides the fact that this argument is not new (it was commonplace in the nineteenth century), it is faced with the following objection: if non-formulated thought is reduced to nothing, we should have no way to perceive it. Furthermore, we could see the whole of philosophy as an investigation into the meaning of words, questioning the categories of language in the name of the categories of thought: this is the case with substance in Aristotle, which therefore is not reduced to the substantive (conversely, "whiteness" is a substantive but not a substance). Finally, if Benveniste were correct, language itself would be impossible. As for the absence of the verb "to be" in a language, this is no way entails the absence of ontology in the culture that speaks it: all human civilizations think the "real" in one way or another. To be precise, it must be understood that an *idea* or intelligible theme is no less rigorous than that of a formulated concept. It is of another order.

Herein lies the difference for us between language and other semiotic systems. All other systems are *translations*, expressions of something by direct modulation of its expressiveness. Dance, painting, music, sculpture, and the like, are invested with an expressiveness which they extend, manifest, and interpret by modulation, according to their proper modes of expression. They are expressiveness itself become dance, painting, music, or sculpture. As in a personality test, the artist can ask, 'if my love, my pain, my peace, my joy, or my contemplation were dance, painting, music, or sculpture, what sort of work would I create?' The idea of translation thus seems quite suitable here: just as one passes by this means from one language to another while preserving the meaning, in non-linguistic systems, the same theme passes from one expressive mode to another while preserving the same expressiveness. Aural, visual, tactile, gestural, rhythmic forms are indeed signs and not the thing itself, in the rigorous sense.[31] But they signify by virtue of the thematic presence inhabiting them, by the direct expressiveness of their qualitative contents in accordance with the proper nature of their respective "materials." On the other hand, language can signify by virtue of its "non-materiality," by its qualitative inexistence (or virtual inexistence) and by its non-inhabitation. Thus dis-existentiated, decoupled from any region of being, it acquires a sort of universality and can signify everything by designation, but this at the cost of a derealization relative to its objects and particularly to other semiotic systems.[32] What remains of music and painting in the discourse of criticism? This question bears not on the semiotics, obviously, but on the semantics proper to each of these modes of expression. It could indeed be said that the "Es ist vollbracht" from the *Saint John Passion* reaches the summit of music, expresses

---

[31] For example, the joy expressed can be that of the artist, that of a joyous person, or yet of a situation, an ambiance, a country, an event: this is the sign's referent. The musical work expressing the joy is necessarily distinct from it: this is the signifier. Finally, the music is not joy per se, but a certain mode of it, an interpretation, the artist's own understanding: this is the meaning. Here we see the three poles of the sign, to which we will soon turn.

[32] Poetry is a unique case in this respect, since its material is not different from "prose." It is thus the most difficult of the arts, issuing a challenge: to make the residual expressiveness of language prevail over its ordinary "mediateness." It cannot fully meet this challenge, but its beauty flowers at the very point of failure. Some languages (Hebrew, for example) have moreover maintained a strong expressiveness.

in a miraculous way the heartrending fullness of death, and its means of expressing this could be analyzed. But the intelligible evidence of this accomplishment is given only in and by the musical execution: the evidence is properly indescribable and yet charged with the purest and most vital meaning. This musical communication is truly something of the essence of Christ's death, of which it performs a sort of hermeneutic presentation, whereas language can only *make us think about it*.

With this last remark, we touch upon the specificity of the linguistic function: "to make one think" is to lead the addressee to reproduce the thought of the speaker. Language is then a mental operation, which means that it is the instrument used by thought in performing its actions (though implying no substantial identification between thought and language). The following question would then demand a response: why is language the proper instrument of the cognitive act?

The body is, naturally, the necessary medium for every process of expression and communication, since by this alone can human subjects perceive one another. What is interior, being invisible, is knowable only in its corporeal exteriorization, by a movement of the body. In this process of manifestation, all degrees are conceivable in accordance with the modes of exteriorization. Among these modes, simple corporeal modification must be distinguished from expressive gesture. The modification of the visible body is generally subtle (redness or pallor due to emotion) but can extend to immobilization, total paralysis of the body and fainting. It indeed makes perceptible the subject's state (fear, pleasure, excitation) but concerns the psycho-corporeal unity indistinctly. The body is not *used* as an expressive medium *by* the psyche, but participates directly and involuntarily in its life and is indissociable from it. The body does not exteriorize emotion, but is rather an integral and formative part of it. This is the minimal degree of manifestation. Expressive gesture is much more voluntary, even entirely so in the arts of mime, dance, theater, or simulation. In these ordinary cases, the voluntary extends and amplifies spontaneous movements: gestures of apprehension, frowning, laughing, postures, and so on. Here the body is truly an instrument of manifestation: it expresses sentiments and passions. It is properly used as a signifying medium relatively distinct from the interior states of the subject. Nevertheless, the relation uniting signified and signifier is that of expressiveness, which is always holistic. This is moreover why gesture *mobilizes* (or attempts to mobilize) the entire body, becoming a more or less disorderly gesticulation. To the violent "movement" of the soul in passion must respond the violent movement of the body. This is the maximal degree of manifestation. There is finally a third state for the subject—thought, the most interior, most voluntary, most foreign to corporeal activity. Being most interior, the process of exteriorization acquires here its full meaning, with the body most necessarily and distinctively playing its role as the medium of manifestation. But also, being most voluntary, most deliberative, most heterogeneous to the body, this act requires the fewest expressive gestures, the minimum of bodily movement, the least visible motion, realizing from within gesture a *rupture* with all corporeal expression, the gesture of non-gesture. Yet, the only invisible movement that the body can perform voluntarily is that of language in the mouth, and the only act the body can accomplish while remaining nearly motionless is speech.[33]

We thus rediscover, through a remarkable confluence, the principle that we identified in our study of signification—semantic extraction. Just as the sign is a sensible entity belonging to the sensible order while being found invisibly captured by the intelligible, so it is for speech. Whereas cries and gestures express directly and instinctively the lived state of the human being and naturally *extends* him, articulated speech breaks with gesture and is posed as essentially non-communicative, as one says of an emotion, foreign in its sensible form to what it signifies.

To speak is primarily to resist the spontaneous desire to cry out, then to substitute for natural expressiveness non-natural signs, which necessarily rely on an agreement between speaker and addressee, on a convention. The conventional, or rather institutional character of spoken language is therefore essential. Not that linguistic signs are completely unmotivated, which is far from the case, but with respect to the constitutive and formal intention of

---

[33] *Langue* [language] in this sense is therefore justly called *langue* [tongue]. True, in German and English, for example, these are two different words: *Sprache* or "language" for discourse; and *Zünge* and "tongue" for the organ. But in fact, *Zünge* and "tongue" are frequently employed for the language of a people, and similarly with *glossa* in Greek, *lashon* in Hebrew, and obviously, *lingua* in Latin.

language, it is as if disregarded. From this point of view, language is a permanent battle against the naturalness of vocal signifiers, a battle never won, because speech requires the use of vocal materials placed at our disposal by the body, and because there is no other way to be rid of natural expressiveness than not to speak: the perfect realization of the intention of language would be silence.[34]

The referent, the object which the signifier makes known and to which it relates, is the more distinguished from the signifier as the latter is more alien to it. In its manifest heterogeneity to the referent, the signifier acknowledges at once its own identity, that of the referent, and that of the meaning relating the two: as a work of lexical institution, meaning is in turn set up as a quasi-entity.

The articulation of the signifying function thereby appears clearly: it is the union of a sign and an object in a meaning. Non-linguistic signs would not have manifested this so clearly, insofar as their constituent elements are less differentiated. This explicit differentiation flows from the predominance in the linguistic sign of designation (referential intention). Other aspects of the structure predominate in other types of signs, either the meaning (for the symbol) or the signified (for the inductive sign). The distinctive characteristic of the linguistic sign is *saying something*

---

[34] Indeed, it is clear that phonemic units themselves already possess a certain natural signification, as recent research has shown (collected by Gérard Genette in *Mimologics*, trans. Thaïs E. Morgan [Lincoln: University of Nebraska Press, 1995], 309–36). As Fabre d'Olivet already observed, "If certain minds attacked by skepticism ask me why I restrict the idea of mother in this syllable aM or Ma, and how I am sure that it is applied effectively there, I shall reply to them that the sole proof that I can give them, in the material sphere which envelops them is, that in all the tongues of the world from that of the Chinese to that of the Caribs, the syllable aM or Ma is attached to the idea of mother, and aB, Ba, or aP, Pa, to that of father" (*The Hebraic Tongue Restored*, trans. Nayán Louise Redfield [New York/London: The Knickerbocker Press, 1921], 93). Similarly, the great linguist Roman Jakobson stated that "the autonomous iconic value of phonemic oppositions is damped down in purely cognitive messages but becomes particularly apparent in poetic language" ("Quest for the Essence of Language," in *Language in Literature* [Cambridge, MA: Harvard University Press, 1987], 424–25). Thus, by using phonemic elements in its constitution, the morphemic chain obscures their natural signification. All human languages could be seen as carting the debris of a universal language, the elements of which are present in each, however transformed. As they evolve, languages are to a certain extent at war with their phonetic substance (mathematical language being perfect but not spoken) at least until they attempt to rediscover the signification of phonemes under the guise of morphemes, poetry being one example.

about something, and this property makes possible not only deceitful speech but also all literature.

We are far from the Saussurean and post-Saussurean tendencies of certain linguists to distance the referent, as an "epistemological impurity," from the rigorous definition of the linguistic sign. Far from it: the linguistic sign is that which objectifies its object. This weight of things which words seem always to drag behind them even causes a sort of "linguistic fatigue," felt by the poet as by everyone in certain inexpressible moments: who has not dreamed of a language free at last, a truly winged speech? Alas, speech can never say nothing—*logos*, our transparent prison.

* * *

The unity of the semiotic field therefore cannot be called into question. And although the linguistic sign is distinguished from others *qua* specific instrument and privileged mode of expression for the cognitive (mental or discursive) act, it can serve as a model for the construction of the sign generally. Further, insofar as this arises from an analysis of the sign—necessarily considering the sign in terms of its constituent elements and structure more than its synthetic functioning—the linguistic sign is even the only model possible, since it offers us precisely the example of such an articulation of distinct elements. To this we now turn.

GENERAL DESCRIPTION OF THE SIGN

The Semantic Triangle

There is nothing original in the triadic conception of the sign arrived at in the preceding analysis. It has been expressed many times, and often (as in Ogden and Richards, on whom the following is based) in declared opposition to the dyadic conception of Saussure. The two models in fact split between them the support of contemporary semioticians and philosophers. We must therefore specify why the former alone appears *philosophically* admissible, even if it requires supplementation on an essential point. A brief review is here necessary.

In Saussure, as we have seen, the sign is defined as a "two-sided unity": signifier and signified.[35] It can be represented schematically in the following way:

---

[35] Saussure, 113.

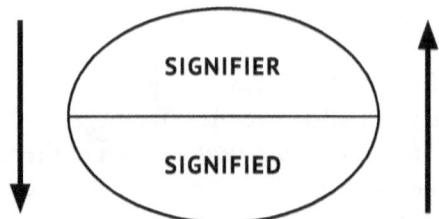

Such a definition is only valid within the closure of the concept of language. The object thus constructed is theoretical, not in the sense that it does not exist, but inasmuch as it exists only from the perspective of linguistic theory and is grasped only by abstraction.[36] Just as we see, not a rectangle, but the surface of a book or a table, we neither perceive the signifier nor conceive the signified *per se*, only sounds and meanings. In the eyes of his disciples, all criticism of Saussure appears to be only ignorance of the precision and rigor of this viewpoint.

However, it is wholly bound up with the distinction between language and speech, or rather the extraction of language from the field of speech within which alone it is given and functions. This is not to contest that a thorough analysis of language would indeed arrive eventually at Saussurean units, these "linguistic molecules," but it is no less true that the opposite course is completely impossible: the real process of language could not be reconstructed beginning from Saussurean molecules, no more than a biologist could reconstruct a being beginning from the macromolecules with which organic chemistry explains its genesis. This is a scientific fact. Though potentially valid within the linguistic system, the Saussurean definition cannot be established as an architectonic principle for human science or philosophy. Such boundless pretension should be strongly denounced.

The second definition of the sign, that of Ogden and Richards, is the work of philosophers and anthropologists who are interested in all forms of the sign (or symbol) and who have observed its real functioning. They therefore cannot accept the Saussurean definition and criticize it vehemently. Saussure is for them the

---

[36] The *Course in General Linguistics* understands signs to be "concrete entities," which is to say, "the signs that make up language are not abstractions but real objects" (102). Yet this terminology is philosophically unsatisfying: many realities, above all in science and metaphysics, can be grasped only by abstraction. They are no less real for that.

victim of his philological formation: the opposition between language and speech betrays an excessive regard for verbal distinctions, and above all, "this theory of signs, by neglecting entirely the things for which signs stand, was from the beginning cut off from any contact with scientific methods of verification."[37] For the Saussureans, by contrast, the referent intervenes only in the act of speech: men using signs can designate things, but signs themselves cannot.

The "semantic triangle" of Ogden and Richards is presented in the following (abbreviated) form:[38]

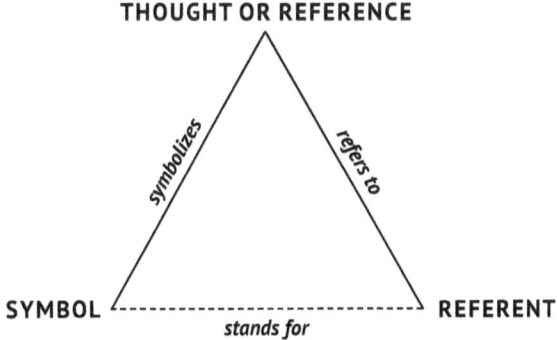

As shown, the "symbol" represents or "stands for" the referent only indirectly, by the mediation of thought, which understands the symbol and so refers to the denoted object.

However, eminent linguists, disciples of Saussure, argue that his definition of the sign is equally triadic,[39] and semanticists of great repute "seem" not to suspect that there could be a contradiction in invoking Saussure, Ogden, and Richards in a single breath. This is the case with Stephen Ullmann, who proposed a simplified diagram of the semantic triangle, reproduced here:[40]

---

[37] C.K. Ogden and I.A. Richards, *The Meaning of Meaning* (Orlando, FL: Harcourt Brace, 1989), 6.
[38] Ibid., 11. The word "symbol" here corresponds to what we call "sign."
[39] Mounin (135–36) attributes these divergent interpretations to the imprecision of Saussure's vocabulary, who had not time to bring the same degree of systematicity to every element of his general linguistics, which seems evident. Nevertheless, he always defines the sign as a two-sided unity, and his posterity (in linguistics as in philosophy) has generally understood this definition as the criterion of a truly scientific semiotics.
[40] Ullmann formulated his doctrine in multiple studies. The first, *The Principles of Semantics* (Glasgow: Jackson, Son, and Co, 1951) does not contain the diagram, but the vocabulary is already the same: *name* is substituted

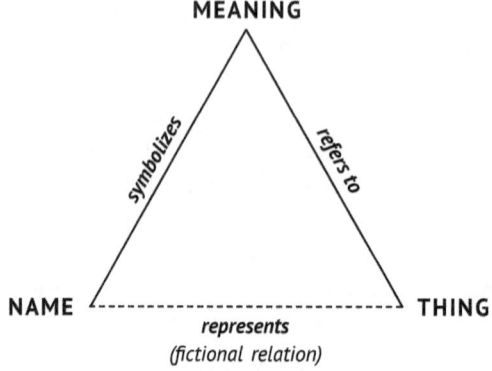

Ullmann explains that the sign has three aspects: first, "the sound system, the formal aspect of the word, as it remains in the state of an imprint inscribed in the consciousness of its users." This is the signifier. Second, "what the signifier calls to mind," for example, in the case of the word *table*, "a more or less schematic image or idea of the furniture." This is the signified. Third, "the non-linguistic element to which the signified corresponds in the consciousness of the speakers ... is the signified *thing*."[41] We nevertheless learn a few pages later that the *thing* must be discarded because it "is not a part of the internal structure of the word."[42]

After this very brief overview of the extreme divergence between conceptions and terminologies and of their tangled lineages, it would seem that the triadic schema is accepted by more or less everyone, because its general truth cannot be seriously challenged, but also (and precisely by virtue of its generality) because it can serve as the basis for very different, even opposed, theories. This is why it can be immediately adopted (the truth being no one's property) and modified or completed according to our own needs. Certainly, the semantic triangle seems to be situated at a less developed level of analysis than that of Saussurean semiotics.[43] But it is for this reason the primary and indispensable

---

for *symbol*, *meaning* for *thought* or *reference*, and *thing* for *referent*. The triangle we give is to be found in *Précis de sémantique française* (Paris: Éditions A. Francke S. A. Berne, 1952), 22.

[41] *Précis de sémantique française*, 20.
[42] Ibid., 23.
[43] But this is not always the case, as is proved by Peirce's triadic conception of the sign, which seems more developed than that of Saussure: cf. C. S. Peirce, *Écrits sur le signe* (Paris: Éditions du Seuil, 1978), particularly the commentary of Gerard Deledalle (the editor and translator), 215–30.

thematization of reality, upon which philosophical reflection can be based. Thus in adopting the semantic triangle, we are not adopting the "philosophy" of Ogden and Richards, which is the antithesis of metaphysics, no more than that of Ullmann, who, in grounding his own definition of the sign, has no hesitation in referring to the reflexology of Pavlov, a theory which enshrines the triumph of pseudo-scientific verbalism.[44] We subscribe to a nearly universal tradition, as will be shown, while yet striving to remain faithful to the semiotic experience as we have described it and to the definition we have taken from it: to speak is to say something about something to someone.

However, and this concludes the preliminary remarks, the debates raised above concerning the definition of the sign are not simply the result of differences in understanding, but also express a difficulty inherent in the object itself: what is the sign's intrinsic makeup? First, though, is the very concept of "sign" not misleading? In seeking to define *the* sign, are we not, as Benveniste criticized in Saussure, supposing that it exists as an object, an Aristotelian substance? What bad philosophical conscience is not pricked in identifying the sign as an "entity"?[45] Is it not the vaguest, most compromised of any term designating a "something"? But how to define this entity? What unifies these semiotic molecules, or even these atoms? A phoneme is a sign, yes; a morpheme, yes. But a word, a proposition, a sentence, a text, a poem, or even an entire book? Why not? And a painting, a symphony, a cathedral, a liturgy? Should we then abandon the concept, however natural? In other words, are there only signifying functions, acts of signification, but not specific structures? If so, then nothing is ever a sign in and of itself, but only usage makes it so. This consequence—which could, strictly speaking, apply to symbolic signs drawn from nature—comes up against the existence of linguistic signs, which are *per se* never encountered in nature and exist only as signs. This is why a consideration of

---

[44] Science is often ready to embrace the least intelligible explanations so long as they exclude the mental—this is called "freedom of thought." There would be much to say on this score concerning the psychology or biology that underlies a great deal of work in linguistics and semiotics. Associationist, behaviorist, and Pavlovian theories play the largest role, despite their having lost nearly all credibility among psychologists.

[45] As in Ducrot and Tudorov, *Encyclopedic Dictionary of the Sciences of Language*, 100.

the sign can find no other point of departure than the linguistic sign (in this respect the "sign of the sign") and, we would add, no other terminus than the symbolic sign. We do not hesitate to follow Plato, who ranked "speech" (*logos*) among the kinds of being;[46] or Meister Eckhart, who said that "what does not participate in being (*esse*) is neither being (*ens*) nor name," not even "word" (*verbum*).[47] At the same time, this "ontology of the sign" should be corrected by an insistence on the inherent inseparability of structure and function. The sign is not only not an instrument indifferent to use but also cannot be effectively isolated from it, no more than the human body from the psychic principle animating and in-forming it. It could not be otherwise. The sign necessarily participates in the nature of its object, in its *dasein*, since it cannot fulfill its function of "notification" if it were not "noticeable," if it were not exposed, identifiable, visible, offered in the passivity and inertia of its materiality to all eventual readers. But at the same time—and this is wholly essential to the sign, as we have argued—its *dasein* "stands for something," ceases to indicate itself alone, to be the appearance or manifestation of itself alone: the sensible being of the sign exists as an act of signification, as a signifying function. This is its hallmark: structure is identified with function, and yet function does not abolish structure.

The "triangular" analysis of the sign is possible, then, but should not neglect the functional nature of its elements, else it fall into innumerable difficulties, as shown only too well in contemporary semiotics. The abstractions of science are legitimate and fruitful on this condition alone; otherwise, they serve only to cause entirely artificial problems. The elements of the semiotic triangle are therefore not "things" needing only to be assembled to produce the sign: reduced to themselves and considered separately, they are no longer even *elements of* the sign. One must carefully guard against the illusion that pursuing analysis to its most basic elements allows us to possess the secret of the whole. Far from it. In themselves, these terms are nothing and explain nothing: this is true of the referent, of the meaning, even of the signifier. The referent in itself, the object "table" for example,

---

[46] *Sophist* 260a, trans. Nicholas P. White, in *Plato: Complete Works*, op cit., 282.
[47] *In Exodum*, n. 167; cited by Alain de Libera, *Le Problème de l'être chez Maître Eckhart—Logique et métaphysique de l'analogie* (Lausanne: Revue de théologie et de philosophie, 1980), 23.

indeed enjoys an objective existence, but bears no relation to the linguistic sign.[48] In itself, the meaning of this word exists under the form of a concept, but neither does this have any intrinsic relation to the sign. As for the signifier, and though this case is more difficult to judge, it could yet be plausibly maintained, at least provisionally, that *qua* pure phonetic sequence, it is only a physical reality without relation to the linguistic sign: hence the babbling of infants, vocal stereotypes in aphasics, or specially coined pseudo-words.

The conclusion emerging from the preceding considerations is that the terms of the semantic triangle define the sign only when considered within their unifying relations. In other words, the sides of the triangle matter as much, if not more, than the vertices, which exist only as results of intersection or as points of articulation.

However, as just implied, this is less true of the signifier. If it belongs to the world of objects, it is nevertheless a very special sort of object, wholly cultural, except of course for its necessarily physical (or quasi-physical) form, lacking which it would no longer be identifiable. And it is therefore with the signifier that we can begin our analysis.

Identification of the Signifier

We depart from the single point on which all semiotic theories agree: the existence of the *signifier*, designating the significant sensible form, which can be a "voice," as it was called in the Middle Ages — that is to say, a phonetic sequence — or any other sensible form. We start with the signifier because, as St Thomas Aquinas said, "the name sign is given primarily and principally to things which are offered to the senses."[49] The sign-signifier equivalence should not surprise us: it is to be found everywhere, not only in Saussure.[50] The medieval grammarian Thomas of Erfurt speaks of "the faculty of signifying... by means of which

---

[48] Whence the surprising attitude of Ullmann, who made this the third vertex of his triangle, then later discarded it as foreign to the sign.
[49] *S. Th.* III, q. 60, a. 4, ad. 1.
[50] In the same chapter where he explains the distinction between the signifier and the signified, Saussure speaks of the arbitrariness of the *sign* where we would expect him to speak of the arbitrariness of the *signifier*, and even writes: "the linguistic sign, or more specifically, what is here called the signifier" (68).

a sign or signifier is effected."[51] The reason for this equivalence is easy to see: to identify the sign is to grasp it as a delimited object, as a recognizable entity. And the element by which alone the sign is identifiable as an entity is evidently by its sensible form, its "body," as is said in printing. It is otherwise more a matter of relations than objects, as we have already observed. Yet this sensible form is only identified as a sign inasmuch as it is significant and not, of course, by itself. Signification, as Thomas of Erfurt said, makes the "voice" (the vocal sound) a signifier. Abstract analysis ending in the isolation of the merely observable element of the sign, its sensible face, leads not to the signifier but to one object among others. It can always be claimed that it is then inseparable from the signified, is already too late in a certain respect. The signifier can therefore not be understood as a sensible element to which is added or associated a relation of signification. This way of seeing things doubtless corresponds to a certain aspect of reality, but only the most exterior. It leads to the insoluble problem of knowing how this association can be made: *"How does signification join itself to voice?"* asks Gilson in commenting on a text by St Albert the Great. "The medieval problematic of the problem remains and... the responses have not been found."[52] But would this not be precisely because the problematic is poorly posed? In reality, as was shown in the phenomenology of semiotic experience, meaning is not associated with the signifier as between one thing and another; the signifier, the sensible face of the sign, is *caught up* in meaning, thereby drawn from the natural circuit, and introduced into a new sphere. We have thus spoken of semantic extraction, the focal point of our doctrine of the sign. This is precisely what is at issue at all levels of the signifying process. The sign is such as it is to the extent that, visibly or invisibly, *it is no longer of this world*.

---

[51] *Grammatica speculativa* I, trans. G.L. Bursill-Hall (London: Longman, 1972), 136 (*"signum* vel *significans"*) [altered]. Recall that the *Speculative Grammar* of Thomas of Erfurt (1350) represents the culmination of a number of previous works and a long tradition that found here its consummation and perfection. This text is so fundamental that Heidegger chose it as the subject for his "habilitation" thesis. It was attributed to Duns Scotus, whence Heidegger's title, *Die Katergorien und Bedeutungslehre des Duns Scotus* (Tubingen: 1916).

[52] Étienne Gilson, *Linguistics and Philosophy: An Essay on the Philosophical Constants of Language*, trans. John Lyon (Notre Dame, IN: University of Notre Dame Press, 1988), 180, n. 6.

We can see clearly the dialectical nature and "diacritical" function of the sign, as Plato put it in the Cratylus.[53] It is something within the world, yet distinguished from it. And this diacritical operation is performed first on the sign itself, or rather the sign is itself the *diacrisis*, the sign of separation and difference. Are we then returning to the Saussurean principle of differentiation? Not at all, for this *diacrisis* has meaning only if it is understood to be the mark of signification, as effect and proof of semantic extraction, and not as the lateral differentiation of units in the linguistic chain. The sign is somehow always second, the sole visible witness of an invisible preexistence, the *trace* of that toward which it leads: there can be true *diacrisis* only between the visible and the invisible, since the sign is by definition always *visible*.

This is not to deny that the sign is identified as such through the cultural (therefore social) experience of its use. To the contrary, as Ricœur has said, "in the last analysis, the sign owes its very meaning as sign to its usage in discourse. How would we know that a sign *stands for*... if its use in discourse did not invest it with the scope that relates it to that very thing *for which* it stands?"[54] Without this experience of use, we would have no awareness of signification, but experience does not produce it *ex nihilo*. It is rather the occasional cause, as shown with Helen Keller: it conditions the manifestation of signification, actualizes it, but actualizes only what was already in potency.[55]

To this must be added the role played by our knowledge of the semiotic system in the cultural identification of the signifier, rendering it yet more dependent upon social institutions. Without this knowledge, many actually significant elements would appear natural and non-signifying, and conversely, natural or non-intentional elements would be perceived as signs: the batting eyelashes or rolling eyes of a Hindu dancer, the twirls of a bullfighter, the shouts of a Tibetan lama, would appear accidental and natural to the profane; conversely, an ornamented letter would disappear beneath its abundant interweaving, a signature

---

[53] "The name is a tool for... dividing being [*diacrisis*]" analogous to the weaver's shuttle dividing warp and woof. *Cratylus* 388c, trans. C.D.C. Reeve, in *Plato: Complete Works*, 107.
[54] *The Rule of Metaphor*, 217.
[55] Culture must be understood as a true agent intellect with respect to the passive intellects it informs. This was explained in *Love and Truth* (50–58) and treated at greater length in *The Crisis of Religious Symbolism* (145–61).

would be reduced to a doodle and pass unrecognized as a sign.

Finally, in the interest of completeness, we must also mention the importance of hermeneutic intention in identifying the sign. It is not sufficient to see the sign, to know through cultural use that it is a sign, and to know its signification: we must understand just what about it should be taken as significant. This or that significant trait in the sign is realized by the hermeneutic intention. For example, in writing, the hermeneutic intention of the reader is entirely different from that of the handwriting analyst, to the point that the latter can study a text for hours without knowing what it says. In this he confers significance on aspects of the sensible form of the sign that another hermeneutic intention would not even notice. This condition of semiotic identification is inseparable from the previous two, encapsulating them in their most general form, since there could be no identification without knowledge of the signification and use of the elements upon which we focus our attention. This does not, however, necessarily come down to an eclipse of voluntary signifying intention in favor of bringing to light a hidden and unconscious signification, as for example in psychoanalysis. The hermeneutic intention should be understood as potentially situated at any possible level, given the signifying intention witnessed by the sign: it can be located below, "placing it under suspicion," as Ricœur would say, and reducing it. It can be at its proper level, as in common usage. It can also be situated above its apparent signification, and this is when the sign becomes a symbol, when the hermeneutic intention reveals the raison d'être of the signifier itself in grounding its own sensible form. As might be guessed, we have here one of the essential elements of a philosophy of the symbol, and what is being said now is only a first approach (which will have to be taken up again) required by the tight interdependence of every aspect of the philosophy of the sign, which makes explanation so difficult. The important thing for now is to remember that all these conditions for identifying the sign (the analysis of which is inseparable from its definition) refer back to the signification outside of which there is no signifier. The sign is thus defined as a sensible signifying reality, a *diacritical form*. Although remaining visible, it is extracted from the order of existents surrounding it and invisibly placed in relation to another order of reality.

How is semantic capture possible? How can a visible form be related to the invisible? This will be considered presently. For the moment, we ask what transformation is undergone by the form as a result of this capture. The answer leaves no doubt: it becomes the *sensible side* of the sign. But this is not a matter of returning to Saussure, for the essential thing is that *there is no other side*. What is in fact the proper operation of signification? Concerning Helen Keller, we said that it is the relation of a sensible form to the object which it would designate. Whereas previously, the sensible form had appeared from within pure perception to be entirely given in the sensible — to perceive an object, Merleau-Ponty said, is to be able to move around it[56] — now, after its capture by signification, we can no longer do so. Something in it invisibly escapes the visible, is as it were "turned around" toward what lies beyond the sensible, and we perceive only its "envelope," its "exterior," its "trace." It is no longer just the sensible *face*, for beyond the sensible, there is no face but a dynamic relation, an *order* for thought to orient itself toward an object.

Such is indeed the hallmark of the sign: *bringing something to mind*, pointing toward an object or referent. Signification arises when we grasp that a sensible reality, which as such is but a part of the total field of the corporeal universe, can exist for some other thing toward which it orients the mind. Even before understanding its signification, we understand that the sign orders thought to intend some distinct object. The sign is therefore a "one-sided" entity, and we know that topology allows for the easy creation of similar geometrical forms.[57] Accordingly, this entity need not have a counterpart that would be called the "signified." In closing the sign upon itself, the Saussurean definition gives the "signified" the same linguistic substantiality as the signifier: it risks making it a linguistic "thing," which linguistics treats as such, an object ultimately even endowed with the power to organize the world

---

[56] For example: "The die is there, lying in the world. When the subject moves round it, there appear, not signs, but sides of the die. He does not perceive projections or even profiles of the die, but he sees the die itself at one time from this side, at another from that"; *Phenomenology of Perception*, trans. Colin Smith (London/New York: Routledge, 2005), 378. Cf. also 392–93.
[57] This is the case in the famous "Mobius strip," a ribbon of paper whose short sides are taped together after twisting half a turn. Such a ribbon has neither *recto* nor *verso*. If it is cut in half along its entire length, there is still but a single ribbon.

according to its own structure. This is why we prefer to keep the traditional term, "meaning," to designate what Saussure called the "signified": meaning is also direction,[58] and we believe the meaning of a signifier always consists in a "manuduction," an act of intentional orientation toward an object. "Signified," however, as a past participle, is applied to the object precisely insofar as it is designated by the sign; such is the stable use of the term *significatum* among the medievals. Gilson states clearly, "When the infant or the adult says *dog* or *knife*, the nouns that he uses signify for him, not the idea of a dog or a knife, but the very things that these nouns designate. It is because we know things that we are able to name them—them, and not the concepts that we form of them."[59]

The signified or designated object is commonly called the referent—to this we now turn.

Identification of the Objective Referent

Reference, the fact of relation between sign and object, is the very essence of the sign. The epistemological schizophrenia claiming to sever the sign from its referent is truly absurd. The sign points toward its object from its heart and with all its being—more, it is this pointing itself. Each sign is an index, else its *diacrisis* would have no raison d'être and would be strictly unintelligible. It could be objected, with Tullio de Mauro, that this is to confound semantics and semiotics, that Ogden and Richards have not understood Saussure,[60] that signs do not signify because they are lifeless instruments *used* by man, and that it is therefore possible to study the instrument independent of use.[61] This conclusion is false and rests on an unsustainable instrumentalist understanding, as we have shown. If it is true that men signify, not words, then we must conclude on the contrary that there are no words independent of signification, and we cannot afford the luxury of studying some instrument called a "sign" which does not even signify. The sign is certainly of all instruments the *least* separable from the function it fulfills, since it is this very function: its *being* is to *stand for*.

---

[58] [Tr: in French, *sens* denotes both "meaning" and "direction."]
[59] *Linguistics and Philosophy*, 143.
[60] Tullio de Mauro, ed. *Cours de linguistique générale*, by Ferdinand de Saussure (Paris: Payot, 1995), 439, n. 129.
[61] De Mauro, *Une introduction à la sémantique*, trans. Louis-Jean Calvet (Paris: Payot, 1969), 28.

The Sign According to Philosophy

In setting up the object as the other "pole" of signification, the first being the signifier, this is not at all a convenience given to itself by the philosophy of the sign: rather, it is simply a necessity proper to any faithful description of reality. There is no sign outside of the fundamental relation by which a signifier is ordered toward an object. It concerns what Frege called "our intention in speaking or thinking."[62] The signified object cannot be understood as the counterpart of the signifier or its correlate. That this view is commonly encountered and conduces to the simplistic conception of language as a glossary is not at all surprising; there are reasons, even beyond the natural tendency to reify the terms of a dynamic relation, which are linked to the existence of a general lexical or semiotic code. But in reality, as the Latin derivation of the word suggests, the signified "object" is the term *aimed at* by the sign. The *meaning* or the orientation of a mental intention is therefore realized in the object. It is obviously not chained to the signifier as the prisoner to his iron ball, and we should never lose sight of the fact that signification is an *act:* there are not words on the one hand and things on the other, but a designative activity of the second by the first. This introduces "play" into reality and manifests the distinction between mind and things.

Yet this explanation would appear faced with a serious objection: signs which, having a meaning, nevertheless seem not to designate any object, either because they cannot exist (a square circle) or because they empirically do not (a concept, a nothing, an emptiness, a chimera, Don Quixote) or again because this cannot be determined (the denotation of the conjunction "and"). This objection is not new, and answers have long been attempted.[63] We will simply make some elementary remarks, showing that the solution involves questioning the objection's own presuppositions.

---

[62] "Sense and Reference," *The Philosophical Review*, vol. 57, no. 3 (1948), 214. Similarly, with Peirce, the *denotation of the object* is the fundamental characteristic of the sign: "A sign is a conjoint relation to the thing denoted and to the mind." C. S. Peirce, "On the Algebra of Logic: A Contribution to the Philosophy of Notation," *American Journal of Mathematics*, vol. 7, no. 2 (1885), 180.

[63] Cf. in particular, the summary of the solution given by "Duns Scotus" (Thomas of Erfurt) to this question: Martin Heidegger, *Duns Scotus's Doctrine of Categories and Meaning*, trans. Joydeep Bagchee and Jeffrey D. Gower (Bloomington, IN: Indiana University Press, 2022), 119–20. And above all, the state of the question in Ricœur, *The Rule of Metaphor*, 217–21.

The first case is the easiest to resolve. It is false to consider the phrase "square circle" as having a meaning. True, the units composing it each have a meaning, but their association does not. This phrase cannot be thought: whoever pronounces it (mentally or verbally) conceives nothing at all. We can see the requirement to distinguish between an apparent and a real meaning, between the appearance of meaning and meaning actually conceived. The former possibility has nothing mysterious about it: it is implied by the autonomy (and so permanence) of the *lexical* functioning of linguistic signs, independent of the intention presiding over their use. What is "thought" in the phrase "square circle" is not the meaning of the *phrase*, its semantic unity, but only the act of its articulation, the simple succession of words that make it up. We are dealing not with a sign but with a *quasi-sign*. It could even be demonstrated that the real referent in such cases is formed precisely through the production of this quasi-sign.

The second case requires a more complex treatment. To begin, we will say that if by "object" must be understood an empirically knowable, physical object, then rare indeed are those objects to which we could justly ascribe a referent; such materialism is untenable. The quality of being a denotable object will therefore be extended not only to corporeal beings but also to ideas, concepts, metaphysical principles, acts, events, emotions, cultural productions—in short, to all that enters into human experience and of which we can have some degree of knowledge.

Should we agree to this extension of the category of reality, a thorny problem remains, at least for some of the examples given: that of distinguishing between sense and reference. In the case of the signifier "ox," we easily see that the referent, the real ox, is distinct from the word's meaning. In the case of historical, social, or artistic realities, one would agree that the signifiers "Baptism of Clovis," "rural depopulation," "Romanticism," and "Cubism" have objective referents distinct from the meanings of these words. But the signifier "concept"? It has a definite meaning: it is the form of the act by which the understanding intends an object. But have we not also defined its referent, and so reduced referent to meaning? Is the meaning of a word anything other than the concept of the thing it evokes in our mind? And Saussure himself, defining the signified (the meaning) as a "mental image," does he not also sometimes call it the "concept"? Having reduced the referent of the word "concept" to the *meaning* of this word, having then observed that the concept is nothing other than the meaning of the signifier generally, we must surely conclude that nominalism is true and that, independent of signs to express them, our ideas have no reality.

However, this conclusion should be rejected, simply in that it is contradictory. What makes a nominalist other than the search for a true understanding of the concept? This is to suppose that there is such a truth, therefore a proper essence of the concept, and moreover that our thought can discover it. But this the nominalist himself specifically denies, since the concept is reduced to the word and the activity of thought to the *functioning* of the signifying chain.

The solution to this difficulty is provided by the scholastic distinction between *first* and *second intention*, which moreover only express the "reflexive capacity" of the human mind. "Intention" (from the Latin *in-tendere*) designates the act by which the mind "tends toward" an object. If we perceive a table, our mind produces a mental act by means of which it conceives what it knows within this perception, an act called the "concept." More precisely, the concept is the *form* of the act by which we think the table. The Scholastics say it is the *formal sign* that makes us know the table. Yet this conceptual sign, this mental form, is not known *per se* in the first intention: it is not known *qua* concept, but makes the table known. In other words, in the first intention, we do not think the concept, we think the table *through* the concept. The concept can itself nevertheless become an object for our thought: our mind need only, by a second intention, *reflect* on the mental act by which it knows the table, objectifying its first intention. This is what we have been doing throughout this presentation. There is a *first* intention only with respect to a *second*.

The concept becoming an object of thought holds no mystery, except that of the mind itself. The reflexive capacity of thought, its possibility of knowing itself, defines its freedom and spirituality. Our thought is not reduced to behavior or functioning. It acts, of course, according to rules and forms that can be described, but it is endowed with self-transcendence, else the description of its functioning would be impossible. "The spirit bloweth where it listeth, and thou hearest the sound thereof, but canst not tell whence it cometh, and whither it goeth."

As shown in the present chapter,[64] the reflexive property of thought accounts for the metalinguistic property of natural (non-artificial) language and is actualized under the effect of the mediateness of language. To ward off the specter of the glossary-language ("one word, one thing") it is unnecessary—and impossible—to reject the linguistic referent. On the contrary, one must accept the referential aim and grasp its true nature. Language, let us repeat, cannot not speak *about* something; the linguistic sign cannot not refer to an object, whether it be a corporeal or incorporeal reality, or even an "emptiness," a "nothing," a "privation."

The mediateness of the linguistic sign, an expression of the mind's reflexivity, is also the occasional, "material," or conditioning cause. The experience of the sign, the original act of the cultural process, realizes object awareness—Helen Keller proves as much. It cannot be bracketed: the referential orientation must be recognized as the mind's birth to self-consciousness as a thinking subject and to knowledge of the world as an objective reality. Certainly, the sign produces neither the being of the mind nor that of the object, yet it is that whereby consciousness imparts to a being the quality of its being an object,[65] its objectivity, or more technically, "objectness."[66] The intention of objectivity is thus inseparable from the sign's nature: it defines the general form of the referential orientation. Now, whether this formal objectivity (objectness) is applied to a real being or not depends on our "experience" of being, not only what actually exists, but also what we take to be possible, in other words, on our *ontology of reference*.[67] Don Quixote is obviously not an empirically observable being, but he is metaphysically a "possible" human, therefore a meta-empirical and exemplary reality of our nature.

---

[64] Cf. *supra*, 113–29.

[65] Alluding to the doctrine of *nāma-rūpa* ("name and form"), Shankara says the same: "the term 'being' [Sanskrit: *sat*, 'that which is'] ordinarily denotes that which is differentiated by names and forms" (*Vedānta Sūtra*, I, Adhyaya 4, Pada 15). Similarly, in Christian theology, the Supreme Name, the Divine Word uttered by the Father, is that *by which* all things are made, and is therefore the principal Sign by whose mediation the possibilities of creation are objectively or distinctly realized prior to their being given separative existence. The objectifying realization performed by the linguistic sign is but the human reflection of this divine and intemporal process.

[66] The use of this neologism to designate the quality of being an object, considered abstractly, allows us to avoid the imprecision of the word "objectivity," which applies also to a mode of knowledge.   [67] Cf. *infra*, 194–204.

There remains the third case, in which the referent is undecidable: what object is denoted by the conjunction "and"? This shows clearly how the rejection of the referent (by the refusal of the glossary paradigm) is in fact conditioned by a "glossarial" understanding of language, and finally by an "atomistic" or "molecular" understanding of reality. To this untenable view, we oppose an understanding of the *architectonic deployment* of the referential orientation, correlative to an architectonic understanding of the order of the world and beings. In this atomistic understanding, only proper nouns would have a referent. But Frege rightly retorts that, if proper names provide the model for reference, we could also consider an entire sentence as a proper name: "the reference is communicated from the proper name to the entire proposition, which, with respect to reference, becomes the proper name of a state of affairs."[68] Similarly, in Benveniste, as Ricœur shows, the word receives its reference from its use within the phrase: "With the phrase, we are connected to things outside of language."[69] But we must go further.

The meaning of a sentence is equally a function of the paragraph in which it is found, itself determined by the section, the chapter, and the part. Nor is this all, for we must also include the book as a whole and its *subject*, which is indeed the primary referent of all the signs it uses. Further, the definition of the referent must also consider the literary *genre* to which the work belongs and therefore also the cultural type. There is truly no endpoint: *from the ground up* in the semiotic system, we encounter only hierarchically subordinated elements, an *architectonic*, in which one element serves as means for that to which it is subordinated, which in turn is itself subordinated to a higher element, and so on. It can seem easier to identify the referent of "ox" than "and," because the referent of "and" is a function of the phrase in which it is employed. But on another level, this applies equally to "ox," which does not exist by itself, and which refers to the order of the world as whole. There are certainly differences among all these modes of reference, but that does not directly concern a

---

[68] Ricœur, *The Rule of Metaphor*, 218; summarizing Frege, "Sense and Reference," 215.
[69] "La forme et le sens dans le langage," *Problèmes de linguistique générale* II, 225. By "phrase" is meant a group of words forming some whole, e.g., "it is raining," "heart of gold," "the cross," "the sun is risen," etc.

philosophy of the sign and does not affect the fundamental law of reference. This architectonic (which is to say, vertical) structure can alone account for the horizontal phrasal structure: words have a raison d'être linking them together only by the superior phrasal unity to which they are subordinated. And there is no possibility of stopping at a first or last element—no sign is purely phrasal, having a meaning only internal to a group of words and deprived of all extra-linguistic reference; but neither is any purely referential, having its meaning only outside of discourse. There is no absolutely proper name.

The architectonic deployment of the referential orientation proves that reference does not at all establish a "solitary" (biunivocal) relation between word and thing. Each referential aim is governed by a superior aim from which it receives its referential value: every sign is caught up in a discourse. Correlatively, denoted objects are no longer posed in atomistic isolation, but form a cosmic "discourse," each referring to every other and all referring to the principial Object, the Divine Referent.

Identification of Meaning, and Discovery of the Intelligible Referent

The signifier is essentially directed toward an object—nothing is more certain. Difficulty arises when we try to identify how this orientation is realized. What is there between sign and referent such that the referent is that to which the sign refers? What indeed *is* reference?

Reference is the act by which a sign is related to its referent. To avoid any confusion with the referent, we give to this act the name "signification," understood in the active sense as the process of signifying an object by a sign.[70] How then is this process possible? It occurs through the *meaning*. By its meaning, the signifier is related to its objective referent.

Frege stressed that we should not confuse the sense of an expression with its denotation, the act by which the referent is denoted. If we consider the statement, "the evening star is the morning star," we are dealing with two different phrases ("evening

---

[70] In ordinary language, "signification" is synonymous with "meaning." This is passive signification, what a sign signifies. The German language uses *Sinn* and *Bedeutung* indifferently for this reason. Such ambiguity in the word is not a problem: it shows that passive signification implies active signification and vice versa.

The Sign According to Philosophy

star" and "morning star") which denote the same object. What explains the difference in meaning? It arises, Frege says, from "the mode of presentation of that which is designated" (*die Art des Gegebenseins*). The same object (the planet Venus) gives itself to be seen first as the "evening star" and then as the "morning star."[71]

For our part, abstracting from the specific implications of Frege's arguments, we will say that meaning is the mediator between sign and referent, to the extent that it is connected, on the one hand, to the signifier, by a lexical institution of the cultural order; and on the other, to the referent, by the mode under which it is presented to us. This definition is evidently just as true for the linguistic sign as for all others. We thus rediscover the triadic conception of the act of signification, represented in the following triangular schema (Schema 1):

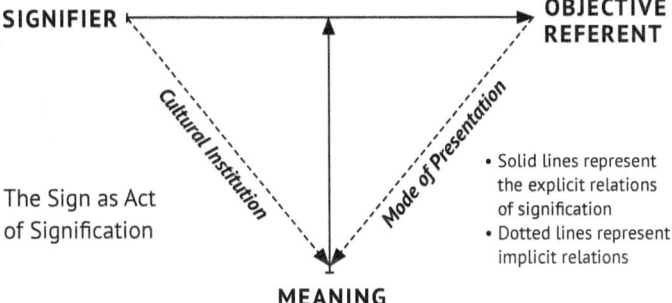

This schema should not make us forget that, in reality, it is only the development of a unique act from which its elements are indissociable. These are not entities which are combined to successfully form the sign. Yet they are distinct, since the signifier is a material or sensible entity, the referent belongs to the world of objects, and the meaning is of the mental order.

If we will now attempt a commentary, let us first remark that the sign has its entire development with a view to signification. It is therefore also by a description of this act that we have any chance of being able to identify the meaning and the relations it maintains with the signifier and the referent. What is happening when we wish to signify?

Every signifying intention is realized by an act which, as such, is voluntary—it is a unique event. This act (or intention) begins

---

[71] "Sense and Reference," 210. (See complementary note, *infra*, 156, n. 78.)

in the referent, in that *about which* it must speak, *but also* from what is to be said about it. It thus finds itself obliged to make use of a signifier, a sensible form, since all communication without exception is sensible. Now, to this obligation, linked to the corporeal nature of the human presence (humans are present to one another through the body) is added another of a different order, the constraint of the signifier's meaning. The signifier as pure sensible form obviously cannot assume the function of signifying the referent, only inasmuch as it is endowed with a meaning. The signifying intention does not invent this meaning, but draws it from the array of signifying forms presented to it by the semiotic system of its culture. It is not free and voluntary, but fixed and determined. Nor is it a unique event, but rather permanent and atemporal. What is important for signification is, first, to select the signifier whose meaning accords with the referent and with what is to be said about it, since it is also by the meaning of the signifier that the addressee can in turn be oriented toward the referent in the desired way. The situation of the addressee is then actually not different from that of the speaker, *relative to the meaning of the signifier*. The latter too must find the referent's meaning. As we have already observed, the sign is an order for thought to orient itself toward a distinct object. This *orientation* is precisely its meaning.

At the same time, and let us take care on this point, signification is *essentially* tentative: it is never confident in the meaning of the signifier it uses. Every act of signification is a risk and a gamble. Not only the addressee but also the speaker wonders what these signs *mean* and if they accord with his signifying intention, orienting the addressee in the proper direction and in the proper way. "Indeed," it could be argued, "we know well that meaning is never wholly determined: a single signifier can have multiple meanings, even without accounting for homonyms. These are listed and enumerated in dictionaries. We should therefore conclude that such meanings are always a function of usage, and that, in the final analysis, they are always determined by the semiotic system." We would reply that such an objection does not account for the real experience of the search for meaning, for the right expression. There are doubtless many cases where language itself speaks in us. Most of our speech acts in daily life are performed unreflectively and as if mechanically, are given to verbal stereotypes functioning almost autonomously. We can even descend into rambling. The reason for this is banal, and that is perhaps why it is little remarked: habit. Of all our learning, there is none deeper and more durable than this. And it is known to involve a determinate structure and the strengthening of cortical areas. From this viewpoint alone can we agree with Merleau Ponty's judgment that "the orator does not think before speaking, nor even while speaking; his speech is his thought."[72] In the same way, highly skilled musicians can play almost instinctively on their instrument and let fly a nearly automatic sequence of musical phrases which seem to obey only their own structural rules—their execution is their improvisation.[73] But it is otherwise when *truly* composing, speaking, or writing, that is, not only designating a referent, but *saying something about* it. The semiotic system we know best would thus be a foreign language.

We often speak to say *nothing*, for a reason other than to say what is actually said: out of pleasure, affection, boredom, to stun, and so on. There have even been attempts to oppose a descriptive language to an emotional language, and denotation can be distinguished from connotation. But denotative language itself is never simply such. The referential orientation, we have said, is essential to the sign. Certainly. However, in responding to its exclusion by Saussure, the referent must not be made essential to the act of signification. For this would be at once to reduce it entirely to denotation and to render it impossible. In fact, and not concealing that here we reach our most important argument, denotation is possible only as a function of the signifying intention, the first and fundamental condition of existence for the sign. We would never have been able to designate things by means of signs had we not first felt a need to *say something about them*. The essential act of language is therefore not to designate things, but to express their essence, at least what we perceive of it. There is *never* pure designation: the most elementary sign of denotation, an outstretched finger, is always already a *meaning*. This is furthermore the teaching of Genesis, which states, "the Lord God formed every beast of the

---

[72] *Phenomenology of Perception*, 209. But it is not possible then to state that "'Pure' thought reduces itself to a certain void of consciousness" (213), precisely because this void of consciousness would be inconceivable if there were no thought without language.

[73] Similarly, a computer can "compose" like Mozart or Bach by reproducing stereotypes most characteristic of their style. But it will never "invent" *Don Giovanni* or the *St John Passion*.

field, and every fowl of the air; and brought them unto Adam to see what he would call them."[74] In other words, to see what he would *say about them*, not only what denotation he would apply to them. This is what we must now consider.

We do not deny that unspoken thought is, as Merleau-Ponty says, a rustling of words, and that we must admit the existence of a "verbal concept" (Kurt Goldstein) or a "linguistic concept" (Ernst Cassirer).[75] We find this idea already in the Scholastics, as St Thomas distinguishes from exterior speech an "interior word, which has an image of the vocal word."[76] And certainly, the work of signification involves "trying" these interior words rustling in the silence. But how can it perform this sorting and testing, how can it reject or accept a given signifying sequence, if not by means of a principle of selection? What is the principle of selection if not the *meaning*? And this meaning, before which all possible signifying sequences pass in review, must not be radically dependent upon any one of them in particular.

Meaning thus begins to appear in its truth, which is not of the linguistic order. That in the name of which signification performs its work of searching for the right signifier, the principle of selection to which it is obedient and which rules out one signifier in favor of another, is obviously not the institutional meaning of the signifier, what we now call its "lexical meaning," since it is awaiting its complete determination, which it receives from its use in discourse as a whole. Besides, how could we rule out and deem inadequate this or that signifier in the name of a not-yet-formulated meaning? It must therefore be recognized that this meaning is no longer the institutional meaning associated with a signifier, but a true *intelligible* or *semantic referent*, transcendent to the semiotic order as well as that of objective referents. For the meaning we seek to signify is not only the meaning of a sign but also, and necessarily, the meaning of *things*.

Relative to meaning as intelligible referent, the lexical meaning given in dictionaries is only a particular crystallization. More precisely, each culture, in the general architecture of its semiotic

---

[74] Genesis 2:19.
[75] *Phenomenology of Perception*, 226.
[76] *Quaestiones disputatae: De Veritate*, Q. 14, Art. 1, Reply; cited by Gilson, *Linguistics and Philosophy*, 74. (*The Disputed Questions on Truth*, trans. R.W. Mulligan [Chicago: Regnery, 1952], 1.172.)

systems, captures and reflects Meaning only from a certain perspective and under some of its aspects. Within a particular semiotic system, a given signifier is therefore the sensible, institutionally determined trace of a Meaning which is *per se* free and inexpressible. The signifier is linked to this Meaning, not the Meaning to the signifier, and this relation uniting the signifier to the semantic referent is precisely the meaning-of-the-signifier, its lexical meaning.[77] It is necessarily limited since, being dependent on a system of formulations, its semantic openness is a function of the ensemble of which it is a part. It nevertheless directs itself toward the intelligible referent, being as it were its emanation and particularization. The very idea of a purely differential semantics, in which the (lexical) meaning would be entirely determined by structure, is simply unintelligible. Neither counterpart of the signifier, nor differential semantic trait, the (lexical) meaning is a particular orientation toward the supreme meaning, the intelligible referent, on the basis of conditions determining the order of signifiers. The culture as ensemble of semiotic systems is therefore as a sort of mirror in which one tries to capture the semantic referent by properly orienting the reflective surface. But the image thus captured is obviously a function of the form of the mirror, of its curvature, its size, its possibility for movement, and its ease of use.

On the other hand, to seek the right expression is not only to seek the signifier for which the (lexical) meaning best accords with what one means, since this process has a raison d'être only if one means something, only if one wants to express the truth or

---

[77] This understanding is found in St Thomas Aquinas, who distinguishes "a threefold word in one who is speaking. There is the word conceived by the intellect, which, in turn, is signified by an exterior vocal word. The former is called the *word of the heart*, uttered but not vocalized. Then there is that upon which the exterior word is modeled; and this is called the *interior word*, which has an image of the vocal word. Finally, there is the word expressed exteriorly, and this is called the *vocal word*." *Quaestiones disputatae: De Veritate*, Q. 14, Art. 1, Reply (Gilson, *Linguistics and Philosophy*, 74). Meister Eckhart took up this doctrine, but with a mystical intention, seeing in the threefold word a symbol of the birth of the Word in the human soul. He wrote in one of his German sermons, "When the word is first conceived in my intellect, it is so pure and subtle that it is a true word, before taking shape in my thought. In the third place, it is spoken out loud by my mouth, and then it is nothing but a manifestation of the interior word" ("Sermon 29," *The Complete Mystical Works of Meister Eckhart*, trans. Maurice O'C. Walshe [New York: Crossroad, 2009], 177). The "word of the heart" is not unrelated to the intelligible referent.

nature of things. The intelligible referent, which is truly a referent in that the (lexical) meaning is oriented toward it, is the "idea it has," the Meaning of the meaning, which underlies the (lexical) meaning as its semantic guarantor and grounds the truth of the objective referent. This latter is all that we can *speak about*, all that we can signify, but if we would say something about it, this is because the simple existence of the objective referent itself is not sufficiently revelatory of its own truth. In signifying the world, man reveals and realizes its meaning. This meaning is therefore necessarily transcendent to the order of objective referents, since it is precisely *this* which the existential conditions of the objective referent prohibit us from manifesting. Its plenitude overflows the inevitable limitations of all formal existence, which can but participate in it in its own way. There would be nothing to say if there were no need to express the essence of beings, if each existent were identical to its essence in the act of being.

We must therefore complete the previous schema with another, no longer triadic but rather tetradic, distinguishing two meanings, placed respectively at each extremity of the vertical axis. This understanding is in a way the exact opposite of the Saussurean, which as we have seen, tends to reduce verticality to the horizontality of differential lateral relations. We represent it in the following way (Schema 2):

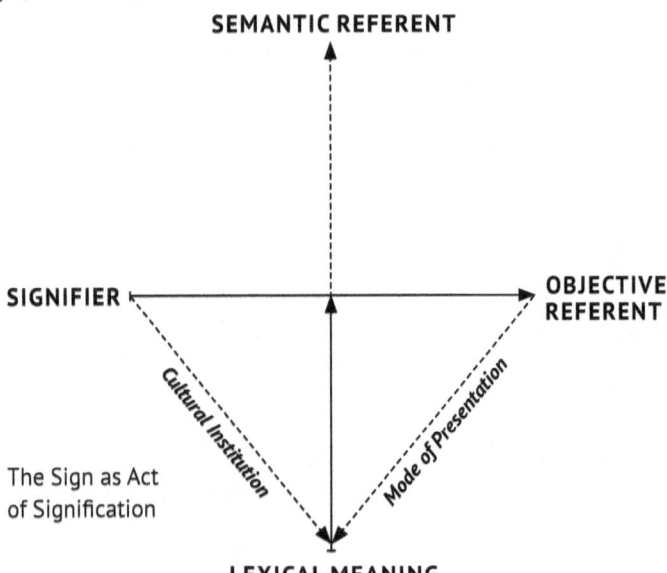

The concept of an intelligible referent, not all consequences of which have been fully developed, doubtless appears rather metaphysical. However, not only does it correspond to the reality of the lived experience of signification, but it also allows us to account for fundamental aspects of the economy of the sign and to respond to Gilson's basic question: how does meaning occur in the signifier?

First, the theory of the intelligible referent alone allows us to understand that semiotic systems, and language in particular, are not glossaries. For a glossarial language, to signify would be to pair the meaning of a sign with a referent in a sort of exclusive biunivocal relation. What apparently justifies this perspective (more crude than totally false) is the stability of the association of signifier and meaning as it occurs in an established language, a stability which appears so strong and so self-evident that it amounts to an identification. Language thus seems to function by itself, and this is what happens where we use the semantic automatism of the signifier in deceptive discourse. But the signifying system can escape the glossary, the horizontal relation automatically uniting its referents, precisely because this horizontal trajectory between signifier and referent is interrupted by a break in continuity, as shown in Schema 2, being traversed by a vertical and transcendent relation. The meaning-of-the-signifier is open (joined) to this transcendence, the intelligible referent, which is at once the normative meaning of the signifier, true meaning of the (lexical) meaning, and real meaning of the objective referent about which the sign speaks.

In a similar way, in the twelfth century, John of Salisbury stated in a formula C.S. Peirce loved to repeat, "adjectives signify one thing and name another. They name singulars but signify universals."[78] This "discordance" could be understood as an imperfection, but this would obviously be an error. The remark presents us with another aspect of the economy of the sign, truly even its most essential. We have already mentioned it many times, particularly in our description of signification, by showing how, in the sudden experience of signification, the order of objective existents, that of human consciousness in its interiority, and the order of signs are differentiated.

---

[78] *Metalogicon* II.10, cited by Peirce, "Sundry Logical Conceptions," *The Essential Peirce, Volume 2: Selected Philosophical Writings* (Bloomington, IN: Indiana University Press, 1998), 281.

Far from constituting a deficiency, the discordance indicated by John of Salisbury is in fact that which makes the act of signification possible. It is because signifiers ultimately express universals that the act of signification can designate singular realities. If the signifying intention were inherently unable to orient itself toward the transcendence of pure semantics, which by definition outstrips equally the order of existents and that of signifiers, there would be no "play" between them, no more than between the visible face of a clock and its works. In other words, by this very transcendence, the signifier and the referent are constituted each in its own order, are distinguished, and so enabled to enter into relation with one another. Without the transcendence of the semantic referent, there would be neither a universe of signs, nor a world of objective and real beings, only signal-response correlations in a closed circuit. Inasmuch as it is the meaning of the signifier as well as the objective referent while being transcendent to both, the semantic referent grounds both their radical distinction and the possibility of their relation.

We will now grasp more clearly the metaphysical condition of the original experience of signification on which we have insisted so strongly. Just as the first cry of the newborn expands its lungs, separates the blood in the veins from that of the arteries, and establishes the exchange of gases with the external air, the experience of the sign posits an objective world before consciousness and reflexive thought. But of course, the signifier as such is not capable of this miracle by which consciousness unfolds and enters into communication with a world of objects. It is the signifier as *diacrisis*, and we do not see how there could be a *diacrisis* if there were no connection to the invisible, no capture of the sensible form of the signifier by the semantic referent. The meaning irrupting into consciousness under the form of the signifying intention, *that which* it seeks to express, belongs neither to the order of the speaking subject nor to that of the object: it is the essence, in itself "not of this world," which the intelligence perceives, or rather by which it is seized. Precisely because this essence is in itself "not of this world," absent by transcendence, the mind feels the need to express it, make it present in the only way possible, by means of the sign. Whoever meditates on these truths will understand that we are here at the heart of the sign's mystery, which itself stands at the heart of the human mystery, the birth of the distinction between microcosm and macrocosm along with the relation uniting (and separating) them: the "semiocosm." In short, culture.

Finally, and this is the final aspect of the economy of the sign that we will derive from the theory of the semantic referent, it is equally the independence of this referent, of Meaning from meaning, that can alone ground the autonomy of the order of signifiers. This autonomy, this *sui generis* consistency of semiotic systems, is required by the original experience of signification. The sign must be something other than things or persons to be the occasion for their common distinction. And it can be so only if it possesses its own subsistence and permanence. How can this self-subsistence be grounded if the signifier is reduced to the pure sensible trace by which it is nothing other than a being of this world, one form among others? What is there, at base, that is stranger than the universe of culture, mediatrix between the reality of the world and that of man, yet whose own reality seems to defy analysis? If the very nature of the cultural order of signifiers defeats our ordinary conceptions, this is because it is somehow not of this world. The universe of signs is traversed from end to end by semantic extraction. The place from which it speaks to us, from which it beckons us, overlooks and so realizes the horizontality of the relation between man and world.

As to the permanence of the semiotic order, it is a reflection, an image, and an effect of the natural permanence of the order of intelligible referents. This permanence is undeniably assured by cultural institutions. Language, in this respect as in so many others, is a clear model: the meaning of words is (relatively) fixed and stable. And this is why they form a true *lexis*, like the rules of arrangements and syntactical constructions, which form another "lexis" just as stable as the former. Generally speaking, these are all systems of signs which can only function, only be used by us, because they receive from this semantic lexicalism as much of their contents and elements as of their constructions and syntax: each employment of a sign occurs on the basis of the meaning *attached to it*. This is true even if the connection between meaning and sign is being established for the first time. There is therefore no doubt that this lexical permanence is a phenomenon of the social order and is related to the existence of a culture.

And yet we ask ourselves, philosophically, how can words have a meaning? What is the ultimate link enabling the association of sensible form and concept? Once we have discarded all pseudo-solutions assuming the problem to be solved, we come to the following: if the detail of its realization is historical, the very *possibility* of such realization implies belief in a self-subsistent, autonomous, and atemporal semantic universe, alone capable of grounding the stability and autonomy of a universe of signs, because it extracts them, from above, out of their horizontal relations and connects them to man and world.

Therefore, and to summarize our entire analysis, signification can occur only by grace of a spiritual universe of intelligible referents which, by the very fact that it is transcendent both to the order of objective existents and to human thought, semantically establishes the sign in its proper and *sui generis* order,[79] independent in its essence from man and world, even if it depends on them as to its historical forms, in such a way that the discovery of significance occasioned by the sign is in turn the original experience in which the universe of things and that of consciousness are distinguished, placed in their proper order, and mutually related.

HISTORICAL REMARKS

Aristotle and the Stoics

One might wonder why our historical remarks on the sign follow its definition, whereas for the symbol they came before. There is a simple answer: the first part of our study involved a

---

[79] This is also the position of Plato, who, we recall, placed the sign among the "kinds of being" (*Sophist* 260a; in *Plato: Complete Works*, 282).

Complementary note to note 70, p. 147:
Modern logicians are known to refuse the identification of *meaning* and *signification*. Signification results from the functioning of signifiers (the "symbol system"); meaning results from the possible relation of signification to reality (the "fact system"). The proposition, "the present king of France is bald" has a signification but no meaning. It is neither true nor false, there being no present king of France to confirm or contradict it. This distinction is obviously legitimate, yet it does not go to the heart of things. There would be no signification if the signifying units had no possible meaning, if they could not be related to a (possible) referent. In any case, two of the terms of this symbol system, "France" and "present," refer directly to reality: the reality of a country that was once a kingdom, and the reality of the speaker's present. Thus, the *signification* of the signifier "present" is its *meaning!* Yet precisely this term and it alone makes this proposition the typical example imposing the meaning-signification distinction. Before 1848, this would not have been the case. It is a valid distinction, but structurally secondary: in the last analysis, meaning grounds signification.

range of terminology given to us within a tradition from which it must be disentangled in order to grasp the symbol's essence. But the second part dealt with the thing itself in its actuality (its existence) as it functions for us. The historical survey can here but (potentially) confirm that we are not thinking "on our own." Such is the primary interest. Secondarily, these remarks will allow us to dispel some widespread interpretative errors ascribing to the binary theory of the sign an antiquity it does not actually possess.

Not infrequently, the Saussurean definition is presented as heir to a long tradition which, beginning with the Stoics, can be found in St Augustine, Condillac, or Wilhelm von Humboldt, to name but a few of the most illustrious references.[80] Here the sign is defined in itself without relation to a referent and therefore situated within a purely semiotic perspective. Unfortunately, so its proponents hold, though this tradition could have led to a true science of the sign, it was stifled by the Aristotelian understanding (sign–meaning–referent) which, apart from the fact that it cannot ground linguistic science, since it allows the intrusion of the non-linguistic, encourages the confusion of words and things as well as an understanding of language as a glossary.

This accusation is groundless, as we have just shown. Rather, only the doctrine of the intelligible referent, inspired by Platonism, can account for the specificity of the signifier as well as that of the semiotic order in general. This doctrine is exactly that taught by Aristotle, notwithstanding linguists who seem ignorant of his most explicit statements. There is not space here to provide proof; we will but refer to the study by Pierre Aubenque on the Aristotelian understanding of language,[81] in which he shows that philosophy explicitly rejects the confusion of words and things based on a triadic concept of the sign. And if they are not confused, Aristotle tells us, this is because "we never speak 'for the pleasure of speaking' but in order to say something." To mean

---

[80] Bertil Malmberg, in particular, made such an argument: "Saussure therefore sides against an Aristotelian tradition going back two millennia for a Stoic line of thought that passes through Alexandria, St Augustine, Humboldt, and Wittgenstein, culminating in the relativism of the linguistic sign in modern structuralist schools," *Signes et symbols* (Paris: A. and J. Picard, 1977), 98.
[81] *Le problème de l'être chez Aristote* (Paris: Presses Universitaires de France, 1977), 94–133.

something is to be directed toward an essence and therefore to presuppose an ontological referent common to the interlocuters, which is the unity and ground of signification. This clarifies the relations among thought, language, and being: "The condition of possibility for thought as an interior discourse and for language as a pronounced discourse is that words have a definite meaning, and what enables this is things having an essence."[82]

We will also say nothing about the Stoics' theory of the sign, despite their driving its most substantial development, except to observe that, despite assertions to the contrary, the *linguistic* sign is for them equally triadic.[83]

The Doctrine of Saint Augustine

Saint Augustine never set himself to construct a general theory of the sign in the scholastic or modern manner. He did lay the foundations in *De Doctrina Christiana*, however, when clarifying the rules of Christian hermeneutics — that is, the interpretation of the signs presented to us in Holy Scripture. In so doing, he created the first synthesis of the semiotic doctrines of Antiquity, being inspired chiefly by Origen but also drawing in part on Stoic teaching. He gives the following general definition: "a sign is a thing which of itself makes some other thing come to mind, besides the impression that it presents to the senses."[84] This definition, though a classic in Christian theology, is nevertheless the subject of great misunderstanding on the part of some contemporary semioticians.

First of all, it is placed in opposition to Aristotle, ostensibly because it demonstrates the importance of communication, upon which Aristotle "sheds no light at all."[85] If this were the case, we might wonder how Thomist and scholastic theology, an unquestionably Aristotelian tradition, could have appropriated the Augustinian definition. In fact, the communicative function and the social importance of language are equally important

---

[82] Ibid., 129.
[83] Cf. Sextus Empiricus, *Against the Logicians*, II.11–12; trans. R.G. Bury (Cambridge, MA: Harvard University Press, 1935), 245. Fr Dominique Dubarle has shown in his unpublished study (*Logistique et épistemologie du signe chez Aristote et les Stoïciens*) that, for the Stoics, only the "epistemological sign" (e.g., smoke as a sign of fire) is dyadic. Cf. *infra*, 183, n. 9.
[84] *De Doctrina Christiana* II.1; op cit., 57.
[85] Todorov, 37.

The Sign According to Philosophy

for Aristotle, St Thomas, and the Scholastics as they were for St Augustine. Commenting on Aristotle, St Thomas writes, "since [man] is by nature a political and social animal it was necessary that his conceptions be made known to others. This he does through vocal sound. Therefore there had to be significant vocal sounds in order that men might live together."[86]

But what is surprisingly modern in St Augustine, it is believed, is the disappearance of the "thing," the referent. Indeed, Todorov writes concerning *De Doctrina Christiana* that St Augustine "does speak of things and of signs in this treatise ... but he does not take the former to be referents of the latter. The world is divided into signs and things according to whether the perceived object has transitive value or not. Things participate in signs as signifiers, not as referents."[87]

This way of viewing the Augustinian positions, at least concerning the referent, seems wholly mistaken, corresponding neither to the text nor to the intentions of the Bishop of Hippo. Instead, it evaluates Augustine in terms of the requirements and criteria of contemporary semiotics, which are hardly to be found among his preoccupations.

The treatise begins with a distinction between signs and things: "All teaching is teaching of either things or signs, but things are learnt through signs."[88] Does this suggest that a quasi-epistemic separation has been performed, allowing for a definition of the sign independent of its referent? Exactly the opposite: for what is the purpose of the treatise? To provide the rules of interpretation for scriptural signs. And how does it begin? By showing us the things of which scriptural signs are the expression, their referents. And these include the Trinity, the Incarnation, the Resurrection, redemption, charity, Christ as the sole spiritual way — in short,

---

[86] *Aristotle: On Interpretation: Commentary by St Thomas and Cajetan (Peri Hermeneias)*, I.i.2; trans. Jean T. Oesterle (Milwaukee, WI: Marquette University Press, 1962), 23. Similarly, Aristotle: *Politics* I, 1253a; *Nicomachean Ethics* IX, 1170b; etc.

[87] Todorov, 40.

[88] *De Doctrina Christiana*, I.iv; op cit., 13. We are not reproducing literally the translation of the "Bibliothèque augustinienne," and we have modified each of our citations when this seemed necessary in order to better express the author's thought. The Latin in this case reads, *"vel rerum est vel signorum,"* which expresses a non-exclusive disjunction (*vel*). It could be rendered either by "and" or "or."

dogmatic truths. Only then does St Augustine consider signs, their exegesis and their interpretation. In other words, the plan is simple: intending to speak of Scripture, St Augustine, far from eliminating the sign's referent, begins rather by setting it out, by telling us *what Scripture speaks about* before telling us *how it speaks about it*. And from the Christian perspective, this is indeed the proper approach. What interests a Christian is not Scripture in and of itself but as a way of coming to know God and His teaching. The Creed is prior to the Scriptures, since Christ is the key to Scripture's meaning, and the Creed summarizes His life and teaching. We know, by faith, of What and of Whom it speaks. We now need to understand how the data of the sacred text are consistent with its Divine Object.[89]

It can therefore not be claimed that the referent plays no role in the Augustinian definition of the sign. Its role is so obvious in St Augustine's eyes, so constitutive, that it can be studied separately without giving the impression of its epistemic isolation. Hardly scientific to force St Augustine to say what he never said or ever dreamed of saying.

This distinction between things and signs therefore does not at all have the meaning it has been given—this much can be granted. Now we must enter into the details of the Augustinian perspective. Things and signs can doubtless be distinguished, but in fact, the only thing that is purely a thing and never a sign is the *Res Divina*, the Divine Thing. In other words, signs are things (else they would not be visible) and things are signs, since all creation can be regarded as a symbol of God. Nevertheless, if all things *can* be signs—such as wood, water, rock, and so on—they are also themselves, and are only additionally signs (through the use made of them by Scripture, though this is done on the basis of a real analogy). There are, however, also objects that are only signs and do not exist for themselves: "Words, for example: nobody uses words except in order to signify something. From this it may be understood what I mean by signs: those things which are employed to signify something."[90]

We can summarize Augustine's theory in the following table:

---

[89] We can see how inexplicable is Todorov's misunderstanding, and yet it is to be found elsewhere, even among specialists. Have the texts been read?
[90] *De Doctrina Christiana*, I.iv; op cit., 13.

The Sign According to Philosophy

Things That Are	In Themselves	For Another
Divine World	Yes	No
Created World	Yes	Yes
Sign World	No	Yes

This table has the virtue of clearly demonstrating that the distinction between signs and things is secondary with respect to that between what exists in itself, what refers to another, and finally that Supreme Other which, being absolute, refers only to Itself. As Fr Roguet has shown, what is most "audacious" in St Augustine's proposal is to make of the order of signs another universe, another world, possessing its own reality.[91] This is the intuition of the "mystery of the sign," which, in Augustine as in Plato, is one of the "kinds of being." What makes something a sign is therefore the property of referring to something other than itself, its referent. The referent constitutes the sign, allows it to be recognized as such (and not necessarily as some mere thing),[92] and particularly the existence of the absolute referent, God, who transforms all other things into signs of Himself.

This interpretation of *De Doctrina Christiana* is confirmed by the text itself. Not merely by accident is the referent mentioned—it is found in many important passages. In Chapter X of Book II, Augustine defines literal and metaphorical signs: "They are called literal when used to signify the things for which they were invented: so, for example, when we say *bovem* [ox], meaning the animal which we and all speakers of Latin call by that name. They are metaphorical when the actual things which we signify by the particular words are used to signify something else." This is the case, for example, when "ox" refers to a "'worker' in the gospel," according to Pauline exegesis (1 Cor. 9:9).[93]

Later, in Chapter VI of Book III, Augustine explains that the Jews "observed the signs of spiritual things in place of the things themselves—not knowing what they related to [*referentur*]."[94]

---

[91] St Thomas Aquinas, *Des Sacrements* (*S. Th. III, q. 60-65*), Appendix II (Paris: Desclée et Cie, 1951), 272.
[92] *The Teacher* X.34; *Saint Augustine: The Teacher, The Free Choice of the Will, Grace and Free Will*, trans. Robert P. Russell (Washington, DC: Catholic University of America, 1968), 47-48.
[93] Op cit., 71.
[94] Ibid., 143.

They nevertheless were able to nurture the faith and the desire to please God, thus preparing the first disciples to receive the message of the Holy Spirit. As he says in Chapter VIII, this is why "Christian freedom has liberated those whom it found enslaved to useful signs—they were, so to speak, not that far away—and by interpreting the signs to which they were subjected has raised them to the level of the things of which these were signs."[95] And in an important and tightly structured development, Chapter IX reiterates that in order not to be "enslaved by a sign," we must "not worship a thing which is only apparent and transitory but rather the thing to which all such things are to be related [*referenda sunt*]." Now, after the coming of Christ, this multitude of signs has given way to but a few, "such as the sacrament of baptism and the celebration of the Lord's body and blood. When an individual understands these, he recognizes with an inner knowledge what they relate to [*referantur*]."[96] It is specifically in knowing the reality they designate that we cease being enslaved by signs, knowing not to confuse them with what they symbolize.

Such is the meaning of the Augustinian doctrine of the sign. We now doubtless better understand the scope of the distinction between *signum* and *res*, which became the cornerstone both of hermeneutic theology (the Old Testament as the *signum* of which the New is the *res*) and of sacramental theology (the sacrament as efficacious *sign* of an invisible *reality*). In vain would we seek here for a prestigious ancestor for contemporary structuralism.

The Medievals

After centuries of oblivion, medieval linguistic and grammatical theories have stimulated renewed interest among scholars. Perhaps never before in the West has reflection on language had such a widespread impact, nor one so intimately linked to the most fundamental questions of philosophy and theology.[97] In this domain

---

[95] Ibid., 145.
[96] Ibid., 147.
[97] These are all the "liberal arts" (grammar, rhetoric, dialectic, arithmetic, geometry, astronomy, music) and their crown, philosophy, itself ordered to theological and spiritual work. This is attested by their depiction on the Royal Portal of Chartres: they "liberate" the human soul by impressing on it an intelligible form making it fit for the reception of divine grace. Dante says this as well (*Il Convivio (The Banquet)*, trans. Richard H. Lansing [New York: Garland Library of Medieval Literature, 1990], II.13).

The Sign According to Philosophy   163

as in others, the "great light" of the Middle Ages never ceases to astonish. Our purpose here is not to write even a brief history of linguistics, so we will make but a few remarks that seem most relevant to the theory of the sign presented above.[98] The medievals certainly did not develop the theory of semantic extraction, at least not to our knowledge. They also never refuted the radical structuralism and functionalism of the moderns. Yet their thought does intersect with ours on one point: the importance they give to the theory of signification. This is what we want to briefly explain.

As Gilson[99] and Chenu[100] would have it, the history of medieval linguistics from the fifth through the fourteenth centuries is that of a progressive victory of logic (or dialectic) over grammar. Ducrot and Tudorov, on the other hand, would convince us that under its most sophisticated form and at the moment of its greatest development, this linguistics "believed in the absolute autonomy of grammar in relation to logic."[101] This difference of opinion serves to highlight the extreme difficulty of the question. Bursill-Hall's work treats of grammar, but a grammar tending toward a logic of language which would be as rigorous and complete as possible.[102] Here the two meanings of *logos*

---

[98] It seems that there is in France no general work on the grammatical theories of the Middle Ages. [The present work had already been completed prior to the appearance of Joël Biard's *Logique et théorie du signe au XIVe siècle* (Paris: Vrin, 1989). We can now also refer to Alain de Libera and Irène Rosier's "La pensée linguistique médiévale," in Sylvain Auroux, ed., *Histoire des idées linguistiques* (Liège: Mardaga, 1992), t. II, 115–86.] Heidegger's study of the *De Modis Significandi* of Thomas of Erfurt (1350), falsely attributed to Duns Scotus, published under the title *Duns Scotus's Doctrine of Categories and Meaning*, contains long quotations in Latin that are often clearer than Heidegger's own writing. We have also used the basic work of Charles Thurot, *Extraits de divers manuscrits latins pour server à l'histoire des doctrines grammaticales du Moyen Âge* (Paris: Imprimierie impèriale, 1869); G.L. Bursill-Hall, *Speculative Grammars of the Middle Ages: The Doctrine of "Partes Orationis" of the Modistae* (The Hague: Mouton & Co, 1971); Thomas of Erfurt, *Grammatica Speculativa*, trans. G.L. Bursill-Hall (London: Longman, 1972); Marie-Dominique Chenu, *La théologie au XIIe siècle* (Paris: Vrin, 1957), 90–107; R.H. Robbins, *A Short History of Linguistics* (London: Longman, 1967), 66–93 (the best available current synthesis).
[99] *History of Christian Philosophy in the Middle Ages* (Washington, DC: Catholic University of America Press, 2019), 312–16.
[100] *La théologie au XIIe siècle*, 100. This is also Heidegger's view.
[101] *Encyclopedia Dictionary of the Sciences of Language*, 47.
[102] Earlier historians see a reduction of grammar to logic, and the more recent ones the reverse reduction: between them, structuralism has altered

meet: reason and speech. This is expressed in the title of Thomas of Erfurt's work, "On the Modes of Signifying: A Speculative Grammar." Not the descriptive grammar of a particular language, but a rational formulation of the general processes of expression at work in all language. And the place where grammar and logic come together is signification, which is established here in its proper and autonomous order, prior to the separation of the two meanings of *logos*.[103] If there is indeed, in discourse, a syntactical articulation of terms belonging to distinct classes of words (the "parts of speech": nouns, verbs, adjectives, adverbs, and so on) together with morphological variations within a word (e.g., the conjugation of a verb) this is because the signification of the word is *modified* by our signifying intention, by the way we see it and how we signify it. The very existence of syntax and morphology, and therefore of language, is a function of this desire to signify different aspects of the referent. All signifying intention is "modal": it only designates its referent because it has something to say about it, only signifies it under a certain mode. And "mode" is also "diversity," different significations and so different signifiers. If there were no modes, there would be only designation, not signification: there would be no language. Thus, to take a classic example, "whiteness," "whiten," and "white" all designate the same "thing," but in the modes of different signifiers. The noun signifies the color in itself, in its quasi-"substantial" permanence; the verb signifies the color by the mode of action it performs; the adjective signifies the color "as infused into and mixed with" the object.[104] The diversity in modes of signification therefore logically explain the diversity in parts of speech and their respective forms.

In other words, signification is a two-stage process, and this returns us to the distinction established by Benveniste between the semiotic and the semantic. First, there is the act by which sounds produced by the voice are transformed into signs by the

---

the very idea of grammar, which ceases to be a (literary) "description of good usage" and becomes a "science of language."
[103] Reason and speech.
[104] We are paraphrasing a text by John of Salisbury, itself summarizing the teaching of Bernard of Chartres: *Metalogicon* III.2; *The Metalogicon of John of Salisbury: A Twelfth Century Defense of the Verbal and Logical Arts of the Trivium*, trans. Daniel D. McGarry (Berkeley/Los Angeles: University of California Press, 1955), 152.

mind. We must indeed begin with the sensible reality of the sign, man as a social animal having no other means of communication. But vocal sound (*vox*) is not itself a sign: it is only an effect of the "throat and lungs."[105] In order to become a sign, a meaning must be given to it, that is, it must be related to a signified reality. This relation, called *significatio* by the medievals, turns vocal sound into speech (*dictio*). This is a real relation which is at once particular, being produced by a *sui generis* act of the intelligence; and yet different from that between, for example, smoke and fire, which does not signify. It is an effect of what Thomas of Erfurt justly calls man's *virtus interpretatia*, his "hermeneutic capacity."[106]

Second, there is the mental operation by which the sign, the already-meaningful and signifying vocal sound, is syntactically articulated, becoming part of a phrase and linked to other words to form speech. Insofar as it is a sign, vocal sound signifies. But as part of speech, it "consignifies": a second signification is added to the first, such that the *vox* is integrated into a group of signs. *Amour* and *aime*[107] have the same signification, but *aime* also consignifies the imperative form and refers to an actually pronounced sentence. This proposition is clearly summarized in the following passage: "the mind imparts a double property to the vocal sound: on the one hand, the property of signifying, which is called signification, by which the vocal sound becomes sign or significant, and therefore formally a *word*; and on the other hand, the property of consignifying, which is called the active mode of signification, by which the (already) significant vocal sound becomes con-sign or con-significant, and therefore formally part of speech."[108]

But signification and consignification not only transform sound into sign and sign into speech; they also govern the "substitutive value," the *supposition*. The distinction between *significatio* and *suppositio*, as well as the relative dependence of the second on the first, was elucidated notably by Peter of Spain.[109]

---

[105] *Duns Scotus's Doctrine of Categories and Meaning*, 77.
[106] Ibid.
[107] [Tr: "love" as a noun and as a verb.]
[108] Ibid., 89.
[109] The treatise, "*De suppositionibus*," in his *Summulae logicales*; cf. Thurot, 375; and Robbins, 77. St Vincent Ferrier also wrote a renowned *De suppositionibus* (1375).

The term *suppositio* is not easy to translate. Maritain renders it as "substitutive value,"[110] but this "dynamic" translation is imprecise. Literally, *supponere* (whence *suppositio*) means "to place beneath." The question is which thing the word "places beneath" itself, which real referent it replaces, which being it "stands for" or represents in the phrase where it is employed. A term on its own does not "stand for" anything, but rather *signifies* a certain essence. For example, the word "man" signifies only the human essence,[111] but in a sentence, and in virtue of the intelligible it signifies, the same word can "take the place" of very different real subjects. It is thereby placed in a relation with an external reality for which it "stands" in the order of language. Take, for example,[112] the same word "man" in the following three propositions: "man [Lat. *homo*] is a word of two syllables"; "the short man"; "man is a species." In the first case, the word "man" stands for itself *qua* word: this is the *material supposition*, which returns us to metalanguage. In the second, it stands for a certain real man: St Peter or St John. When not the word but an individual is short, we have the *personal supposition*. Finally, in the third case, the word stands not for individuals but for what they have in common: this is the *simple supposition*, as it concerns simply what the term itself means and not the concrete being in which it is realized.[113]

The doctrine of *supposition* and its distinction from *signification* corresponds, in its own order, to the modern distinction between sense and referent.[114] But what must be emphasized here is that the substitutive value remains dependent on the term's signification, on what we have called its "intelligible referent." Does it follow, as is often said, that the predominance of signifying modes leads us to a sort of psychologizing of grammar and logic, and thus of metaphysics? By no means. The *significatio* which the mind gives to the vocal sign has reality not only as a mental activity,

---

[110] Jacques Maritain, *Formal Logic*, trans. Imelda Choquette (New York: Sheed & Ward, 1937), 60.
[111] Hyacinthe-François Dondaine, in *Somme Théologique: La Trinité*, t. II, note 78 (Paris: Desclée et Cie, 1950), 342.
[112] Used by Ockham in his commentary on the *Book of Sentences*; cited by Fr Vignaux, "Nominalisme," *Dictionnaire de thélogie catholique*, t. XI, col. 737.
[113] These three types of *suppositio* essentially reflect, within the "substitutive" order itself, the three elements of the linguistic sign: signifier, referent, and meaning.
[114] Also, connotation and denotation, and intention and extension (Robbins, 77).

or nominalism is inescapable. We must here distinguish between an active mode of signification (the act by which a *significatio* is given to the *vox*) and a passive mode (which is the signification itself, given by the mind). Passive signification, the "meaning," expresses a property of the thing, an intelligibly signified objective quality;[115] it is not a mere psychic event. In reality — and now we can fully articulate the general doctrine of the Modistae — there is diversity in the modes of signification (corresponding to the different grammatical categories) because there is diversity in the modes of intellection of things (*modi intelligendi*), which is itself a function of diversity in modes of being (*modi essendi*). This doctrine is therefore fundamentally realist: being itself actualizes the intellect according to the particular aspect in which it gives itself to be comprehended. Thomas of Erfurt explains that the modes of signification are not "fictions" (*figmenta*): "they must find their radical origin in some property of the thing." And as the intellect needs an external agent in order to be in act, "when it gives to the sound the quality of being a sign under a certain active mode of signification, it is necessarily under the effect of a certain property of the thing, some mode of being."[116]

There is an active and a passive mode of signification, or as we would say today, signification as activity and signification as semantic content or meaning. In the same way, there is also an active mode of intellection, which is the intellect insofar as it grasps the mode of being, and a passive mode, the mode of being itself insofar as it is given to the intellect — the intellect as intelligible content, the essence of the thing *within* the intellect.[117]

Signification therefore functions in the following way: some mode of being determines an act of intellection, containing in itself a particular intelligible form and providing the ability to signify it by a vocal sign, whose meaning it is. As we can see, the whole process depends on the mode of being, on some quality of the being as revealed to the intellect, and this returns us to the intelligible referent. The *modus essendi*, the intelligible referent, lends unity to the signifying process: the concept is the mode of being *within the intellect*, and the meaning is the mode of being *within language*, having become significant, understanding that there is more in the

---

[115] *De modis significandi* I.1b; Heidegger, 90.
[116] II.2a; ibid., 91.
[117] III.3a; ibid., 95.

being than in the intellect and more in the intellect than in the linguistic sign. Thus in the twelfth century, Alain de Lille stated, "it is necessary to know that there are three elements: the thing, the intellect, and language...[but] the nature of the thing in itself is fuller and broader than the intellect: there is more in the thing than it grasps, and this is why the intellect remains outside the thing. Similarly, the intellect is fuller and broader than speech: we intellectually perceive more than we can express."[118]

The fundamental semantic triangulation continues to reappear in one form or another, along with the operation of signification by which the intellect discovers itself to be the revelation of the world's modes of being, a proposition leading directly into the metaphysical and religious order. It would indeed be false to see any of this as purely "linguistic."[119] At the terminus of its perfect formalization, it is certainly only a matter of "*grammatica.*" But had we been able to retrace the history of the doctrine, we would have been able to demonstrate the important role played by theological debate.[120] Confronted by the supreme task of "speaking God," language here reveals most clearly the modal nature of signification, thereby giving "modism" its true meaning. St Thomas demonstrates this in the following text, on the question of knowing if "God" and "Godhead" can be employed indifferently,[121] which serves to bring together all the themes of our investigation: "Now although 'God' is really the same as 'Godhead,' nevertheless the mode of signification is not in each case the same. For since this word 'God' signifies the divine Essence in Him that possesses it, from its mode of signification it can of its own nature stand for Person. Thus the things which properly belong to the Persons, can be predicated of this word, 'God,' as, for instance, we can say 'God is begotten' or is 'Begetter.' The word 'Essence,' however, in its mode of signification, cannot stand for Person, because it signifies the essence as an abstract form."[122] It therefore cannot be said that "The Essence begets" or "is begotten."

---

[118] *Summa* n. 9; Chenu, *La Théologie au XIIe siècle*, 99.
[119] This is why the current favor enjoyed by the Modistae is somewhat specious.
[120] This is precisely what Chenu does in his chapter on "Grammaire et théologie," op cit.
[121] God is all that He is, so His essence (Godhead) is identical to His existence; a particular man, however, is not humanity.
[122] *S. Th.* I, q. 39, a. 5.

The Sign According to Philosophy

What has been said will presumably allow for better comprehension of similar texts. The bearing of these distinctions can be better appreciated by noting that they assume their most radical metaphysical significance with Meister Eckhart, in his distinction between God and Godhead. But even in St Thomas, their influence was able to inflect the official Aristotelianism of his teaching. The relation established by the process of signification between the mode of being and a signifying audible form is so powerful that it threatens the received teaching on the arbitrariness of the sign. Thomas, commenting on Aristotle, defines the linguistic sign as *vox significative ad placitum*: "vocal sounds signifying according to convention."[123] And yet this institutional quality of the sign can be combined with an essential correspondence between signifier and signified: considering whether the Name of Jesus is suitable for the Incarnate Word, St Thomas replies, "A name should answer to the nature of a thing. This is clear in the names of genera and species... The names of individual men are always taken from some property of the men to whom they are given."[124] Aristotelian "rationalism" is thus caught up in a general context of symbolic correspondences in which the entire Middle Ages participated, which the rigor of scholastic definitions should *never* cause us to forget, the two being able to coexist without any contradiction.

The Doctrines of India

§1: **Classical Hinduism.** Like the medieval doctrines, Hindu linguistics witnesses both to a permanent metaphysical concern and to highly sophisticated technical preoccupations, principally in the domain of phonological analysis, where with Pāṇini (fifth century BC) and his commentator Patanjali (third century BC), India attained an unsurpassed degree of perfection. Among the *vedanga*—"auxiliary disciplines of the *Veda*," analogous to our "liberal arts"—grammar (*vyākaraṇa*) is considered primary. If John of Salisbury called it the "cradle of philosophy,"[125] Pāṇini considered it to be the "mouth of the *Vedas*."[126]

---

[123] *Peri Hermeneias* I.iv.6; Oesterle, 39.
[124] *S. Th.* III, q. 37, a. 2.
[125] Cited by Jolivet in *Histoire de la philosophie*, Pleiade, t. 1, 1458.
[126] *Pāṇiniya–Shiksha*, v. 41; cited by Jean Canteins, *Phonèmes et Archétypes* (Paris: Maisonneuve et Larose, 1972), 84, n. 1. Whoever desires to become

Beyond Tantrism, to which we will dedicate a more extended study, three types of meditation on language can be found in Hinduism: that of the pure grammarians, like Pānini; that of the philosophical grammarians, such as Bhartrihari in the fifth century; and that of the pure metaphysicians, as with Shankara in the eighth. These doctrines have been well studied in the West, and we will say very little about them.

Most address the question of the "arbitrariness of the sign," the absence of relation between the word (*shabda*) and its referent (*artha*). Unlike Buddhism, each school affirms the reality of such a relation. For *nyāya* (logic), this relation is conventional, but it is a convention (*samketa*) established by God (*Ishvarasamketa*),[127] and therefore enjoying a kind of eternity. For *mīmānsā* (Vedic ritual exegesis), the relation of word and thing is eternal and uncreated, like the *Veda* itself, which is uttered timelessly. With more precision, Patanjali explains that the link (*sambandha*) established by God[128] between *shabda* and *artha* is *nitya*, that is, "permanent" yet not properly eternal: the name is indeed arbitrary, "but the *system* of the *shabda*, the *artha*, and the functional link uniting them is nevertheless unchanging."[129]

However, for many grammarians, up to the eighteenth-century Nāgeshabhatta, the Lord as logothete does not act irrationally, and the link he establishes between *shabda* and *artha* "should be understood as illuminating a preexisting connection."[130] This is why, before accounting for this connection, the grammarians formulated the doctrine of the *sphota*, whose sound evokes the idea of "explosion" or "bursting." The "meaning of the word" preexists its audible utterance (*dhvani*). This is proven by the fact that it is contained in none of the audible elements of the word but is manifested to consciousness — in a "sudden explosion" — only after completion of the entire utterance,[131] like the invisible peak

---

acquainted with the "Science of Letters" should read this work, which is astonishing on a number of levels.

[127] *Nyāya Bhāshya* II, l. 55; S. Radhakrishnan, *Indian Philosophy* (London: George Allen & Unwin, 1948), v. II, 107.

[128] In his role as "logothete," legislator of names; cf. Plato, *Cratylus*, 389a; and Genesis 2:20.

[129] D.S. Rueg, *Contributions à l'histoire de la philosophie linguistique indienne* (Paris: Éditions de Boccard, 1959), 56.

[130] Ibid., 9.

[131] Louis Renou, *L'Inde classique* (Paris: Adrien Maisonneuve, 1985), t. II, 80.

The Sign According to Philosophy 171

of a mountain appearing when the sun lights upon it.

The *sphota* (the "soul of the sound") is in fact the grammatical translation of a metaphysical theory: it is identified with the Divine Word, the eternally uttered Sound. This teaching is found also in St Thomas Aquinas and Meister Eckhart, as we have seen.[132] It leads to a genuine theology of the Word, which lies, as Jean Canteins has said, "at the confluence of grammar and metaphysics."[133] This is especially the case of Bhartrihari, who in his *Vākyapadīya* ("Words and Sentences") develops the doctrine of the "God-Word," the "Theo-Logos" or *shabdabrahma*: "That beginningless and endless One, the imperishable Brahman of which the essential nature is the Word" is He who is the underlying reality of every signifying entity.[134] In consequence, "Speech and meaning, being the two halves of the one *Atma* [*Brahma*], are not distinct and separable."[135] The dominical institution of names only illuminates this eternal connection, yet it is indispensable, for in its absence—that is, without Tradition—we could have no knowledge of them.[136]

We will conclude by referring to Shankara, who certainly knew the work of Bhartrihari (the "Plato of India"[137]) and who commented on the distinction between *sphota* and *dhvani*: the latter is ephemeral and varies according to pronunciation, while the former is imperishable.[138] Even more fundamentally, we find here the importance of the intelligible referent as key both to the connection *and* the distinction between word and thing, *shabda* and *artha*. As he says, "it is with the essence that the words are connected, not with the individuals, which, as being infinite in number, are not capable of entering into that connection."[139]

§2: Kashmiri Tantrism and Shaivism.[140] The word "Tantrism"

---

[132] Cf 151, n. 76; and what we have called the "lexical meaning" (Saussure's "signified" and the Stoic *lekton*).
[133] *Phonèmes et Archétypes*, 84.
[134] I.1; *The Vākyapadīya*, trans. K Raghavan Pillai (Delhi: Motilal Banarsidass, 1971) 1.
[135] II.31 [Tr: altered].
[136] I.23. Here we see the union of *logos* and *mythos*.
[137] Madelaine Biardeau, *Théorie de la connaissance et philosophie de la parole dans le brahmanisme classique* (Paris: Imprimerie Nationale, 1964), 144, n.1.
[138] *Vedānta-Sūtra* I.3.28; trans. George Thibaut (New York: Dover, 1962), 206–7.
[139] *Ibid*, 202 [Tr: altered].
[140] The essential study here is that of André Padoux, *Recherches sur la symbolique et l'énergie de la parole dans certains textes tantriques*, Publications de

is used to designate the metaphysical, spiritual, and ritual doctrine expounded in those texts bearing the name *tantra*, a word evoking the symbolism of weaving.[141] Orientalists often see it as a relatively late religious movement, breaking with Vedic and Brahminic tradition. That there was such a rupture is not the opinion of Tantric adherents, who assert the Vedic and traditional authority of their doctrine.[142] As Guénon writes, "To tell the truth, it is more a question of a 'spirit,' if one may so express it, which in a more or less diffuse way penetrates the entire Hindu tradition in its present form, so that it would be almost impossible to assign it precise and well-defined limits within the latter."[143] This doctrine is considered uniquely adapted to the difficult conditions of the present cyclical age.

Within *tantra*, it is important to note especially those grouped under the name of "Kashmiri Shaivism," who relate to the Absolute primarily in its aspect as Shiva,[144] arising toward the end of the ninth century AD in northern India. Of their writings, those of Abhinavagupta (tenth-to-eleventh century) are certainly among the high points of universal metaphysics.[145]

The "philosophy" of *trika* (so-called because of the predominance of triads at all levels of analysis) foregrounds in its metaphysics the Divine Energy (Shakti), figured symbolically as the wife of Shiva. (In the West, we would speak of a god and his consort.) This Shakti is not considered a reality distinct from Shiva. We are indeed beyond all dualities and even their common source in Being, the first ontological affirmation, symbolized by

---

l'Institut de Civilisation indienne (Paris: Éditions de Boccard, 1963).
[141] Cf. René Guénon, *Studies in Hinduism*, trans. Henry D. Fohr and Cecil Bethell (Hillsdale, NY: Sophia Perennis, 2001), 65.
[142] Padoux, 45.
[143] *Studies in Hinduism*, 64.
[144] The *Trimurti*, or "Triple Manifestation" (of the Lord, *Ishvara*) includes three aspects: *Vishnu*, preserver of beings; *Brahma* (in the masculine), creator of beings; and *Shiva*, destroyer and transformer. These divine aspects correspond to the level of the (quasi-divine) archangels in Abrahamic tradition.
[145] Beyond the above-cited work of Padoux, we have made use of the *Paramārthasāra*, a Sanskrit text edited and translated by Lilian Silburn (Paris: Éditions de Boccard, 1957); as well as the *Vijnāna Bhairava*, also edited and translated by Silburn (Paris: Éditions de Boccard, 1961). These two texts provide particularly clear explanations of the thought of Abhinavagupta. See also: *The Trantrāloka of Abhinavagupta*, ed. R.C. Dwivedi and Navjivan Rastogi, 8 vols.

the number 1. The energy of the Absolute, *Maha-Māyā* or *Maha-Shakti*, is not really distinct from the Absolute Itself, *Paramashiva* or "Supreme Shiva." This is indicated clearly in the *Vijñāna Bhairava*: "Since there is never any difference between Shakti (Energy) and the Lord of Energy, and between the attribute and the possessor of the attribute (substance), therefore the supreme Shakti is not different from the supreme Self (*parātman*)."[146]

1) The "Supreme Word." Starting from this supreme degree, which is in truth no degree at all, Kashmiri Shaivism describes the theogonic and cosmogonic process in terms of the formation and manifestation of the word, based on the ontological correspondence between the first and second. This correspondence accounts for the central role of the word and its symbolism in Tantrism. It also explains, in turn, the divine and cosmic power of the ritual use of a sacred word, particularly in incantatory prayer, the process of reintegration into the divine being inversely analogous to the process of manifestation.

The essential idea that can be gleaned from these complex and extensive descriptions[147] is that the "Supreme Word," when it is produced from within the undifferentiated unity of the Divine Energy, causes the appearance at once of the Absolute's Self-knowledge, making Him the Lord of creatures, and of the knowledge of the innumerable multiplicity of the possibilities of creation. It is as if, by the emergence of the primordial Word, *Paramashiva* (the Absolute) "became conscious" of the distinction between Himself and the uncreated archetypes of all things. Shiva is consciousness (*chit*) or knowledge, and this consciousness includes two aspects: an aspect of "pure light" (*prakāsha*) and one of "awareness" (*vimarsha*). *Prakāsha* is Shiva, *vimarsha* his Shakti. But this energy of consciousness could not be distinguished from

---

[146] *Shloka* 18; *Vijñāna Bharaiva*, trans. Bettina Baumer (Varanasi: Indica Books, 2002), 16 [altered]. Ananda Coomaraswamy refers to this doctrine as the "divine biunity" (*Selected Papers, Vol. 2: Metaphysics*, ed. Roger Lipsey [Princeton: Princeton University Press, 1977], 231–40), and it is articulated by René Guénon, a Shankarian, in *The Multiple States of the Being* (trans. Henry D. Fohr [Hillsdale, NY: Sophia Perennis, 2001], 12). Curiously, one can find a statement of the same biunity in St Paul, in one of the most "theological" passages in the Epistle to the Romans: by means of visible things, we can intellectually grasp two aspects of God, "his eternal Power and Godhead" (1:20).

[147] Which should not at all be taken to imply any "becoming" in the Divine Principle.

the pure light were there not *vāc* or *Paravāc*, the "Supreme Word," which by its very manifestation as it were "reveals" the "energy" making it possible, such that one cannot isolate *vimarsha* from *vāc* nor indeed from *prakāsha*. As Padoux writes, "The word is that by which the universe is created, by which He sustains it, in which He reabsorbs it. Living consciousness is inseparable from the Word: as in this world, according to the aphorism of Bhartrihari which he takes from Abhinavagupta, there is no reflexive consciousness, no idea, which is not accompanied by the Word."[148] And as he goes on to say, there is therefore a manifestation "first within the archetype, in potency, under a purely energetic aspect."[149]

2) *The Logo-Cosmogonic Process.* But upon this intra-divine or theogonic process follows the cosmogonic. This process (and we are here following Padoux) can be described as an exteriorization, a progressive condensation, of the energy of the Word, considered as the energy of sound. The primordial sonic vibration (Shiva's Shakti) is condensed and, passing through a first resonance (*nāda*), becomes a "drop" (*bindu*) of sonic energy, divides, then gives birth first to the matrices of phonemes (*mātrikā*), and finally to phonemes (*varna*) and words. This sonic process is "signifying" (*vāchaka*) and so implies the appearance of the "signified" (*vāchya*), the world of objects (*artha*) and significations expressed by signifiers.[150]

We see that the steps of the cosmogonic process are rigorously parallel to the steps of phonematic emanation. When they describe these steps, from the purely interior and silent word, indiscernible from idea; through the language of the subtle mind, already formulated yet not audible; to articulated speech and

---

[148] Ibid., 69. In Christian language, *Paravāk* corresponds to the Divine Word, insofar as it contains in itself all the possibilities of creation, considered in a state of undifferentiated immanence.

[149] Ibid., 71. In the same way, as we have shown in *Love and Truth* (299–309, 326–36), the Holy Spirit, as "hypostatic maternity," can be seen as the very receptivity of God, in the unity of which the Father "begets" the primary Image, the first symbol of Himself. It is in this "Beginning" that God first creates the "Heaven and the Earth."

[150] Padoux, 73. We should mention that André Padoux published a summary of his doctoral thesis with Éditions du Soleil Noir in 1980 [English translation: *Vāc: The Concept of the Word in Selected Hindu Tantras*, trans. Jacques Gontier (Albany, NY: State University of New York Press, 1990)]. This work provides the only complete outline of phonematico-cosmogonic emanation and the doctrine of the *mantra*.

sound, Abhinavagupta and his disciples are also and without distinction describing the steps by which the world is created. These are traditionally three in number, leaving to one side *Parāvāc*, the Supreme Word, principial synthesis of undifferentiated creaturely determinations, itself "anterior" to creation "in the Principle" of Heaven and Earth. This principial "creation" would correspond, on its face, to the phonematic emanation called *Pashyanti*, the "Visionary." But *Pashyanti* corresponds also to the appearance of the intelligible world (*fiat lux*). It encompasses at once the "relative" aspect of the Non-Manifest and the highest degree of manifestation, the principial creation and the world of *Buddhi*. *Pashyanti* is said to be the "supreme non-supreme," and it is called "the visionary" because within it first appears the desire for sight, the root of subject-object duality, though we are here still within the "subject." At this stage, the archetypes (creaturely determinations) are qualitatively distinct from one another and no longer considered in the undifferentiated unity of the pure *Logos* (*Parāvāc*).

The second stage is called *Madhyamā*, the "Intermediary" (Word). It corresponds to the mental state and therefore to the subtle world (*sukshma*). Here we depart from the Informal and enter into formal manifestation, in the same way that in speech, "synthetic understanding" gives way to the elaborated mode of discursive language (in "phonemes, words, and sentences"). At this level, the distinction between language and thought arises, as also that between the linguistic sign ("what expresses," as Abhinavagupta says) and the objective world ("what is expressed"). However, this is a distinction only "in thought," as the linguistic signs are here still mental: this is the stage of the internally articulated word. It involves *antahkarana* (the internal organ), a term which comprises the three *tattva*: *buddhi*, *ahamkara*, and *manas*.[151]

---

[151] The mention of *buddhi* might be surprising, since the intellect relates to informal manifestation and *madhyamā* is of the subtle order. This question is very complex: let us say that it concerns precisely the point of connection between spirit and soul, the universal and the individual, the aspect of *buddhi* that "is engaged" in the individual being and "becomes" *ahamkāra*. (The word *ahamkāra* is formed from *kāra*, "maker"; and *aham*, "I"; whence the translation, "I-maker.") Individual consciousness is also knowledge (*qua* consciousness) and is therefore related to *buddhi*, while being of a subtle or psychic nature insofar as it is individual. It is a reflection of *buddhi* on the surface of the animic waters. Cf. Michel Hulin, *Le Principe de l'ego dans*

Thus the subject begins to distinguish the external and internal worlds, both within himself and by means of the internal word.

We come finally to *Vaikhari*, the "Gross" (Word).[152] This is the culmination of the cosmogonic as well as the linguistic process. What expresses (the signifier) and what is expressed (the objective referent) — linked by the signification bestowed by the word upon the object — are really and physically distinct, which also implies that the corporeal world exists in its proper exteriority, since it is designated by spoken linguistic signs. There is then a correlation between phonemes, the audible elements of language, and the elements of objects.

Finally, we would emphasize that each of these stages includes three aspects, corresponding respectively to *Pashyanti, Madhyama,* and *Vaikhari*. For example, there is a gross aspect to the Visionary, a pure sound with "a resonance as light and beautiful as a series of musical notes, not divided into phonemes."[153] This teaching of Abhinavagupta (*Tantrāloka* III.236–47) means that *Pashyanti, Madhyamā,* and *Vaikhari* are not only three successive stages in a logo-cosmogonic process, but are also three permanent modalities of all manifestation, corresponding to the three states of deep sleep, dream, and waking.[154]

3) Invocatory Reminiscence. We will say nothing of phonematic emanation, which describes in detail the particular signification of each of the fifteen phonemes as they pass from one state to another. This science is fundamental for everything concerning the knowledge and efficacy of the *mantra*. We will observe, however, in a remarkable similarity to Biblical teaching, that the transcendent emitting energy is symbolized by AHAM, the "supreme great *mantra*" (*paramahāmantra*).[155]

---

la pensée indienne (Paris: Éditions de Boccard, 1978).

[152] Padoux translates this as "Displayed," which he says "expresses one of the possible meanings of the Sanskrit" [Tr: In the English edition, Padoux explains that, while "Displayed" is how he renders it in French, "Corporeal" is his preferred English translation (*Vāc*, 216 n. 115)]. The audible (or written) word is indeed always linearly expanded or "displayed." This is Saussure's "linearity principle": a sign always follows another sign. "Gross" has here the sense of "material."

[153] Padoux, 202.

[154] The same goes for the anthropo-cosmological tripartition, as we have shown in *Love and Truth* (96). Cf. the concepts of the gross body, the subtle body, and the spiritual body.

[155] Padoux, 286. *Aham* means "I," "Me," "I Am." Padoux relies here on a

To conclude, we would like only to mention what is for us the most essential aspect. The ontological correlation (not to say identity) uniting the cosmogonic and phonematic process—the phases of universal manifestation and of the manifestation of speech—should be grasped in all its truth, not regarded only as an ingenious metaphor, or worse, as oriental ingenuity. It means that every act of speech, and particularly the invocation of the Divine Name, which is speech par excellence, not only retraces the cosmogonic process, but also effectively participates in this process. In our deepest ground, where speech develops and germinates, a ground to ourselves unknown, that is, to ordinary consciousness—in this ground, we are always present in the Origin of things and beings, and therefore in our own Origin. And this is why it is said, "whosoever shall call upon the Name of the Lord shall be saved." From this perspective, man is the being of invocation, since he is the being of the word, the only living being endowed with language.[156] And this fact itself, the manifestation of speech in man, "proves" that he is the being of invocation. This is what etymology seems to suggest: the word *mantra* is comprised of the root *man*, signifying properly human thought, and the suffix *-tra*, which is used to form words referring to instruments,[157] whence the meaning "instrument of thought" (cf. the concept of "theme of meditation"). But the *Trika* is even more explicit, since it relates *-tra* to the root *trai*, "to save," "to deliver." Whence the celebrated Tantric aphorism, "The *mantra* is so-called because its nature is thought (*man*) and deliverance (*tra*). It is indeed omniscient thought and deliverance from transmigration."[158] By pronouncing the divine *mantra*, due to the ontological correlation we have indicated, we actualize the supra-conscious "memory," borne within the heart of our human substance, of

---

text of Abhinavagupta (*Tantrāloka* III.203). He cites as a scriptural foundation this verse from the *Brihadāranyaka Upanishad* (I.4.1), which states that "In the beginning this (world) was only the self, in the shape of a person. Looking around he saw nothing else than the self. He first said, 'I am.' Therefore arose the name of I." *The Principal Upanishads*, trans. S Radhakrishnan (London: George Allen & Unwin, 1953), 163.

[156] Despite what is affirmed by the uneducated, there is no animal language in the proper sense of the term: cf. Benveniste, *Problems in General Linguistics*, 49–54.

[157] Padoux, *Recherches sur la symbolique de la parole*, 293.

[158] Ibid., 294.

the cosmogonic process by which it has itself passed in coming into existence. In the vibrations of the *mantra* is heard the direct audible echo of our own archetype, to which we are recalled and with which, by God's grace, we are identified. In this archetype, we are finally delivered from all accidental conditioning. The mysterious relation uniting invocation, remembrance, and deliverance is hereby revealed. Abhinavagupta writes, "Memory, a recalling to mind, is at the root of all the modalities of existence; verily its innermost nature is the mantra... Know that as such it is called supreme reality [or essence]."[159]

But in that the archetype actualizing the invocatory remembrance is one with the Supreme Word, from which it has in truth never departed, to this extent, "he who remembers is none other than the supreme Lord."[160]

* * *

In these doctrines can be easily recognized the essential themes of signification, metaphysically transposed, and of the revelatory role of speech in the awareness of self and world. We obviously could have expanded on this, gathering other texts taken from other cultural milieux, but the ideas in their essence would have been unchanged. Enough has been said in order to demonstrate the agreement among traditional doctrines concerning the sign. After these historical remarks, then, it remains to take up the description of the symbolic sign, the primary objective of the present work.

---

[159] *Tantrāloka* V.137–39; Padoux, *Vāc*, 397–98.
[160] Abhinvagupta, *Ishwarapratyabijnāsūtra Vimarshini*, 1.4.1; Padoux, 397.

CHAPTER VI
The Symbolic Sign

SPECIES OF THE SIGN

Ground of the Distinction between Species of the Sign

THE FOLLOWING DESCRIPTION EXCLUsively concerns sacred symbolism. Certainly, the word "symbol" is used to designate objects belonging to other domains, for example in mathematics or logic. But for reasons already given, and to which we will occasionally return, it is within the field of sacred symbolism that symbolic entities reveal their essential truth.

We will next note that, in speaking of the symbolic sign, we are thereby placing the symbol within the category of the sign as the genus of which the symbol is a particular species. This point seems hardly debatable. We have certainly opposed the sign to the symbol many times,[1] but the same goes here as for the Aristotelian definition of man as a rational animal: whatever the relevance of contrasts between man and animal, it remains the case that man *qua* living being is a mammal, even though from another perspective he surpasses animality and therefore transcends the category entirely. Symbol and sign can be similarly contrasted: insofar as it is a symbol, it nevertheless exercises a signifying function and therefore belongs within the semiotic category, yet from another perspective it surpasses this category and is therefore something more than a sign, perhaps even a quasi-sign. In other words, if we naturally consider man from within the animal kingdom, we naturally consider the symbol from within the semiotic field. Only here have we any chance of observing the functioning of symbols, even if just to note that they transcend this field itself.

This is the place to recall what was said at the beginning of this analysis, that structure independent of function is unintelligible. In the biological order, it might be possible to subsume

---

[1] Cf. *supra*, 61–62 and 63–64.

man and ape within a single category based on simple anatomical considerations—the morphological resemblances are obvious. Nevertheless, these can equally be misleading: a whale is not a fish, nor a bat a bird. In any case, this is obviously impossible for semiotic entities, which present such a variety of forms that, based on appearance alone, one could not even determine if they even belong within the category of signs. On the other hand, as for the animal kingdom, morphological resemblances are misleading and cannot serve as the criteria for differentiating species: though the cross on a traffic sign and that on a coat of arms or a priest's vestments can be morphologically indistinguishable, no less are they two essentially distinct semiotic entities. It follows that (1) the signifying function alone, and not the semiotic entities it includes, defines the category of signs; and (2) particular species of the semiotic genus are distinguished by the diverse modes according to which they exercise the signifying function.

In distinguishing the different species of sign, we are therefore led to inquire into the variations of which the signifying function is capable *a priori*. This requires defining it at the greatest level of generality, in its simplest and most abstract form. The preceding analyses reveal this to be the following: the signifying function consists in orienting thought toward an object (the referent or signified) through the meaning attached to a signifier. In other words, it is characteristic of the sign to make us think of something other than itself. This definition of the signifying function is essentially that given by Augustine (following Origen) and taken up by the entire scholastic tradition: "a sign is a thing which of itself makes some other thing come to mind, besides the impression that it presents to the senses."[2] The signifying function therefore involves establishing a relation between a signifier (or semiotic entity) and a signified (*signatum, res significativa*, referent). We will set everything else aside for the present, retaining only these two terms and the relation uniting them.[3] They can be quite different in nature: from the formal perspective we

---

[2] "*Signum est res praeter speciem quam ingerit sensibus, aliud aliquid ex sa faciens in cogitationem venire.*" *De Doctrina Christiana* II.1; trans. Green, 57. Cf. *supra*, 158.
[3] We therefore do not have to consider the intelligible referent, which relates to intention (what is meant) as well as the content of the signifying function, only the latter's simple *form*.

have taken, they are characterized entirely by the relation that makes one the signifier and the other the *signatum* to which it refers. It is therefore only the relation itself that varies, not in that it relates the signifier to the referent, but rather the manner of their relation. What causes such a variation, reflected in the different modes of signification? It can only be the ground of the signifying relation itself, the rationale relating the signifier to the referent. And this relation is active: the signifying function is an act of designation. It has a ground or rationale, which determines the mode by which the signifier designates the *signatum*. Such are the sufficient elements for a theory of the signifying relation: the ground provides the "why," while the mode provides the "how," but it sometimes happens, as we will see, that these are identical.

Having said this, note there are three possible grounds for the signifier's referential act: causal power, traditional institution, and ontological correspondence. To better demonstrate our thinking, we will take the distinction between the different types of signs presented in scholastic treatises as a point of departure.[4]

The Inductive Sign and the Institutional Sign

According to these treatises, there are two types of signs: natural signs, where signifier and referent have a natural relation, such as tears and sadness, or smoke and fire; as well as institutional (arbitrary, or *ad placitum*) signs, where signifier and referent are related "by human or divine choice," as in the linguistic sign. To these can be added the mixed sign, which "comes partly from nature and partly from institution." This third type is what mainly interests us, since it concerns sacramental and therefore symbolic signs, which would thus arise from convention while yet being grounded in the nature of things.[5] This is the case, for example, with the water of baptism and the symbolism of sensible elements, which is why Christ instituted them as the matter of the sacraments.[6]

---

[4] For example: Désiré Barbedette, *Philosophia scholastica* (Paris: Berche et Pagis, 1934), t. I, 26–27.

[5] "Sign," *Dictionnaire de théologie catholique*, t. XIV, col. 2054.

[6] St Augustine distinguishes also between what he calls the *signa data* (given signs) and *signa naturalia* (natural signs). He likewise combines the two in sacramental signs, which are signs *given* (by Christ) due to their *nature*: "The divine will, which permanently established the relation between signifier and signified, found grounds for its choice in the nature or action of a sign"

This classification, though not false, is somewhat schematic, and so does not avoid confusion. We will return shortly to the concept of the mixed sign; suffice it for now to register some disappointment at being limited to characterizing such an important category of signs as a mixture. This is not to deny that the symbol is both institutional and natural. But perhaps we should wonder what this means for the sign itself. Moreover, and this is the question we want to address first, in saying that the symbol is a mixed sign, we are necessarily considering it as a natural sign to which institutional election is added. But is this indeed possible, if we define the sign as we have and as illustrated by the examples given above? How can fire, animal tracks, baptismal water, and the oil of holy chrism all be placed in the same species? Is not the rationale (the ground) by which smoke signifies fire different from that by which water signifies the instrument of purification? This is an important question, leading us to introduce a distinction within so-called "natural" signs.

Considering the examples given by St Augustine in *De Doctrina Christiana* (II.2) — smoke as a sign of fire, tracks as a sign of a passing animal, the cries of an infant as a sign of its desire — it seems that we are faced with what the Stoics called the *semeion*, which they distinguished from the *semainon*, the linguistic sign. Fr Dubarle[7] rightly translates *semeion* by "epistemological sign," as what characterizes this type of sign is to increase our knowledge by allowing passage from the manifest and apparent to what is hidden, even invisible. This is essential, as it allows us to escape from the order of naïve knowledge (basically ignorance) and ascend to the hidden truth of things: the presence of milk in mammals is thus a sign that there is an infant, sweat is a sign of pores, and tracks of passage. We are dealing here with what medicine called semiology and what would today rather be termed symptomology. This is a vast field, and one that Aristotle did not fail to address, either from a logical point of view (the sign as proof or argument) or from a noetic (in physiognomy, for example, movements or lines of the face as signs revealing states

---

(*De doctrina christiana*, II.3) [Tr: Translated from the French]. St Thomas also takes up this doctrine: "From their very nature sensible things have a certain aptitude for the signifying of spiritual effects: but this aptitude is fixed by the Divine institution to some special signification" (*S. Th.* III, q. 64, a. 2).

[7] *Logique et épistemologie du signe chez Aristote et chez les stoïciens*, 32.

of the soul).[8] Setting aside the different distinctions that can be introduced in this species of sign,[9] we should remember that it does not only concern the order of profane knowledge but extends also to the religious: these are the "divine signs" of revelation, sensible effects by which man is "brought to a certain degree of supernatural knowledge of the objects of faith."[10] In the Old as well as New Testaments, miracles and marvels are used to testify to the power of God and so reveal or confirm His active presence.

Seeking now to grasp the ground of the signifying relation involved in all these cases, we see that it is basically a matter of causality, giving this term a somewhat broad meaning. The sign is an effect which, through its observable existence, testifies to its unobserved or unobservable cause. Causality here can be understood as either efficient cause (fire as cause of smoke) or else as condition of possibility, that *without which* the effect could not occur, rather than that *by which* it occurs (as in a miracle as a sign of the divine). Whatever the case, what predominates is the cause considered in its power, its efficacy. The sign-effect is a sort of excess, an overflow, which requires a causal reality (unobserved or unobservable) to give itself away, expand "outward," and thus reveal its indisputable presence. The sign-effect announces the existence of a cause, some *thing*.[11] But what is revealed about the cause? Nothing, or nearly so.[12] Smoke does not resemble fire, nor tracks passage, nor God a miracle. To a certain extent, it could even be said that the relation between sign and signifier is as surprising or unexpected as in the case of the institutional sign. This is why the designation "natural" sign does not seem sufficiently precise. One could doubtless describe the relation of

---

[8] *Prior Analytics* II.27; *Rhetoric* I.2 and II.25.
[9] The Stoics, for example, distinguished between the commemorative sign or "reminder" (*hypomnestikon*) and the revelatory or "indicative" sign (*endektikon*), according to whether, in the former case, the association between the signified and its signifier was once clearly observed (the connection between smoke and fire) such that the presence of the sign suffices to remind us of the thing signified; or, in the latter case, the signified is unobservable (for various reasons), and the sign can only indicate it or reveal its invisible existence (Cf. Sextus Empiricus, *Outlines of Pyrrhonism*, II.97–102; trans. R.G. Bury [Cambridge, MA: Harvard University Press, 1933], 213–17).
[10] *S. Th.* II–II, q. 178, a. 1.
[11] The word *chose* [Tr: "thing"] comes from the Latin *causa*.
[12] Analogously, for Aristotle, induction leads us to a thing's existence, but not to knowledge of it (which requires a deductive syllogism).

smoke to fire as natural, but this description would be applied with much more difficulty in the relation of tracks to a passing animal, and rather unfortunately in the relation of a miracle to God, where we would rather speak of the supernatural. And yet the signifying mode is unquestionably the same in all three cases: a miracle signifies divine power just as smoke signifies fire, by its character of being an effect, a contingent reality requiring a sufficient reason. Note that so-called "natural" signs are never wholly so, else it would not be a sign. Smoke is a sign of fire only if the fire is invisible or occurs in unusual circumstances. The miracle or marvel therefore realizes an essential aspect of the sign: more than any other, it shows the necessity of causality, and demonstrates more specifically the dimension of causal *power* through the marvelous and unforeseeable character of the observed effects.

It is fair, then, to assign causality as the basis for this category of signs, due to the necessity of some cause relating signifier and signified. As to the mode according to which this relation is effected, it could hardly be defined otherwise than as induction. "Induction," indeed, in Latin, means *to conduct toward*. This is exactly what the sign-effect does, which for this reason is called the *inductive sign*. We obviously leave to one side all questions related to the nature of induction, which concerns logic or philosophy of science, in the same way that we did not broach the distinctions established (or not) by semiotics between the index and the signal, as well as all other types of inductive signs.[13] These do not directly concern us here. We will just observe that the inductive sign satisfies the general fourfold schema of the sign we have previously described. For example, in the case of smoke and fire, the signifier is smoke, the objective referent is fire, the meaning (allowing passage from one to the other) is the experiential knowledge that fire is the cause of smoke, and the intelligible referent is the general notion of causality considered in its metaphysical reality. This latter far surpasses the simple determinism with which it is often identified, since it implies the unity of a transpatial and transtemporal cosmic "theme" or "idea," of which "step by step" physical determinism is only the

---

[13] These questions are outlined in Jeanne Martinet, *La Sémiologie* (Paris: Seghers, 1975), 49–51.

observable trace and which, in its principial and metacosmic root, is nothing but the creative power of *Natura naturans*.[14]

We are now able to approach the institutional sign.[15] We will not dwell on it, since we have spoken in detail about the linguistic sign. Nevertheless, a few remarks are necessary, which will lead finally to the symbolic sign. First, as we have suggested, this species of sign does not make a distinction between mode and ground, at least not if we hold to purely formal definitions. The idea of a pure convention is indeed that of a relation which would be its own ground: "it is so because we have decided it." Pure convention is foreign to the nature of the terms it places in relation—lacking knowledge of the convention, the referent could not be discovered simply by examining the nature of the signifier. *Why* is the institutional signifier related to its *signatum*? Because the semiotic system has decided it will be. *How* are they related? By institutional and known semantic conventions. Now, and this will be our second remark, can we not see in this institutional character the reason that the linguistic sign could serve as an example for the analysis of the signifying function in general? As we have already pointed out, whenever the signifier is not related to the signified *inherently*, due to its nature, the signifying function acquires at once a certain autonomy and self-existence, by which it appears in its own right. And this entirely conforms to the definition of convention we have just recalled. The signifying function is no longer buried within the naturalness of the signifier, but is presented and manifested in its irreducible actuality. Moreover, in comparing the institutional to the inductive sign, we will see that only the first truly performs a signifying function, whereas in the second case, the signifying function is nothing other than a causal relation *in reverse*. Nevertheless, and for our third remark, as we have repeatedly observed, there is no such

---

[14] We are indebted to the distinction between determinism and causality in the teaching of Raymond Ruyer. In his work, *Du fondement de l'induction*, 2nd ed. (Paris: Alcan, 1916), 97–102. Jules Lachelier has made an argument similar to the one we are sketching here. Finally, we can confirm the relation of the problem of induction to that of the symbolism of nature in the study Louis Millet has dedicated to *Symbolisme dans la philosophie de Lachelier* (Paris: Presses Universitaires de France, 1959) and the Neoplatonic inspiration of his thought.

[15] We prefer "institutional" to "conventional," as this term better expresses the relation to an institution, that is, to culture and tradition.

thing as pure convention. To the extent that it is the work of someone, a primordial legislator, whether an Adam logothete or God Himself, that is, a being who could not have acted without sufficient reason (freedom excluding the arbitrary), semantic convention necessarily participates in a certain naturalness.[16]

THE SYMBOLIC SIGN, TRANSFORMATIONAL UNITY OF THE INDUCTIVE AND INSTITUTIONAL SIGNS

We are thus led to a third species of sign, the symbolic. Must we define it in the Scholastic manner as a mixture resulting from a combination of the two preceding species? This is undeniably true, but remains formal. Either the symbolic sign results from a simple mixture of the inductive sign and the institutional sign, but then it is only an assemblage with no proper reality, and there is then no longer a symbolic sign *per se*; or this combination realizes an original synthesis of the inductive (the natural) and the institutional,[17] as is evidently the case, but then the elements constituting it undergo a radical transformation making them capable of coalescing in a unique and irreducible entity, despite what in them was previously contradictory. We must show what this transformation involves, not settling for an external definition. Such is the present task of an analytic of the symbol. To better demonstrate this twofold transformation, we will present two examples where it occurs clearly: the *semeion* in the Gospel of St John, where we see the inductive sign become symbol; and Rublev's icon of the Trinity, where the institutional sign in its turn undergoes the same transformation.

The Semeion in St John

The inductive sign, as we have said, is a natural sign. It announces that there is something to know, which we do not see but which the visible sign effectively reveals. It therefore relies on the idea that both the effect and its cause belong to the order of nature considered as causal power, but it does not give knowledge of the cause. Even in the case of miracles and marvels, only the power of God is revealed, not His essence.

---

[16] This doctrine agrees with that of St Thomas; cf. Roguet, *Les Sacraments*, 296.
[17] This means that the symbol essentially realizes a synthesis of nature and culture.

Actions belonging necessarily to an acting subject (*actiones sunt suppositorum*), observation of an action implies the existence of a (perhaps invisible) actor, of whom this action is the effect. To know the essence of this actor, however, we must go beyond simple observation, the simple apprehension of the inductive sign. Of the four questions distinguished by Aristotle — "the *fact*, the reason *why*, *if* it is, *what* it is"[18]— the inductive sign concerns only the first and possibly the third, given the existence of deceptive signs.[19] Induction is essentially performed in the mode of a sign, and the inductive sign does not lead to true knowledge, which requires grasping intellectually the *why* of the effect in the cause's rationale or essence.

Yet this is exactly what the symbolic sign asserts. It does not preclude that the signifier be understood as the effect of a cause which it reveals by its very existence, but asserts further that the effect is the image of its cause, that the cause does more than signal its *existence* through the index of its effect; rather, it manifests its own essence within the effect itself, due not to causal power but to exemplarity, that is, the effect's participation in the essence or form of the cause. In other words, from the standpoint of the symbolic sign, the effect is not *essentially* distinct from the cause, only existentially so, which means, from this point of view, that there is no purely and exclusively inductive sign. It is our way of understanding the sign, then, our intellectual gaze, which makes it alternately an inductive or a symbolic sign, a sign of true knowledge and not only of existence. At any rate, this is so when we consider things from the perspective of symbolism, where the inductive sign is but the extreme lower limit of the symbolic sign. There is no longer an irreducible difference between them, and this is why the inductive sign can be transformed into the symbolic sign. But as we see, this is also on condition that we pass from an Aristotelian to a Platonic etiology, from efficient to participatory causality.[20]

---

[18] *Posterior Analytics*, II.1, 89b, 22–25; trans. Jonathan Barnes, *Complete Works of Aristotle, Volume 1: The Revised Oxford Translation*, ed. Jonathan Barnes (Princeton, NJ: Princeton University Press, 1984), 147.
[19] See in particular Robin's analyses in *Aristote* (Paris: Presses Universitaires de France, 1944), 52–59.
[20] Aristotle undoubtedly maintains that the form (or essence) is the (exemplary) cause. But his doctrine does not provide for an account of this form's causal power.

It appears that St John can help us in this transition. Certainly, the "sign" (*semeion*) frequently encountered from the Evangelist's pen almost never loses the signification of "miracle" or "wonder," testifying, in the eyes of those who can truly enter into direct knowledge of the mystery of Christ, that an indisputable divine power is present in this man. This interpretation must be held firmly against an exegesis anxious to excuse itself for the rationalist impropriety of a faith founded thus on thaumaturgy, and which would easily transform all miracles into pure "symbols," fruits of the primitive community's pious imagination. This is impossible. The texts are absolutely explicit about this, and we should take them for what they are and with their clearly expressed intention of presenting us with a man invested with wholly extraordinary powers. Such, moreover, is the proof Christ gives to the messengers of St John the Baptist come to question him on behalf of their imprisoned master: "Go your way, and tell John what things ye have seen and heard; how that the blind see, the lame walk, the lepers are cleansed, the deaf hear, the dead are raised, to the poor the gospel is preached. And blessed is he, whosoever shall not be offended in me" (Luke 7:22–23).

Before coming to the Johannine text itself, however, it must be observed that the word "power" in the New Testament, almost always in the plural (*dynameis*), is found only three times on the lips of Christ and is hardly used except by witnesses to miracles.[21] Further, St John never uses it in his gospel, which knows only *semeion* to express this idea. What then does this word mean from his pen?[22]

An explanation can be provided by a phrase, traditional in Jewish literature, frequent in the Acts of the Apostles and the epistles of St Paul, which John uses once: this is the formula, *semeia kai terata*, in which the wonders are linked to signs. This phrase translates the Hebrew *'otot we-mophetim*. As Dodd notes, if the singular *mophet* signifies a miracle, the singular *'ot* translated by *semeion* does not imply the idea of the wonderful or marvellous: "it is used by itself for a pledge or token, between man and man

---

[21] It is indeed by the word "miracle" that French Bibles translate the Greek *dynameis* (Matthew 7:22, and so on). But *miraculum* is absent from the Latin New Testament, which renders *dynameis* by *virtutes*.
[22] We are here following the analyses that C. H. Dodd dedicated to St John's symbolism in *The Interpretation of the Fourth Gospel*, 133–43.

The Symbolic Sign 189

or between God and man."[23] What an astonishing confluence! This was precisely our definition of *symbolon*. The equivalence of *semeion* and *symbolon* was already noted in the case of the bronze serpent in the Septuagint, with the latter term explicating the former.[24] And this is no doubt one of the sources of the symbolic dimension of the Johannine "sign."

But there is perhaps another. Philo of Alexandria does not associate *symbolon* only with *allegoria*, as we have already pointed out;[25] there are also many instances of the *semeion-symbolon* couple. Concerning the trees in Paradise, for example, which are "pleasant to the sight" and "good for food," Philo explains that the first formula is "the *symbolon* of the contemplative" and the second is a "*semeion* of the useful and practical."[26] We are certainly dealing here with a more technical and intellectual sense than in St John, but it is proof at least that in the time at which the gospel was written in Greek, for the public to whom it was addressed, a *semeion* was indeed truly a symbolic sign.

However, philology alone does not ensure that the *semeia* in St John "are for him to such an extent the immediate epiphany of the thing itself—Christ's divinity—that the faith resulting from the *semeion* is for him tantamount to a 'vision' of Christ's glory and of God's glory in Christ."[27] More profoundly, this comes from the metaphysics implicitly structuring his gospel.[28]

Such an implicit metaphysics is expressed through the symbols St John uses and the way he speaks of them. Even without alluding to the sacramental and liturgical background which gives the mention of water, bread, and wine their signification

---

[23] Ibid., 141.
[24] Cf. *supra*, 20–21.
[25] Cf. *supra*, 17–18.
[26] *Legum Allegoriae*, I.58; cited by Dodd, 142.
[27] Balthasar, *The Glory of the Lord*, v. I, 134.
[28] This formulation could give rise to some objections, the partisans of a certain Christian existentialism seeing in metaphysics only a conceptual betrayal of what is addressed first of all to our very being: Christ wants to save us, to liberate us, not teach us philosophy, which moreover seems incompatible with the eminently concrete nature of the Semitic spirit. His words are impulsive presence, not speculative description. But we must choose: either metaphysics is pure vanity, and the case is closed; or else it sets forth the truth, and its message is the truth of being, that is, it says intellectually what is said concretely and directly in the Holy Scriptures. The refusal of metaphysics expresses, in the exegetes above all, the narrowness and even falsity of the understanding they have of it.

as religious symbols, we should note the insistence with which St John speaks of the *"true* light" (1:9): "true," here, means "real." And if there is a true vine, a true light, a true bread (which came down from heaven), there is also a merely apparent light, vine, and bread, which have but the shadow of reality. And what can these be if not sensible realities, such as we know them, shadows — but also images — of intelligible realities? Did St John know Plato? Difficult to say. But, as Dodd argues, "in any religious philosophy the conception of a *kosmos noetos* in some form or other was assumed — the conception of a world of invisible realities of which the visible world is a copy. It seems clear that the evangelist assumes a similar philosophy. His *phos alethinon* is the archetypal light, of which every visible light in this world[29] is a *mimema* or symbol."

But conversely, this participation in the eternal or celestial archetype is what grounds the reality of visible beings. "Bread, vine, water, light, are not mere illustrations or analogies. A vine, insofar as it is a vine at all, bodies forth the eternal Idea of Vine; except in so far as it does so, it has no significance, indeed properly speaking no existence."[30] The Platonic nature of all sacred symbolism could not be better expressed. And what goes for cosmic realities applies equally to historical events, deeds, gestures, even the names of places — such as the pool of Siloam, where Jesus sends the man born blind to wash, which John tells us (9:7) must be "interpreted" (*hermeneuetai*) as meaning "Sent" (*apestalmenos*), referring to Christ himself, as *Chiloah* (Siloam) in Hebrew designates an "aqueduct" that "sends" water into a pool.[31] The acts of the Incarnate *Logos*, such as the miracle at Cana, the multiplication of the loaves, the healing of the man born blind, all of which St John calls "signs," are essentially

---

[29] This is how John designates the light of the sun (*to phos tou kosmou toutou*, 11:9).

[30] Dodd, 139–40.

[31] What a difference between patristic hermeneutics, which sees in Christ's mixing mud with his saliva to anoint the eyes of the blind man a symbol of the creation of man, of the Incarnation of the Word, or of the union of nature and grace; and that of modern or contemporary exegetes (Erasmus, Lagrange), who interpret it "psychologically" as a testing of the man's faith, with the rational and scientific justification that this process would only deepen his blindness! There is in this such a "petty bourgeois," "Renanian" spiritual flatness, such an absence of the sense of divine realities, that we might be surprised such a thing as the Christian religion even still exists.

symbols, due to what Dodd calls the "intrinsic unity of symbol and thing symbolized."[32] And so history itself has substance and reality only through the eternal and sacred incarnated within it. St John's thought does not vacillate between a fabulous and unrealistic "symbolism" and a historicizing literalism. He simply ignores such an oscillation, so essential to Western hermeneutics at least since the so-called Renaissance, wherein one can affirm historical reality only against symbolism, and symbolism only against historicity. He would not even have understood this.

We can conclude that the inductive sign is transformed into the symbolic sign by conversion of the meaning of its naturalness. The naturalness of the symbol is no longer grounded in the order of causality: "nature" here is *essence*, the *nature of things*. Efficient causality is certainly not lost from view, but is absorbed in a deeper relation—the ontological participation of the visible in the essence of the invisible, by and in which it becomes the latter's manifestation and epiphany.

The Rublev Icon

We should now account for the transformation undergone by the institutional sign in becoming a symbol. Let us only say (and we will return to this crucial point) that far from being opposed to the naturalness of its ground, the election of the semiotic entity as a symbol by cultural institution relies on it, expresses and authenticates it. The signifying function no longer obscures a threatening naturalness, but rather realizes this latter by allowing itself to be borne by it into full flowering. This is what we will now briefly demonstrate.[33]

Let us consider Rublev's famous icon, "The Trinity." We find within it the following elements: colors; natural objects (a rock, a tree, the sky); works of art (a temple, a stone table, a cup, robes, scepters); people (three angels seated around the table, making certain gestures); geometrical forms (circle, octagon, rectangle, triangle, cross); dynamic relations between these elements (a circular movement starting from the left foot of the person on

---

[32] Dodd, 140.
[33] We could have also studied the Johannine *semeion* on this point and come to the same conclusions. However, it would perhaps be more instructive to consider a relatively late (fifteenth century) pictorial work, in which the Christian cultural system is therefore expressed in full force, than a founding text in which that system is expressed in a nascent state.

the right, sweeping along the rock, and leading to the angel on the left; the direction of the gazes of the three angels; and so on); value relations among the colors (through contrasts, or else by the rhythmic repetition of colors within different forms); relations of proportions (for example, the body of each angel being four times as large as the head, whereas natural proportion is seven). All these elements are symbols, and so the question is, why and how do these signs signify what they signify? There can be no doubt as to the answer: by institution. Tradition, the Christian cultural system, determines the significance of each of these symbolic entities.[34] Human beings with wings signify angels, halos signify sanctity and glory, scepters signify royalty, the lamb originally contained by the cup signifies the immolated Christ, etc. Lastly, tradition also teaches us the synthetic signification of the work: it is a representation of the Trinity.[35] Yet this information raises some difficulties: what are angels doing in such a depiction? And the tree in the midst, the rock, the temple, the table, the cup? Let us consider the cultural institution. We learn that it is a representation of a scene from the Old Testament, the appearance of YHWH to Abraham at the Oak of Mamre in the form of three men (or three angels) whom Abraham provided with a meal.[36] We therefore find ourselves presented with a Christian reinterpretation of a pre-Christian event, in which the Christian cultural system sees the proclamation, the figure, the type, the symbol, not of a future event, but of a dogmatic truth only revealed later.

This reinterpretation is not at all surprising. Quite the opposite: such a process is commonplace in the Christian tradition. But in this case, a few comments are necessary. First, an icon is not written with the specific intention of interpreting the Old Testament, as a work of exegesis. The path is rather somewhat the reverse: it

---

[34] Among commentators on this "icon of icons," we refer to Paul Evdokimov, in *The Art of the Icon: A Theology of Beauty*, trans. Steven Bigham (Redondo Beach, CA: Oakwood, 1990), 243–57; and, partly drawing on Evdokimov, Abbé Henri Stéphane, *Introduction à l'ésoterisme chrétien* (Paris: Dervy, 1979), 164–69. The major work remains Leonid Ouspensky's *Theology of the Icon*, trans. Anthony Gythiel (Yonkers, NY: St Vladimir's Seminary Press, 1992).

[35] The role of cultural institution is not limited to fixing significations, but also determines the cultural use of the icon and, above all, consecrates it. We will leave this question to one side for now.

[36] Gen. 18:1–15.

is meant to presentify a spiritual reality—even, as here, a divine reality—and for this it uses elements taken from Holy Scripture, already reinterpreted, introducing them into a completely different semantic universe. The crossing of the Red Sea prophecies baptism, but is not really baptism; the sacrifice of Isaac prefigures that of Christ, but is not to be identified with it. In these two cases, and in many examples of typological hermeneutics, we find ourselves *within* sacred history. With the scene at the Oak of Mamre, on the other hand, we leave history behind. YHWH manifesting Himself under the form of three angels is already a true revelation, not a figure, of the Trinitarian mystery.[37] Consequently, as a further comment, the interpretation of the Christian cultural system does not involve giving a secondary meaning to a reality already in possession of one, but rather reveals what, from its own point of view, is the fundamental meaning of that reality, what it always was, but which could not be seen because the Revealer—Christ, the Hermeneut par excellence—had not yet appeared. The Trinitarian mystery is eternal and therefore present to all time. Only its revelation is historical. It was proclaimed at the Oak of Mamre, accomplished and grounded by Jesus Christ, source of the tradition, logothete of the Christian cultural system, *institutor* of the signification given by this system to all its semiotic entities. But at the same time, this Christic *institution*, as we have said, introduces the semiotic entities into another semantic universe; they enter into a vertical relation of ontological correspondence with the realities they symbolize. It could even be said that they are prophetic figures, yet they are no longer prophecies in time, but rather *prophecies in being*. This is why we said that the purpose of the icon is to *presentify* a divine reality, make it somehow present to us, or rather make *us* present *to it*, to the extent of our contemplative receptivity. From the perspective of their semantic transfiguration, symbolic entities are no longer historically situated: the Oak of Mamre is identified with the Tree of Life and finally with the World Axis; Abraham's home is identified with the Church and finally with Mary, its celestial prototype; the table of the meal becomes

---

[37] Jewish commentators evidently interpreted the three men as three angels, justified in part by the verses following, which speak of two angels (19:1). For Rashi, they were Michael, Gabriel, and Raphael. Cf. *La Voix de la Thorah*, a commentary on the Pentateuch by Elie Munk: *La Genèse* (Paris: Samuel et Odette Lévy, 1976), 180.

that of the eternal sacrifice of the Lamb "slain from the foundation of the world";[38] and so on for the rest. As we see, the significations of each element are layered on three hierarchically ordered planes: the human and natural plane, the Christic and supernatural plane of the work of salvation, and finally the divine and metacosmic plane. Each of these is in ontological correspondence with that which is immediately superior to it and of which it is a manifestation and presentification. A single prototypical nature, essence, or reality is expressed on three different levels, along with all the intermediary levels these represent synthetically, a unity of essence crossing and unifying all the degrees of being or reality. This is as it were "proven" by the unicity of the semiotic (or signifying) entity, since it is always the same symbolic form that is visibly offered to the Christian who contemplates the icon. Yet it is as though, to the degree of their contemplative receptivity, in a sort of silent penetration, behind each mystery one more elevated and luminous is unveiled. The knowledge the mystic eye thus gleans from the sacred work is like a motionless progress drawing us further into the secret of its ineffable beauty. There is for each signifier, then, a plurality of referents, and this plurality is not accidental but is instead *entirely essential* to the symbol. This important observation requires development if we wish to grasp its full significance.

SEMANTIC POTENTIALITY OF THE SYMBOL AND ONTOLOGY OF REFERENCE

The Symbol Signifies by Presentification

We will briefly confirm that the symbolic sign is at once an institutional and a natural sign, specifying that, far from being contradictory or simply additive, these two aspects merge and even reciprocally condition one another. This, to our mind, is the logic of the symbol. But this logic is so synthetic (definitionally so) that it is quite difficult to demonstrate analytically all its implications. The essential plurality of referents can nevertheless be of some assistance to us.

We begin with the idea of the naturalness of the symbolic signifier, since this governs everything else. In the example of the Trinity icon, clearly, and we have stressed this, the signification of the work is to be found *within* the work itself, we would even say

---

[38] Revelation 13:8.

on the work itself. Whereas the reading of a text virtually excludes the perception of the concrete forms of the written signs, here, the intelligible vision is instead primarily and essentially the perception of a sensible form, a perception as direct, as immediate, as naïve, as attentive, as loving as possible. The colors and forms must be allowed to sing freely in their inexhaustible reality. One of the major obstacles to the "meaning" of the icon is actually the semantic desire, an abstract will to mentally grasp a signification when one should simply look.[39] Ultimately, the naturalness of the signifier therefore identifies it purely and simply as a being of nature, which as such seems to fall totally outside the symbolic order. How then—faced simply with a rose, a tree, a swan, a man—are we to know that it is a sign? This is perhaps rare in Christian symbolism, but is common in that of the Far East, particularly Chinese and Japanese painting, which has pushed the art of the natural to an unequaled perfection. Has the *diacrisis* of the sign not here entirely disappeared? Cultural institution becomes necessary to alert us to and teach us the semiotic function of the sensible form, thereby liberating it from semantic silence.

Cultural institution makes symbols speak. It should therefore be considered a true hermeneutic, or rather one of the major chapters in the history of the hermeneutics of symbols. We will attempt to treat this more systematically in the following article. For now, being primarily interested in the symbolic sign, we will simply raise the most important issue this function of cultural institution poses with respect to the symbol's signification: is a fatal contradiction not introduced into the symbol itself? If culture assigns the referent, how can we maintain that the symbol signifies inherently? And if it does, what is the point of cultural institution (in other words, hermeneutics) assigning its referent?

To respond to this objection, we must consider the mode of signification proper to the symbol—what we have called "signifying by presentifying"—and distinguish this from the linguistic mode, whose widespread use tends to impose it as typical of all signification. As we have shown, to speak is to speak *about* something:

---

[39] We speak only of the initial phase. This is not to exclude the necessity of a "mediation of the eye," a hermeneutic tour of the work, imposed by the work itself. Marcel Lamy demonstrates this in a magisterial study, titled *L'œil médite: Note sur deux chapiteaux du Portail Nord de l'église Notre-Dame du Cunault* (1982, typescript).

the relation to the referent is structural for the linguistic mode of signification. What we have referred to as its "designativity" or "mediateness" ensures that it forms the matrix of all objectifying consciousness—the experience of language is the origin of our discovery that there are objects before us *and* that they are not ourselves. Moreover, consider the Bible's very explicit teaching in the second chapter of Genesis: it is in naming beings and objects that Adam discovers that there is nothing in the world akin to him.

The relation to the objective referent, constitutive of the linguistic mode of signification from the philosophical perspective, is popularly seen as a fixed and biunivocal relation between words and things—the "glossary" conception of language rightly rejected by Saussure. Scientifically, we are forced to realize this relation in artificial languages functioning according to the ideal norm: one signifier, one referent. Having done so, we forget the intelligible referent, forget that to speak is not only to *speak about* something but also to *say something about* it. Although the vertical relation to the intelligible (or semantic) referent is primordial, it is as if obscured by the horizontal relation to the objective referent. The signifying function appears entirely realized in the designative function, and this is why language can be misleading; conversely, when the semantic referent comes to dominate over the objective referent, it appears as poetry, "language within language."

The symbolic sign clearly breaks with the mediateness of the linguistic sign and instead manifests the greatest possible predominance of the semantic referent—"possible," that is, compatible with the nature of the sign. To speak as we have of a "*suspension of the referential orientation*" is to assert that every signifying function is necessarily realized in designation. But there is another mode of signification, which is realized in presentifying. This mode is proper to the symbol, as its purpose is to make the semantic reality (dare we say) "substantially present." What signifies within it is the very naturalness of the signifier. The signifying function is exercised here on the basis of the symbol's own existential presence, which presupposes, as the ground of this signifying mode, an ontological correspondence between semantic and symbolic being.

This is not the place to develop all of what such a ground and such a mode implies *metaphysically*,[40] namely, that in the

---

[40] This will be developed in *The Metaphysics of the Symbol*, the last panel of our triptych. [Ed.: Never written as such, see *supra* 73, fn. 12]

last analysis, for a symbol to signify by its own naturalness, the cosmos must be naturally symbolic. But we should understand that precisely because it signifies by presentifying, and therefore *inherently*, the symbol speaks only under the operation of hermeneutics. The necessity for interpretation, far from contradicting the "self-semanticity" of the symbol, presupposes and realizes it. Remember that language is its own interpreter: it speaks *about everything* and therefore *about itself.* But without exception, it does not inherently "sensify," as Ruyer would say.

Semiotic Reference and Symbolic Reference

Our analysis of the symbol should therefore direct us to the following assertion, which should finally be stated clearly: *a symbol has no semiotic referent.* This is the conclusion suggested by the foregoing, as it alone fits with our conclusions. The semiotic referent is that proper to the semiotic entity, which we have called the objective referent, and designates the sign in its activity of signification, that its function is *essentially* to designate. Two features characterize this semiotic reference, which the present comparison with symbolic reference allows us to underline, though we have already more or less explicitly referred to them in our analysis of the sign.

The first feature is that, not only does discourse speak *about* something, but in so doing, it indicates the order of reality to which its object belongs, either directly or by implication. In neither case is there symbolism, properly speaking. Ordinarily, the *ontology of reference* of discourse is taken to be the world of common experience, the sensible world as well as the universe of mental activities and moral, political, social, and other realities. This property of language is a consequence of the role played by the experience of signification in the awareness that there is a "world," an order of objective and permanent reality: in semiotic reference, to posit an object is also to presume a world of which that object is a member. Typically, then, the intelligibility of discourse is predetermined by the idea that the *ontology of reference* is that of ordinary life. Nor, generally, is there symbolism when discourse itself indicates that its ontology of reference is not that of common experience, as in abstract language, such as that of philosophy and theology; and in the language of fiction, such as that of the novel. It might be objected that there are cases where language explicitly asserts its symbolism—often in poetry, and more so in the Holy Scriptures.

But to declare a language symbolic is precisely to abolish, not suspend, ordinary or direct reference; it does not determine reference. For example, when Christ proclaims that He is speaking in parables, that is, in a symbolic form,[41] He still does not indicate the degree of reality to which one should refer in grasping His meaning; and without exception, He leaves His listeners at the mercy of their own hermeneutic. From this perspective, explicitly symbolic discourse is no different from that which is so implicitly. The latter is found whenever the literal meaning is "impossible," when discourse, which only uses signs with ordinary reference, bars this reference as in conflict with its laws, at least within the understanding of our empirical logic. Thus in Genesis, the narrative of the Fall of Adam is necessarily symbolic: we are told of a tree, for example, something which belongs to common experience, but a Tree of the Knowledge of Good and Evil does not conform to any that we know.[42] This confirms *a contrario* that the symbol has no semiotic referent, even when it makes use of the linguistic sign—the latter's most basic property (to have a defined referent) is used to signify that we are dealing with a symbol.

The second feature characterizing semiotic reference is its effect on the sensible reality of the signifier, which it causes to disappear as such. We hardly need dwell on this, having mentioned it more than once. Once the (written or spoken) linguistic sign is understood, it is literally no longer perceivable, at least in the positivity of its sensible existence. It is as it were swallowed up, absorbed by the signifying function. To read is not to perceive, and is even to not perceive. On the other hand, the symbolic sign persists as such and survives all hermeneutics. Semiotic reference absorbs the sign, and necessarily so, since the sign is such only insofar as it has a referential orientation—it is essentially transitive, essentially turned toward its complementary object. Yet the symbolic sign is essentially *intransitive*, for the very reason that it is not required to submit to the law of semiotic reference in exercising its signifying function, but need only be what it is.

---

[41] Many disputes have arisen concerning whether parables should be included among symbols. Their conclusions have never seemed decisive, even if they have highlighted certain clear distinctions.

[42] We have examined this question in a series of articles in *La Pensée catholique* (July through August, 1984) and reprinted in *Un homme, une femme au Paradis* (Geneva: Ad Solem, 2008), chaps. 4, 5, and 6, and in *Aux sources bibliques de la métaphysique* (Paris: L'Harmattan, 2015), chap. 12.

The Essentially Multiple Orientation of the Symbol

This comparison leads us into the presence of the symbolic signifier, into the plenitude of a sensible reality that seems to have absorbed or obscured the signifying function. In the last analysis, and after the unfolding of every consideration, the original ground of any symbol remains a natural being existing before us, just as it is—water (of baptism), tree (of life), gold (of a halo), cup (of salvation), dance (of Shiva), black stone (of the Kaaba). It will be objected that there exist abstract symbols—numbers in Pythagoreanism or the Kabbalah, musical rhythms in sacred dances, geometrical relations between symbolic elements, such as in architecture. Even simple concepts, such as the act by which the mind utters an interior word, which is taken in Latin Christianity as symbolizing the generation of the Son. Can a sensible reality still be spoken of here? Indeed it can, extending the domain of the sensible to include interior and purely intellectual perception. The preceding examples are symbols not insofar as they are abstract, as operations of the mind (what Descartes called their formal reality), but rather insofar as they are contemplated in their actual nature, as pure essences or qualities (what he called their objective reality), in the *opacity of their mental presence*.[43] In Pythagorean number theory, the *quality* of 1, 2, or 3 is the symbolic signifier, not the quantity they represent.[44] Similarly, the relations comprising a network of

---

[43] The opacity of the symbolic sign will rightly, if not without ambiguity, be opposed to the transparency of the linguistic sign. We have pointed out this opposition on several occasions. The Russian Formalists have themselves spoken of a "perceptibility" of the symbolic sign, particularly in the poetic domain. Jakobson writes of the "opacity" of signifiers in the poem (*Questions de poétique* [Paris: Seuil, 1973], 14). But the opposition between opacity and transparency is ambiguous because, from another perspective, one could just as easily speak of the opacity of the institutional sign, which signifies nothing *inherently*, whereas the symbol *inherently* allows something of the signified reality to shine through due to their participative identity. It is in fact not the linguistic sign that is transparent, but the signifying function, as we have amply demonstrated. Transparency and opacity do not apply to the conventional sign, only to the symbol, which unveils (transparency) even as it veils (opacity), as with everything belonging to *Māyā*.

[44] Can we indeed speak of quality for any given number? Beyond a certain point, they seem to lose their "individuality." Yet number symbolism actually considers only the first ten and reduces all others to these through various processes, which themselves have symbolic significance. The source of our knowledge on this subject is, in the West, the presentation given by Nicomachus of Gerasa in his *Introduction to Arithmetic*, which Jeanin Bertier

symbols are themselves seen as qualitatively expressive, and are often reducible either to numbers (as in relations of proportion) or geometrical figures (relations of position). Whatever the symbol under consideration, then, its symbolic substance is always grounded in what is naturally given in the signifier.

Does this mean that the symbolic sign is entirely without referent? Many semioticians lean toward this conclusion, but if this were the case, it would no longer be a sign—which it nevertheless is, as demonstrated by all traditional cultures. Two considerations could lead in this direction: first, Western intellectuals generally believe that there is no other reality than the corporeal world, and so a sign without reference in this world is a sign without referent *tout court*. Second, language is given predominance over all other categories of signs, even when discussing symbolism, despite symbolic language being unproblematic, as we will see shortly. And for our part, in speaking of the symbol, we are careful to guard ourselves from thinking primarily of discourse. Insofar as the referential aim defines the linguistic sign, to consider the symbol exclusively within the framework of language is to see it as a semiotic entity failing to satisfy this condition. But once its ontology of reference is no longer conceived on the model implied by common experience, nor its referential orientation on the model of linguistic reference, then it becomes possible, even necessary, to speak of the symbol's referential function.

The referential orientation of the symbol is therefore beyond doubt, but it is determined neither implicitly, as in the case of the most ordinary language; nor explicitly, as can sometimes occur. In these conditions, the only remaining option is to understand this referential orientation as essentially multiple—"essentially," meaning constitutive of the symbol's essence. Such was the conclusion established from the example of the Trinity icon. But to speak of a multiplicity of referents is in fact to understand the signification of the symbol as essentially potential, in other words, that the symbol is, in its essence, a semantic potentiality. The linguistic sign no doubt also has a certain semantic potentiality, since (with the exception of artificial languages) the meaning of a signifier is not absolutely determined: there are many possible

---

has published in an annotated translation (Paris: Vrin, 1978). The clearest article is by René Guénon, "On the Production of Numbers," *Miscellanea*, trans. H. D. Fohr et al. (Hillsdale, NY: Sophia Perennis, 2001), 42–50.

meanings. This should not be surprising. The differences between the linguistic sign and the symbolic sign, metaphysically, are of degree rather than kind; each realizes in its way one of the two major poles of the sign, the linguistic sign realizing more particularly the signifying function, and the symbol realizing more particularly the signifier as such. However, the potentiality of the linguistic sign is taken to be an accident, not part of its essence, as with the symbol. This is in fact an imperfection, a defect in the signifying function, even as it makes possible the use of language, as we have already noted. On the other hand, the semantic potentiality of the symbol constitutes its proper perfection.

Semantic Unity and Transcendence of the Symbol

We could formulate this in the following way: the plurality of referents for a linguistic sign results in different meanings, whereas the meaning of a symbol is almost always unique, or rather is *one*, across the plurality of referents. One can certainly always speak of a plurality of meanings for the symbol, and we do so ourselves: this is due to the fact that ordinary language does not clearly distinguish meaning from referent, which is particularly appropriate to the linguistic sign. As we have shown in our analysis of the act of signification, the referent is taken as the starting point from which to select a signifier in such a way that the lexical meaning is almost entirely inflected, modified, and invested by the referential function. To take the simplest case, the meaning of the signifier "table" is determined, on the basis of its lexical possibilities, by the referent it would designate: a piece of furniture, for example, or a moral code (tables of the law). Insofar as the linguistic signifier is conventional, it is always secondary with respect to the object it denotes.

But the symbolic signifier is primary, and this for many reasons, of which at least one is obvious: the object it denotes outstrips our ordinary knowledge, or better, the referent of the symbol is not an object, a "thing" endowed with a well-defined and identifiable existence within a spatiotemporal frame. It is therefore no longer this referent which determines the meaning of the symbol, modifies, inflects, or invests it, but rather the *one* meaning of the symbol is as it were "capable" of a plurality of referents which it indicates in a synthetic and potential manner, and which hermeneutics is tasked with *unfolding*.

A moment's reflection will convince us that it could not be otherwise. On the one hand, indeed, simple referential plurality is equivalent to pure semantic dispersion: in this case, the symbol could signify anything whatsoever, which is the same as signifying nothing at all. On the other hand, if hermeneutics determines the meaning of the symbol considered as pure potentiality of reference, such that the symbol loses its ontological primacy, it becomes, *qua* symbol (that is, *qua* significant sensible form) a *product* of interpretation. The symbol would simply be a given sensible form transformed by hermeneutics into a symbolic sign. But in this case, it would no longer be a symbol, whose essential characteristic is to signify inherently. We must therefore hold that the symbol has a single meaning which is *given* in the symbolic signifier itself, but that this meaning is not the inherent signification of any particular referent: this is precisely why we have spoken of a semantic potentiality, which calls for hermeneutics in order to unfold the different degrees of its ontology of reference. We see that plurality of referents and unicity of meaning are mutually implicated. If the symbol inherently had a determined multiplicity of meanings, this would mean that it necessarily points toward a determined multiplicity of referents. It would thus lose its symbolic quality and be transformed into a lexical code.[45] The essential polysemy of the symbol would disappear, since as Aristotle saw, an accidental polysemy is arguably equivalent to monosemy.[46] But between strict monosemy (in artificial languages) and determinate, numerable polysemy (in natural languages), there is room for a semantic potentiality. Such a "meaning" is not the signification of one or more referents, or more precisely, it is a meaning not insofar as it is signified, as with the linguistic sign. Rather, it is a meaning *absolutely*, so to speak, an intrinsic semantic reality. The plurality of referents is

---

[45] This can indeed occur in symbolism, for example in that of alchemy or astrology, which is inevitable to the extent that symbolism becomes a technical language for the communication of information. However, it is always possible to rediscover the symbol beneath the code, and possibly even to correct the form of a symbolic sign whose natural foundation has been forgotten. In this way, Titus Burckhardt suggested replacing the normal sign of Mars (a circle topped by an arrow) with a circle topped by a cross, which would become the exact inverse of the sign of Venus. *Alchemy: Science of the Cosmos, Science of the Soul*, trans. William Stoddart (Baltimore, MD: Penguin, 1971), 78.
[46] *Metaphysics* Γ, 4, 1006b.

thus only the other side of the symbol's semantic unity, or better, *its indifference to any determined ontology of reference*. But this single and absolute meaning, which exists inherently, is nothing but the symbolic signifier itself in the unity of its own nature, an autonomous and irreducible semantic presence.

It must nevertheless be observed that the meaning's indifference to its referent is possible only if this is understood as following from the symbol's transcendence. The symbolic meaning is naturally foreign to a determined order of referents only because pure intelligibility, pure semantics, surpasses any given ontological degree. And such surpassing consequently implies multiple degrees of reality: to transcend an order, or rather a hierarchy of multiple orders or degrees of being, is at once to awaken us to consciousness of this multiplicity. Again, the symbol does not reveal this multiplicity to us by pointing toward it, as does the linguistic sign, though this is exactly how it is usually spoken of. It does not transitively indicate it, but implies it, presupposes it by its very existence. It is indeed itself a natural existent, which however does not belong, *qua* symbol, to the order of known existents. It is not quite even an existent, rather a semantic presence. Or perhaps it would be better to go as far as saying that the symbol converts every existent into a semantic presence, teaches us to renounce the philosophical fiction of a natural existent, self-sufficient and enclosed upon itself, and to see in things only the manifestation or incarnation of a meaning. The symbol threatens the Aristotelian ontology of individual substance, to the extent that this ontology is something other than a provisional cosmological approximation and thinks to found metaphysics on the world of common experience, because this is seen to be incapable of accounting for the reality of the symbol. In other words, challenging the unicity of the existential order would have no real effect if it did not occur within this order itself. Metaphysical discourse can challenge the pretensions of those who limit reality to what is revealed to the senses, provoking nothing but contrary assertions. But as we will demonstrate in another work,[47] the symbol is, by its very existence, an implicit metaphysics, the silent witness to "something other," the proof of an essential ontological alterity. And existence cannot be refuted.

---

[47] *The Crisis of Religious Symbolism.*

This is not merely to say that the symbol witnesses to this or that "other world," but more radically, that it awakens us to consciousness of every possible "other world." Everything transcendent reveals the finitude of the order it transcends: it is the vertical revealing the horizontality of the planes it traverses. Yet to discover that the world is finite is to at least potentially discover the innumerable multitude of other worlds, and more profoundly, what lies beyond every world. Thus we see that the symbol, as semantic transversal, realizes what was begun in the act of signification: we have demonstrated that the discovery of signification was the original experience in which the distinctive knowledge of the world as an objective whole finds its root. The symbol now elevates us to the awareness that this whole is finite, else it would not be whole. It shows us that to think and posit *the* world is to think and posit *a* world, and therefore to open us to what lies beyond it. The symbol is therefore *fundamentally salvific*.

HERMENEUTICS IN ACCORD WITH THE SYMBOL—MEMORIAL AND ANAMNESIS

We have to this point defined the specific traits of the symbol: naturalness of the signifier, semantic potentiality and plurality of ontologies of reference, and transcendent unity of its meaning. These account for the non-contradictory character of its definition as a mixed sign, at once natural and institutional. Our question was, what must the symbolic sign be for its naturalness to be in accord with institutional election? We must now pose the opposite question: what must this election be in order to accord with its fundamental naturalness? But as we have suggested many times, this arises from another, more general question, which must now be asked in its own right: what hermeneutic is in accord with the symbol? And first, are there not many forms of hermeneutics, which perhaps must each conform to it in a particular way? When we proposed considering cultural institution as a hermeneutic, it could already be understood that we were giving this term a much more general meaning than it has ordinarily, defined as knowledge of the rules governing the interpretation of the Holy Scriptures (exegesis designating more precisely the application of these rules).

But if we observe, on the one hand, that there is hermeneutics wherever there is a symbol, and that, on the other, symbols are encountered everywhere, as much in the great "Book of Nature" as in the Scriptures or sacred forms, we will be led to envision a universal hermeneutics, of which the preceding would form no more than a particular branch: the term would designate all of humanity's relations with symbols, whatever they may be. Thus understood, universal hermeneutics is essentially nothing other than symbolic *culture.*

Culture, precisely, in its most direct sense, will serve as our guide in distinguishing three forms of universal hermeneutics— which refer to domains not at all mutually exclusive but rather intersecting and ordered to one another.

"Culture" means primarily to work the earth: according to Littré, it is the whole of the operations proper to obtaining plants needed by men and domestic animals from the soil. We can distinguish in these operations three different areas of activity: first, planting (or sowing) the plants in the soil; then, growing them to full height; and finally, harvesting them and making them fit for consumption, by which they are transformed into animal matter.

Institutive Hermeneutics

The first operation, planting or sowing, always involves taking a plant or seed, separating it from the collection of all plants generally and integrating it into a particular grouping, in a determined soil, according to a proper arrangement and in new relations with other plants.

This operation appears to be a quite accurate image of what cultural institution—tradition or religion—performs with respect to the symbol. Symbols preexist institution, since they are ultimately always beings of nature. It is proper to tradition, first, to choose from the theoretical set of possible symbols some symbolic entities (and this is why we have often spoken of "election" in this respect) and to insert them within a particular whole, that of the tradition in question, order them relative to one another according to determined symbolic constellations, and make them serve the tradition's specific uses. It could be said that the purpose of this first hermeneutic form is not to invent the symbol's meaning but to fix it, determine it, and consecrate it. By the symbol's semantic fixture, we must understand that every religion officially "declares" the symbols it employs by fixing their signifying function within the tradition, such that each religion possesses its own symbolic vocabulary whose terms are grouped according to defined constellations. This planting in the soil of a particular tradition truly "institutes" its symbols, by making them privileged means of expression for the institution. This fixture, which is opposed to the "volatile" and universal character of the symbol, is operative — and can be discerned — in the Holy Scriptures, traditional arts, and ritual forms. It entails a limitation of the symbols' meaning, or rather an accentuation of certain semantic aspects at the expense of others which remain, if not latent, at least marginal. For example, in Christianity, the symbols of water, the cross, and the serpent will develop above all the significations of purification, of sacrifice, and of deceit, while other traditional employments develop different semantic aspects. This can be called the "determination" of symbols, which emphasizes that their meaning is inherently limited, whereas fixture corresponds to the other face of the same limitation, which considers it relative to the human community making its own use of these symbols. Finally, the consecration of symbols, a consequence of fixture, then of determination, confers upon them a spiritual power, the capacity to place the use of the symbol in contact with the Spirit, or better, to realize the symbol's property of communicating with the Spirit. This is religion's raison d'être. Every religion presents itself as a manifestation of the Spirit, or if you will, as the place where the Spirit consents to manifest itself. It is the guarantor of this manifestation, thus requiring faith in its testimony, and promises that a given symbolic form actually has the power to communicate the Spirit to us, provided we fulfill the necessary conditions. This guarantee of the spiritual power of symbolic entities is certified by their consecration. Moreover, that this power is conferred upon the symbol by consecration does not mean that it comes from outside, for we could always maintain that it only restored an efficacy that the symbol had lost or held within itself virtually. Such is the first form of hermeneutics, which we name "institutive." Observe that, of the three operations we have attributed to it (fixation, determination, consecration) the first defines institutive hermeneutics alone, while the others already introduce the two remaining forms, which we have called "speculative" (or intellective) and "integrative" — true indeed, as we have said, that these different forms are mutually implicated and intersecting.

Speculative Hermeneutics

The second hermeneutic corresponds to the second phase of agricultural labor, that of growth. We have characterized it as the complete development of the plant to full maturity. In the same way, speculative hermeneutics should, at least in principle, unfold the symbol's entire semantic potential. We must perhaps admit that the semantic exhaustion of the symbol belongs to what lies beyond all speculation—that is, of all hermeneutics, given their close connection: the speculative is the proper form of hermeneutics, its form par excellence, in the same way that speculation, and especially metaphysics, is almost always, at least in practice, a hermeneutics of symbols and of the Holy Scriptures.

We just saw that institutive hermeneutics is in accord with the symbol's own semantics insofar as it only involves rooting it in the soil of a particular tradition. For speculative hermeneutics, the conditions for accord are different and even the reverse: if the institution of a symbol particularizes a sign which is in itself virtually universal, in speculative hermeneutics, by contrast, the particularity of the symbol meets the necessity and universality of intellection. There is therefore no speculative hermeneutics in accord with the symbol except that which recognizes within it a content in accord with the nature of the intellect. One could say that such is the first postulate of this hermeneutic. In other words, prior even to unfolding any meaning from the symbolic entity, this hermeneutic presupposes an affirmation concerning the entity's nature. The symbol realizes a concrete metaphysics of sensible forms—it is a concretion of the *logos*, in the same way that metaphysics is an intellectual unfolding of the *mythos*. It can be proven, and we will attempt to do so, that any other potential hermeneutic leads either to contradictions or to reductions incompatible with the nature of the symbol.[48]

That the symbol is a concrete and implicit metaphysics is precisely what was established by our entire analysis of the symbolic sign, demonstrating that the symbol signifies by presentifying, by making its meaning present by its very existence as a formal reality. The symbol is a concretion because it is a corporeal reality or natural form, and this concretion is metaphysical because the natural form signifies inherently, is endowed with a *semantic ray* surpassing

---

[48] *The Crisis of Religious Symbolism*, 379–89.

every determinate *physis*. Everything that has been said about the semantic potentiality and unity of the symbol as a presence within our world of something not of this world, leads us directly to a metaphysics of the degrees of reality. This metaphysics, implicit in the symbol, becomes explicit in speculative hermeneutics.

The primary act of the intellect is the knowledge of being. The intellect is a function of reality, or rather the sense of reality, as the eye is the sense of the visible. In the same way that red and yellow have meaning only for the eye, not for the ear or the tongue, reality, being, has meaning only for the intellect.[49] Or again, the intellect is in essence ontologically referential, is that which "perceives" being. Yet there are degrees of this perception, for the intellect does not grasp being as such, only as enveloped within an intelligible. Being orients the intellective aim, but the aim itself, what the intellect itself grasps in its act, or rather that by which it is grasped, is an intelligible enclosed in being as the condition or root of its reality. As we have seen, there are for Aristotle four sorts of questions: "the *fact*, the reason *why*, *if* it is, *what* it is."[50] Arab and Christian scholasticism particularly emphasized the importance of the latter two, which relate more immediately to metaphysics, and which concern existence and essence, or being and intelligibility. The fact that the question of being is posed proves that the intelligible is not necessarily enclosed in being, but that the former can be thought apart from its existential reality, and therefore that the intelligible inherently overflows a determined degree. Indeed, the question could not be posed if we could think *only* intelligibles whose existence is known immediately, for then we would have no experience of an intelligible whose existence is in question. The only existents of which we have immediate and direct knowledge, taking only common experience, are corporeal. The question of being therefore presupposes that this class of existents is in reality a determinate degree, or what comes to the same thing, that the response to this question is necessarily a function of the fullness of our knowledge of reality, the ontological horizon of our intellect.

In other words, if the intellect poses the question of being, this is evidently because it is the desire for and directedness toward being, the sense of being which seeks its object as its proper good

---

[49] We have outlined this position in our philosophical anthropology, in Chapter 7 of *Love and Truth* (121–24) as well as other works.
[50] *Posterior Analytics* II.1, 89b, 22–25; trans. Jonathan Barnes, 147.

and beatitude, but also because it is conscious of a multitude of possible degrees of being, and it can therefore not identify being with corporeality. In fine, the intellect is inherently the sense of *being* as such, but it can generally only experience *qualified* being, and more specifically *corporeally* qualified being. For the intellect to understand is therefore explicitly to situate its object within a determinate ontological degree consistent with its essence.

Returning now to our hermeneutical problem, we will see how the act of interpreting the symbol conforms to the nature both of intellection and of the symbol due to the doctrine of the degrees of reality, since on the one hand, this doctrine is implicit and concretized in the symbol, while on the other, the work proper to the intellectual act is precisely to explicate and posit it in itself: the intellect realizes the perfection of its nature by interpreting the symbol. But we understand also that each interpretation will be a function of its understanding of reality and the different degrees it allows within the latter.

We can therefore now state the proper task of speculative hermeneutics without risking misunderstanding: it assigns to the symbol its ontology of reference, establishes the order of reality to which the symbol refers, and this is obviously first a function of what the intellect recognizes as real. The preconception of reality determines hermeneutics, which many hermeneuts and semioticians do not in the least suspect.

The intellect, as we have briefly tried to demonstrate, finds in itself the doctrine of the degrees of reality, or rather the requirement for such a doctrine. But as for the determination of these degrees, knowing what they are and how to identify them, this can only be arrived at by *reflecting* on corporeal reality and by *listening* to the teachings of the metaphysical tradition, which in the West is broadly represented by Platonism. The intellect's openness to reality is therefore in turn a function of its fecundation by Platonism, but a Platonism "confirmed" by reflection on the sensible world, for according to a formula we read somewhere in Muhyiddin Ibn Arabi, "the seven heavens are on earth." The contemplation of the corporeal world can itself offer to the intellect, enlightened by metaphysical tradition, the occasion for recognizing the different degrees of reality, at least synthetically.

We will illustrate these considerations concerning speculative hermeneutics with the help of René Guénon's interpretation of the symbol of water in *Man and His Becoming According to the Vedānta*.[51] The occasion is provided by a passage from Shankara's commentary on the *Brahma-Sūtras* (also called the *Vedānta-Sūtras*), where the Master declares that the Self is no more affected by its reflection in the individual soul than is the sun by the movements of its reflection on the water.[52] Guénon relates this to Genesis, which says that the Spirit of God moved upon the face of the waters (1:2) and also speaks of the separation of the "upper waters" from the "lower waters" (1:6–7). "If the symbol of water is taken in its general meaning, then the sum of formal possibilities is described as the 'lower waters' and that of the formless possibilities as the 'upper waters.'"[53] Note the expression, "its general meaning." There is indeed a single signification, yet this is applied to different degrees. It could be stated as follows: metaphysically, water is the symbol of the possibilities of creation; cosmologically, it is the plastic and passive principle, the (non-material) "*materia prima*" of which all things are made, which fills all forms while taking the form of none, and so remaining virginal with respect to each. Formal possibilities concern the corporeal and psychic (subtle) world, which is characterized by the presence of form as condition of existence, which is to say that the beings of this world must be limited and distinguished from one another by their individual form in order to exist. Informal possibilities concern the spiritual (angelic, intelligible) world, in which beings need not be clothed in a limiting individual form to exist and be distinguished from one another, but rather subsist and are differentiated by their proper and intrinsic "quality," as red is distinguished from blue and not as one pine tree from another.

Guénon continues, "It is also worth noting that the word *Maïm*, which means 'water' in Hebrew, has the grammatical form of the dual number, which allows for its conveying, among other meanings, the idea of the 'double chaos' of the formal and formless possibilities in the potential state." After which we pass to another degree of reality, leaving the macrocosm for the divine world, the domain of metaphysical principles: "The primordial waters, before their separation, are the totality of the possibilities

---

[51] Trans. Richard C. Nicholson (Hillsdale, NY: Sophia Perennis, 2001), 50, n. 8.
[52] II.3.46–53; cited by Guénon, 48.
[53] [Tr: Guénon translation altered.]

of manifestation, insofar as the latter constitutes the potential aspect of Universal Being, which is properly speaking *Prakriti*.[54] But there is also another and superior meaning to the same symbolism, which appears when it is carried over beyond Being itself: the waters then represent Universal Possibility, conceived in an absolutely total manner, that is to say insofar as it embraces at the same time in its Infinity the domains of manifestation and non-manifestation alike." The Waters therefore symbolize, (1) at the supra-ontological level, the infinite limitlessness of the Divine Reality; (2) at the ontological level, the universal protoplasmic substance; (3) at the intelligible level, informal possibilities; (4) at the subtle level, formal possibilities; and (5) at the corporeal level, the element designated by this name. At each level, it is always the same symbol, and further, it is always essentially the same meaning, the same theme, the same semantic potentiality, for the Ontological Waters are nothing other than the Supra-ontological Waters as limited to Being—that is, the primordial ontological determination or affirmation, which as such is distinguished from negation. The Informal Waters are nothing other than the Ontological Waters as limited by their manifestation or exteriorization in the created world. The Formal Waters are nothing but the Informal Waters as limited by their mode of individual existence. And the corporeal waters are nothing but the Subtle Waters, relatively coagulated by the spatial condition affecting them. This means that corporeal water, in its most immediate essence, is nothing but Universal Possibility as known and made present here below, as much as our conditions of existence allow. This essential and underlying identity, in spite of all existential discontinuities, is expressed by the symbolism itself, which we can then appropriately describe as a semantic transversal: the essence of water is one and identical, yet the degrees of existence "intersecting" it are so distinct as to admit no possible (ontological) comparison between them.

This ontological incomparability between the degrees of Reality means, for example, with respect to Infinite Being, that all of

---

[54] *Prakriti* in Samkya philosophy designates primordial Nature, the original Womb from which all things arise: she is the consort of *Purusha*. But in Vedānta, which is the perspective Guénon adopts, *Prakriti* is an aspect of Being as Creator and Lord (*Ishvara*). To speak of a *potential* aspect of pure Being, as Guénon does, is problematic.

creation, considered in itself, is as if nonexistent. But it means also, and conversely, that within a determinate degree, the higher are imperceptible; it is as if *they* were nonexistent. The relation between a higher degree and a lower is not reciprocal. All the lower degrees of being are contained within the degree immediately above them, which is the case pre-eminently for Principial Reality, which is moreover not a degree (or is so only from the perspective of the lower) and which contains the whole within itself. But all lower degrees ontologically exclude the higher degrees—inclusion from the higher to the lower, exclusion from the lower to the higher. As St Thomas Aquinas says, God sees the world "in Himself."[55] This all-encompassing "vision" is God's Knowledge of all things, enclosing all things within its orbit and thereby realizing their unification in the Principle. Consequently, it cognitively extracts them from their proper mode of existence, since it is precisely by this mode (being a particular limitation of Infinite Reality) that they are distinguished and separated from the Principle. To exist is to "stand out" (*ex-sistere*) from perfect Reality, and thereby to fall towards nonbeing. If this fall were to reach its terminus, it would be annihilated, and existence could not "take place." Existence is therefore paradoxically possible only because this fall toward nonbeing is as if arrested by a contrary attraction: this is the action of the Divine Knowledge, realizing the unity of all things in the Principle through their archetypes. Here we see that knowledge is converted into being to the very extent that being is converted into knowledge. In other words, the ontological coherence of created beings is of a semantic (or cognitive) nature. God's knowledge of secondary realities prevents their pure existential dispersion, their annihilating pulverization: *esse est* percipi, *a Deo*. The different degrees of reality should moreover not be considered fixed and unmovable: on Jacob's Ladder were seen "the angels of God ascending and descending." It is only for the purpose of exposition that we represent these degrees as immutable regions, however accurate this may be in certain respects. But we should not forget that they are the site of a *permanent conversion* of being into knowledge and of knowledge into being, and this for all possible degrees.[56] If we

---

[55] S. Th. I, q. 14, a. 5.
[56] We think here of the illusion of scientism in the nineteenth century, which considered the (material) corporeal world as a stable given and

represent the divine gaze as a ray of knowledge given color by each archetype as by a prism, we could say that whenever this ray meets a given degree, it halts and gives birth to a being (thus converting knowledge into being) which receives the image of the archetype transmitted by the ray and returns it to its origin (thus converting being into knowledge).

As it stands, this metaphysics of the degrees of reality suffices to reveal an essential aspect of the symbol—the symbol as memorial.

The symbol indeed appears as a memorial in the eyes of speculative hermeneutics, the memorial of the all-encompassing knowledge of God. It is itself the memento and memory of this knowledge's continuing presence, semantically wresting each thing from its plane of manifestation. What metaphysical discourse develops abstractly and with great difficulty, the symbol realizes in its very being. It is itself the confirmation of this knowledge, without which we will always risk forgetting. There is not a word in the preceding description which cannot be applied to the symbolic sign, though with the difference that the symbol appears as an implicit realization of this metaphysics, or better, expresses it by its own existence. In other words, we are awakened to consciousness of the implicit symbolism of natural beings by the very existence of the symbols explicitly communicated and presented by cultural tradition. The symbol is therefore, within our world, truly the memorial of the metaphysical nature of the cosmos, the memorial of the universal presence of the Logos.

But this is not all. The symbol is not simply immanence: it is an immanence calling for transcendence. The archetype's presence within the symbol is semantic, revealing its autonomy relative to all conditions of determinate existence and thereby invoking an unconditioned reality. With this point, then, we leave the domain of speculative hermeneutics for that of the *integrative*.

Integrative Hermeneutics

We related this third form of hermeneutics to the third operation in agriculture, in which the products of the soil are harvested and submit to those transformations making them fit for direct

---

foundation. The world was explored, excavated, searched, and divided, with the thought of one day discovering an ontological terminus, a definitive endpoint, *solid ground*. But there is obviously no such thing. Cf. our *Symbolism and Reality*.

consumption, or else to industrial treatments (threshing wheat, for example, before processing into flour). But the agricultural work proper stops at this point. Integrative hermeneutics also includes such a preparatory phase, but it goes further, because if the consumption and assimilation of the plant no longer pertains to agriculture, the ritual "consumption" of symbols and their mystical and spiritual "assimilation" does belong to integrative hermeneutics. We give it this name because it involves the symbol's integration into oneself, or rather integrating oneself into the symbol, for these are but two sides of a single process. The symbol thus becomes our very being, edifies our spiritual body, while it finds through us the fulfillment of its deepest truth. This is at once the end of hermeneutics and of the symbol: the latter disappears in this transformation insofar as its qualities are perfectly realized—that is, insofar as man truly rises to the supra-archetypal source of all symbols, to the Center whence all semantic rays emanate. Symbolic integration still belongs to hermeneutics, then, because to truly understand the symbol, which is its proper task, is to know that the symbol itself leads and beckons us to such a union.

The intellect is the desire for reality, the search for what is at once intellection and being. The symbol *presents* exactly such a synthesis since it is meaning made presence. Becoming symbols ourselves, our very existence becomes a meaning. By the symbol's grace, the intellect's hope finds fulfillment; the most secret instinct propelling knowledge toward the objectivity of being is thereby realized. But also, and conversely, integrative hermeneutics fulfills the symbol by obeying its deepest semantic orientation. As an objective memorial, it is but the visible trace and witness to the unitive knowledge of God. And the signifying function is thereby revealed for what it is—an *anagogy*, which is precisely the action of *leading toward the higher*. The symbol is an ascension. It is the call projecting the essences toward man, the song of the intelligible spheres descending to us that we might ascend to them. To understand a symbol is to ascend this celestial ladder, this cosmic memorial of the one and only Reality, this vertical trace painted by the divine brush on the canvas of the universe.

The hermeneutic of the symbol as memorial is discovered also to be an anamnesis. The symbol is a memento of the essence, a call and divine song playing for "he that hath ears to hear," in the words of the Gospel. It should therefore awaken the echo and memory of the essences sleeping within the intellect, for its intrinsic content is the original light of the Logos which "lighteth every man that cometh into the world." The key to the "hermeneutical problem" is therefore to be found where memorial meets anamnesis. The symbol's song awakens the corresponding intelligible vibrations within the soul. Without the symbol, they would remain dormant: yet without the soul's vibrations, the symbol's song would remain unheard and as if silent. Or again, symbols are like notes played on the strings of a guitar, the soul of man as hermeneut is like the hollow body resonating and so making them audible.[57]

Such, in brief outline, is the doctrine of the three forms of hermeneutics consistent, each in its own way, with the symbolic sign. It seems possible to speak here of a reciprocal realization: the symbol realizes hermeneutics, with hermeneutics in turn realizing the symbol. The symbol comes first, a priority not *de jure* but *de facto*, insofar as there is for man no other starting point than the state in which he currently finds himself, the psycho-corporeal. In a certain respect, everything begins with the body, and it is even true that *"nihil est in intellectu quod non fuerit in sensu,"* yet only given Leibniz's correction, *"nisi ipse intellectus."*[58] The symbol realizes hermeneutics by its very existence, which, never forget, is always given within a culture and a tradition. It elicits hermeneutic activity because necessitating it, because it presents itself to the intellect as a natural being mysteriously wrested from the order of nature, an enigma, a *diacrisis* and sign. Hermeneutics realizes the symbol in turn as its consummation, not only as the unfolding of its virtuality or potentiality, but as the necessary medium by which the symbol can fulfill its purpose, can find its raison d'être: the anagogical ascent of man to the Principle, and through man, of all creation to its Creator. For the symbol is a sign because it signifies to someone: the symbol

---

[57] In a violin, the wooden dowel which unites the front and back plates and transmits vibrations is called the *âme*, the "soul" [Tr: in English, "soundpost"].

[58] *New Essays on Human Understanding* II.i; trans. Peter Remnant and Jonathan Bennett (Cambridge: Cambridge University Press, 1996), 111. To the symbol's *de facto* priority corresponds the priority *de jure* of the intellect, which applies to a certain extent to hermeneutics as a whole insofar as it leads to true intellection.

is the presence of the One in the many that the many might be made present to the One.

These reflections on the relations between hermeneutics and the symbol lead to a striking conclusion, underlying everything which came before but now appearing in its own right: the symbol is itself a hermeneutic. Logically, it could not be otherwise: for the symbol to be realized by hermeneutics, it must itself be a potential or implicit hermeneutic. We have indicated as much in saying that the symbol is a concrete metaphysics (insofar as metaphysics *just is* hermeneutics, at least in a certain respect). In other words, when speaking of a hermeneutics of the symbol, it should be noted that the genitive has two senses: objective, that hermeneutic having the symbol for its object; and subjective, the hermeneutic proper to the symbol. And this, in the final analysis, is the basis of the accord between symbol and objective hermeneutics. For what is at issue? Not the hermeneutics incorporated into the linguistic sign, whereby, as we have said, the linguistic sign explicitly denotes its own ontology of reference. This denotative hermeneutic is, in fact, simply another way of indicating the meta-semiotic property of language. Rather, what grounds their accord is that the symbol is itself a hermeneutic of objective reality: by its own formal existence, it is already an interpretation of what *is*, a "word" about the world, a way of understanding and expressing it. Prior to any interpretive discourse, symbolism's use of natural forms, elements, colors, beings, and the like, is itself already an interpretation of nature. Objective and explicit hermeneutics has only to develop this primary and founding hermeneutic, which will remain within it, through all its deployments, as the radiant source of its intelligibility. So if, from a certain point of view, the symbol has become a hermeneutic, then from another, hermeneutics itself always remains symbolic.[59]

---

[59] This doctrine of the symbol as hermeneut of reality is developed in Chapter XI of *The Crisis of Religious Symbolism*.

CHAPTER VII

The General Structure and Organization of the Symbolic Order

DIAGRAM OF THE SYMBOLIC SIGN

WE RETURN NOW TO THE GENERAL diagram of the sign in order to indicate its modification by the symbol, in conformity with its essence.

We proposed adding a fourth term to the triadic schema of the sign (signifier, meaning, referent) — the intelligible referent, which is indispensable in accounting for the act of signification. The symbolic sign gives primary importance to the intelligible referent; it becomes the dominant pole to which all else is subordinated. It is nothing other than the essence or archetype, the primordial determination of principial Being, of which the symbol is itself the manifestation on the plane of natural forms. This intelligible referent is therefore also the ultimate objective referent, that reality finally designated by the symbol. There is doubtless something analogous in the case of the linguistic sign, but in an implicit or inchoate state.

On the other hand, as we have seen, the symbol does not point to an objective referent. It denotes only secondarily, under the action of hermeneutics, and this absence of denotivity is the most striking character of the symbolic sign, transforming the whole orientation of its structural schema. The symbolic signifier is not oriented toward an objective referent, but presentifies an intelligible referent. The meaning of the symbol is no longer the quasi-autonomous and independent mediating relation uniting signifier and referent, themselves equally autonomous. It is a *vertical ray measuring the distance or separation between intelligible referent and signifier*. In other words, intelligible referent and symbolic signifier are essentially one but existentially distinct, according to the degree of being. The symbol's meaning is then nothing other than the trace of their essential unity across this existential interval. It should therefore be represented by a vertical that is but the unfolding of a higher point, the archetype or intelligible referent, through to a lower point, the corporeal symbolic signifier, which would be its terminal endpoint. We say "terminal endpoint," which might sound redundant, because each point along the semantic ray can be considered an end of this unfolding, insofar as it is determined by an encounter with a given degree of reality, and this for man does not go beyond the corporeal state, which is terminal in every respect. This representation has some interesting consequences, from which we should not shrink back: in particular, each point along the vertical can be considered a signifier relative to all that is immediately higher than itself, and so the concept of the symbol can be extended beyond the sensible world. Also, if the signifier is essentially identified with the intelligible referent, the reverse is no less true: the archetype-referent can in certain respects be considered a signifier, even the perfect signifier, since it is naturalness par excellence. And this signifier-archetype is thus the ultimate symbol of what, paradoxically, can in no way be symbolized. To be more precise, if not clearer or more explicit, we could say that this ultimate "symbol" is Being itself with respect to trans-ontological Reality.

And finally, we should note the presence of a new element in the symbolic sign, which was not needed for the linguistic sign: hermeneutics. Hermeneutics was not absent from the linguistic sign, but was not apparent in itself, because it was as if hidden and implied in all the functional elements of language, particularly the denotative function. It could even be said that language (excepting symbolic language) is the system that inherently implies its own hermeneutic, which returns us, as noted earlier, to the metalinguistic property, that by which it designates its own ontology of reference. If hermeneutics must be taken into consideration in the definition of the symbolic sign, this is just because it inherently requires hermeneutic explication. From this perspective, we could say that the symbolic sign is defined as a sign to be interpreted, though specifying that this is not causal but rather a consequence of its nature: hermeneutics does not make the symbol, the symbol makes hermeneutics.

The task of objective hermeneutics is to assign the symbol's referent; our understanding on this point is clear and has been developed at length. However, at the two extremes of the semantic ray, it could be said that hermeneutic and referent are identified: at the highest level, the intelligible referent *qua* essence and archetype is the synthesis at once of all other referents and all intellection; and at the lowest level, the symbolic signifier, belonging by nature to the first degree of being, represents the first possible referent, and at the same time realizes by its existential presence the first hermeneutic of reality.

In principle, however, the hermeneutic act depends solely on the intellect, and so on an extra-symbolic source. We observed above that the symbol possesses a *de facto* priority over the intellect, because the corporeal is always our starting point. But the intellect possesses *de jure* priority — not chronological, but logical — over the symbol, simply because it could not be otherwise. All true intellection, all "evidence" inherently implies its own ground. That is, true intellection is always *per se* first, having inherent necessity, even when it is in fact second. It receives its light directly from the Logos, so to speak. As Lagneau says, "To think is to think order," to which we must add that intellection is equally informed by the metaphysical tradition to which it belongs by virtue of its historical and geographical situation. Based on this twofold authority — the "light drawn from the Logos," according to St Thomas, and its being informed by metaphysical tradition — and under the influence of the symbol's presence, the hermeneutic act unfolds through elaboration of the different degrees of reality to which the symbolic sign can refer.

Finally, an analytical diagram of the symbol should equally account for the essential role of cultural tradition, as this is how the symbolic sign is presented to us. Metaphysical and cultural tradition are one, or more precisely, cultural tradition has two aspects, an "essential," sapiential, intellectual aspect; and an "existential," formal, concrete aspect — the two (ideas and forms) being inextricably intermingled.[1] Tradition, always extending

---

[1] There are countless cases in point here. India presents us with a metaphysical tradition inseparable from cultural, scriptural, or plastic forms. The metaphysics of Guadapada or of Shankara are as "Hindu" as the *Veda* or the dance of Shiva. In Christianity, apart from the prologue to St John's Gospel, the metaphysical tradition is Platonic or Aristotelian, the cultural

more or less from the beginning of time and forming the very continuity of human civilization, will be adequately represented by a horizontal line.

We arrive at the following:

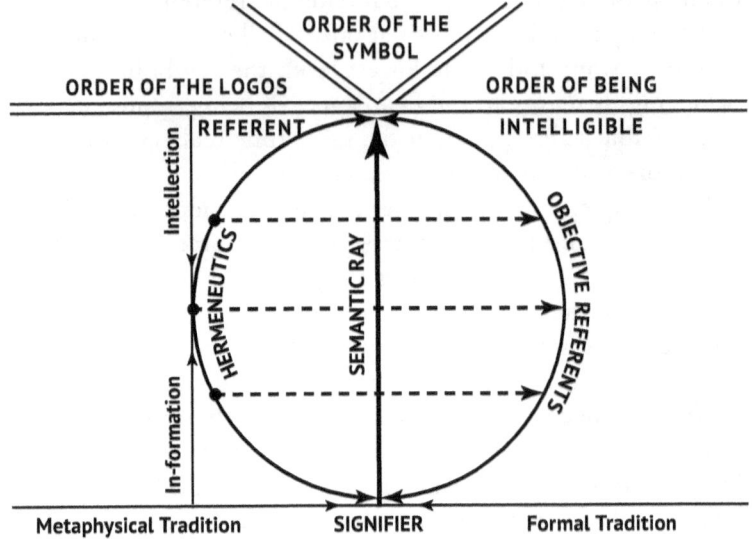

CLASSIFICATION OF SYMBOLS

Rejection of the Linguistic Model

It is evident that symbolic classification still awaits its Linnaeus. In Chapter I, we indicated the attempt by René Alleau,[2] the most systematic, to our mind, though he multiplied the different classes of symbols to such a degree that it lost any interest and became simple enumeration. Our proposed classification has no such pretension, and even has serious deficiencies. We seek only to introduce a little order into a field whose scope and diversity defies analysis.

---

forms partly Jewish. In Greece, it seems that the intellectual tradition, at least with Pythagoras or Plato, is also of a different origin than the religious or mythological tradition. In other cases, the Native Americans, for example, the intellectual tradition hardly exists *per se*, which does not in any way indicate its absence — far from it. The existence of an elaborated metaphysical tradition is not itself a criterion of superiority, but can to the contrary be the result of "saving what can be saved" in an age of profound incomprehension. This is what Plato suggests in his Seventh Letter: theoretical discourse is the last resort for teaching truth (326a–b).

[2] Cf. *supra*, 7–9, referring to his book, *De la nature des symbols*.

We do not at all discount the possibility of a satisfying classification in this area. Yet the utility, if not the necessity, of even an imperfect classification is hardly debatable. This utility seems twofold, at least for a minimal classification such as ours: on the one hand, a classification provides as it were a confirmation of the general definition of the entities contained in the set of classes—across the multitude of its forms, the symbolic sign is indeed always the same. On the other hand, a classification allows us to delineate the entire field of symbolism. In particular, it allows us to relate to the general category of symbols those elements often not considered as such, an oversight which causes great distortions in the theory of symbolism, as if a biologist were to develop a general theory of reproduction based on the observation only of sexed beings.

This error occurs, for example, whenever the symbol is defined in terms of language alone, as often happens. A simple observation of facts shows such reductiveness to be untenable: the vast domain of visual forms, colors, music, chants, dances, ritual gestures, clothing, processions, sacred architecture, statuary, customs, artisanal techniques (weaving, forging, ploughing)—this vast domain does not have lesser scope than that of symbolic language or the Holy Scriptures. On the other hand, the study of linguistic symbolism alone does not allow us to identify what is proper to the symbol: in so defining the symbolic sign, we risk attributing to it characteristics belonging rather to language itself, or at least to symbolic language, that is, to the symbol's effect on language, as if heat were defined only by the expansion it causes in metal. An example of this distortion of the issues can be seen in the arguments developed by Todorov in *Symbolism and Interpretation*.[3]

The author does note a certain arbitrariness in reducing symbolism to symbolic language,[4] but he thinks this can be justified. For him, symbolic language appears wherever there is *indirect meaning*. (This moreover partially takes up the *philosophical* arguments of Ricœur.) And there is indirect meaning wherever the direct sense is inapplicable, wherever it is not *pertinent*.[5] It must therefore be interpreted symbolically. This leads him to offer an example of the "symbolic functioning of language," that of

---

[3] Trans. Catherine Porter (Ithaca, NY: Cornell University Press, 1982).
[4] Ibid., 15–16.
[5] Ibid., 28–30.

a rabbinical commentary on a verse in the Torah which states that even animals will be rewarded by God: "if it is so for a beast, how much more rightly then for man will God not withhold his reward?"[6] This has an indirect meaning: that God will reward the animals (the direct meaning) signifies *a fortiori* that He rewards man (the indirect meaning). The same reasoning can be found on the lips of Christ, concerning the lilies of the field clothed by God more gloriously than Solomon. But where is the symbolism? It takes a great deal of goodwill to see in this rabbinical commentary a "symbolic functioning of language." It cannot even be said that the reward given to the animals by God is the symbol of that given to man, except in a very weak sense. It is an argument, not a symbol.[7] Such a truly inconclusive example does not demonstrate that the symbol is constituted by indirect meaning, though this is always present in symbolic *language*; rather, the indirect meaning's grounding in the nature of the direct meaning makes the latter the symbol of the former. However, language essentially presents us with a rhetorical process, that of the indirect meaning—possible or necessary, as the case may be—and not the naturalness of a signifier.[8] And this is why the linguistic mode of presentation

---

[6] Ibid., 39.

[7] Todorov recognizes this, though he thinks it can be avoided: "Let us set aside the device of *a fortiori*, or qal wahómèr, which is essential in the rabbinic gloss, and retain the overall result: the signifier of a single proposition leads us to knowledge of two signifieds, one direct and the other indirect" (40).

[8] We cannot think of taking Todorov's arguments point by point, as they deserve. We will make but two comments, one general, the other more specific: first, a large portion of the examples analyzed have, to our mind, nothing to do with symbolism. Second, where they do concern symbolism, the author often makes inexplicable errors in reading comprehension. On the subject of St Augustine's commentary on the anointing at Bethany, during which Mary (the sister of Martha) washes the feet of Christ with a precious perfume (John 12:1-8), Todorov argues that this is for St Augustine "an *in absentia* contradiction" (i.e., did not take place) and therefore must be interpreted symbolically (99). But Augustine says nothing of the sort, which would be inconceivable for a Christian. In the text cited by Todorov, Augustine says, "No person in his right mind should ever think that the Lord's feet were anointed by a woman with precious ointment *in the same way* as the feet of self-indulgent and evil men are anointed at the sort of banquets which we abhor. A good perfume signifies a good reputation: anyone who enjoys this through the deeds of an upright life anoints Christ's feet in a figurative sense with a most precious perfume by following in his footsteps. Again, what is generally speaking wicked in other people is the sign of something great in one who is divine or a prophet" (*De Doctrina Christiana* XIII.12.18; trans. Green, 152–53). The negation ("no person . . . should ever think") bears

obscures the truth of the symbolic sign. Symbolic language is not particularly problematic *with respect to the symbol itself*, though it is obviously otherwise for language generally. The linguistic symbol is not distinguished *as symbol* from any other symbolic sign, the only difference being that in the linguistic mode of presentation, it is "spoken," while in other modes, it is shown: whether a cow is painted on canvas or named in speech, its symbolic reality undergoes no change.[9] At most, we could hold that, language being the most denotative of semiotic systems, it refers more directly to the natural cow and its symbolism than painting, which, possessing its own sensible reality, primarily signifies itself and refers to the natural cow only indirectly. The spoken cow thus more explicitly brings into play the natural symbolism of cosmic forms, and consequently poses the question of the historicity of what is said; while the painted cow, possessing its own sensible reality, suffices to bear the weight of the symbolism independent of any reference to its living model. The pictorial symbol belongs more directly to the universe of symbolic forms, while the spoken symbol belongs more directly to the symbolism of the forms of the universe. The painted cow can therefore potentially be presented in stylized ways which explicitly signify its character as a symbolic sign, which could hardly be the case with the spoken cow, except where its designation is accompanied by description. Yet in any case, we must always return to the cow itself and its proper symbolism, as can be seen in those "bestiaries," particularly that of Louis Charbonneau-Lassay, which were assembled by combining the representations of statuary, painting, medallions, jewelry, fabric, and of all symbolic objects, the designations of the Holy Scriptures.[10] As St Thomas

---

on the *manner* and not on the fact of the anointing. Moreover, after having cited this text in his commentary on St John (*In Joannis Evangelium* I.6, PL XXXV, col. 1760), St Augustine writes, "We have heard the fact, let us seek the mystery" (*factum audivimus, mysterium requiramus*).

[9] It must be clarified, however, that there is one important case where the linguistic mode of presentation is the only one possible: in symbolic narratives (myths) which are recounted as *story*, which is to say, a series of actions, for there is no other way of presentifying it but language. A myth can perhaps be mimed or danced, but it can be known only *in the telling*. This would go toward demonstrating that language is as essentially ordered toward action as toward the knowledge of beings.

[10] Louis Charbonneau-Lassay's work, *Le Bestiaire du Christ*, was reissued by Éditions Arché at Milan in 1975 (Desclée de Brouwer, 1940) [English edition: *The Bestiary of Christ*, trans. D.M. Dooling (New York: Penguin, 1992)]. It

said, summarizing the whole Christian tradition, these are "the things signified by the words which can be themselves signs of other things," and not the words themselves.[11]

True, language can itself be interpreted symbolically. But neither in this case does the symbolism proper to language as such pose a particular problem. It is always a matter of the symbolic signification which can be clothed in the sensible forms of speech by virtue of their "naturalness": for example, we can consider the order of words in a sentence, the number of times they are repeated,[12] the symbolism of vowels and consonants, their numerical value, the permutation of syllables, their symbolic decomposition, and in written language, the shape of letters. The Kabbalah is known to have especially elaborated such reflections. But they are not absent from the Latin Middle Ages, as evidenced by Joachim of Fiore.[13]

Extension of the Symbolic Field

The foregoing remarks lead to an important observation relative to the classification of symbols: the symbol must not be confounded with its mode of presentation, which is tantamount to saying that it must be distinguished from the particular domain that makes use of it and is thus its bearer. If it is true, as we have shown for symbolic language, that the mode of presentation does not change the nature of the symbol, then the grounds for classification must be sought in the symbols themselves, not the domain in which they are employed. Otherwise, there would be as many classes of symbols as there are modes of presentation, or possible

---

was said that Charbonneau-Lassay had also intended to compose a floriary and a lapidary. As it is, while perhaps too historical, his monumental study (997 pages) remains unparalleled.

[11] *S. Th.* I, q. 1, a. 10.

[12] We note on this subject a very thorough study by François Quiévreux, "La structure symbolique de l'évangile de saint Jean," which appeared in the *Revue d'Histoire et de Science religieuses* (t. XXXIII, 1953, 123–65). He established the existence of a numerical symbolism in the disposition and repetition of the same term within a single phrase or a single passage.

[13] See especially the extraordinary figures, of great symbolic richness, in which Joachim de Fiore condensed all his theological and mystical thought: Marjorie Reeves and Beatrice Hirsch-Reich, *The Figurae of Joachim of Fiore* (Oxford: Oxford University Press, 1972). On the symbolism of letters and phonemes, the most penetrating studies are by Jean Canteins: *Phonèmes et archetypes* (Maisonneuve et Larose) and *La voie des lettres* (Albin Michel).

domains of use. This would appear to be the basic flaw in the classification proposed by René Alleau in his work, *De la nature des symboles*. Despite the great expertise of this scholar of traditional (and modern) sciences, it must be acknowledged that differentiating seventeen classes of symbols (or rather synthemes)[14] leads ultimately to differentiating seventeen domains where the symbol is used. For example, he distinguishes numismatic, topological, chronological, didactic, and other synthemes, but they are in every case the same kind of sign, the only difference being that they are found on a medallion, on a map or diagram, on a clock, or in a treatise on astrology or alchemy. On the other hand, considering this classification closely, we see that it is not homogenous, with the author juxtaposing these seventeen classes without thought for certain semiotic disparities, in this case depending on the signs themselves and not their domain: for example, philosophical synthemes (signs of recognition for members of a philosophical school) and semiological synthemes, having to do, for example, with the symptoms of a disease, and which actually belong to the category of epistemological or "inductive" signs.

Furthermore, the domains employing symbolism are many, even indefinite, for religious man can always invent a new mode of expression. In a traditional civilization, there is not a single area of human activity that does not make use of symbols. We should include here not only the arts (in the modern sense, such as chant, music, painting, sculpture, architecture, dance, poetry, theater) but also all the crafts (weaving, tailoring, carving, smithing, pottery, glazing, bookbinding) and even the techniques of agriculture, decorating, cooking, down to the art of serving tea. We should also add social rituals, not only rites of passage (birth, maturity, marriage, death) and rites of commercial exchange, but also rites where members of social groups are presented to one another, at once in active relations—celebrations, rules of etiquette, table manners, greetings, and so on—and for individual recognition—professional and corporate dress, habits of class, coats of arms, flags and banners, decorations, etc. There are also rites governing the relations among different social groups which make heavy use of symbolism, particularly warfare. With martial

---

[14] Recall that for Alleau, symbols unite man to the divine, while synthemes unite man and man. Yet symbols are also and necessarily signs of union and recognition—the cross, for example.

arts, the science of horsemanship, the art of archery, we enter into a vast domain of religious rites, from prayer to the symbolic recitation of the great founding myths, the Holy Scriptures and epics, down to the minute details of processions, circumambulations, and liturgies—the Sacrifice of the Mass, *pujā*,[15] or the Peace Pipe ceremony—which govern the activities of humanity across the whole surface of the earth in "waiting on the Lord," ordering their gestures and words. But this still has not yet sketched the entire field of symbolism, for we must further consider its extensive use in the traditional sciences: metaphysics (think simply of the symbolism of Plato's Cave), theology, cosmology, astrology, alchemy, numerology, geometry; as well as in medical and divinatory practices, not to mention magic and theurgy, and finally, at the lowest degree, the different forms of sorcery.

The Nature of the Signifier as Principle of Classification

Such are the major domains constituting the field of symbolism: art, craft, society, religion, science, technology, each susceptible of being subdivided into more specific areas and combined with others. All bring into play a vast array of symbols, which are not always identifiable as distinct units and often appear more as constellations. They can certainly be organized in different ways, and scholars of the symbol have proposed many systems of classification, depending on the principle adopted. Some of these are highly detailed,[16] though none are satisfying or enjoy unanimous approval among scholars. They are related variously to a psychological principle (Durand, Freud, Jung), a sociological principle (Dumézil and the tripartition of social functions), to a cosmological principle (Bachelard and the quadripartition of elements), or to a combination of these.[17] As we see it, these systems of classification, all of which have their merits, imply a certain theory of the symbol. This is their value, but also their weakness. It seems possible to establish a *positive* classification,

---

[15] The Sanskrit word *puja* means "cult," "act of adoration."

[16] We are thinking particularly of Gilbert Durand, in his *The Anthropological Structures of the Imaginary*, trans. Margaret Sankey and Judith Hatten (Brisbane: Boombana, 1999), 52–64.

[17] An outline of the different systems of classification can be found in the introduction to Jean Chevalier's *Dictionary of Symbols* (Paris: Seghers, 1973) t. I, xxxv–xli. [Tr: the English edition does not include Chevalier's introduction.]

that is, relying only on the observable data of the symbolic field. But no matter the domain, no matter the use made of the symbol, no matter the motive leading to its employment, no matter the peoples using them, the time or the place—all symbolic entities and all constellations of symbols have a "visible face," whatever the nature of this visibility: the signifier. The different classes of symbols are therefore distinguished based on the nature of the signifier. This should not be surprising, since as we have shown, a symbol is above all the presentification of an essence in the nature of a signifier. Every symbol is an entity belonging to a certain degree of existence, signifying all the superior degrees by ontological correspondence. On the other hand, we should not forget that the symbol is addressed to man as he is: such is its raison d'être. Accordingly, these are the different modes of being or of reality which human consciousness knows or experiences, and which can be used as signifiers, points of departure for the symbol's anagogical ascent. Everything that is real for normal human consciousness can be taken as symbolically significant, and by "normal," we mean that consciousness possessed by each person in their normal state of existence. Our conclusion is not only consistent with the preceding analyses, but also imposes itself with a certain obviousness: given that symbolism consists in taking a reality from one order to signify another in a higher order, clearly there would be as many classes of symbolic elements as there are modes of reality for the being instituting the symbolic relation—that is, for man. In other words, the *material* forming the symbolic signifier is necessarily borrowed from the diverse modes of reality of which man is conscious, and as a result, the classes of symbols will vary according to the nature of this material. This seems to be the principle of the primary or most elementary classification of symbols, but it does not preclude that other systems could perhaps be superimposed on it or, perhaps, make different distinctions. As we have acknowledged, no system is perfect, and none can exhaust the field of symbolism or order it in any definitive manner.

For normal human consciousness, there are three modes of reality: as perceived, as conceived (or thought), and as felt, or rather as lived. The real is what we perceive with our senses, or what is inseparable from that perception. It is what we think with the mind, what we live with our consciousness, inwardly or outwardly. Obviously, man being a single being, these three modes interpenetrate: the perceived is also thought and lived, and similarly for the others. However, it is legitimate to distinguish them according to the predominate mode of reality which polarizes consciousness and around which all else is organized. In perception, consciousness of reality is given by perception itself, or in any case, is given along with perception, what is thought and lived being present also by implication—perceived reality is what is objective and external. Conceived reality is what is objective and internal, or rather, the objective as posited independently of a determined spatiotemporal framework. Lived (felt, enacted) reality is what is subjective, existential—if you will, *human*, for there is indeed also animal perception, and what is thought or conceived (not, obviously, the mental act itself) is undetermined and universal. But it is subjective while being at once internal and external, including sentiment and affectivity as well as gesture and activity. In this respect, the lived realizes a sort of synthesis of the perceived and the conceived, or rather, it is as if an intermediate mode. This mode of reality is often forgotten, yet the lived is indeed real, even if its subjective character seems in contradiction with the objective and stable character normally attributed to reality. But *practically*, it is even instinctively our primary concern, as modern psychology abundantly demonstrates.

We should now observe that consciousness of reality is always twofold. Reality—what is perceived, thought, or lived—manifests in two forms: either as being, substance, and unity; or else as relation. Thus, in the case of perceived reality: we know beings such as trees, horses, water, the sky, stones, and the like with our senses, but also, however indirectly, we know the relations which hold between these beings or substances, particularly their relations of coexistence and succession or of ordered movements and rhythms—that is, space and time, which are the conditions of existence for perceived reality. True, these relations are not given in themselves: we see neither space nor time, which in themselves are but concepts. But we do perceive extension and duration, at least in a certain respect, as a *continuum* given along with things themselves and linked to them, either in their mutual presence or in their movement, development, and processes.

In the same way, what is thought is given under the form of abstract terms, of objective units: either such concepts as man, animal, matter, and triangle, or under the form of relations, such as order, position, size, quantity, and opposition.

Finally, the lived also features a duality of analogous aspects: inwardly, it consists essentially in affective themes, identifiable in their singularity, such as love, hate, joy, sorrow, anger, or pity. Outwardly, it consists in all forms of activity, which are inseparable from the body and can be abstractly reduced to a relational schema: the model here is gesture, which is a relation (or complex of relations) performed by the body. Affective and enacted reality are opposed in a certain respect: a feeling is real while it is being felt, gives shape to some nature. On the other hand, gesture or action is real to the extent that man realizes it, makes it exist. Action has man for its creator, and yet reality is normally understood to be that which is independent of us, imposing itself upon us. However, the reality of an action is also that norm, model, or structure which the action incarnates in time and space. In any case, the felt and the enacted have this much in common: both are lived, indeed *are* our lives.

The Three Fundamental Classes of Elementary Signifiers

We are therefore led to distinguish six types of material which can compose the symbolic signifier, grouped in three distinct categories, yielding six types of elementary symbolic signifiers and three fundamental classes. The designation of these three classes poses some insoluble difficulties, and what we have settled on here is but a stopgap.

For the perceived, we can define the class of concrete, natural, or macrocosmic symbolic components: these are all the symbols consisting either in a being of nature, a corporeal being, as in floriaries, bestiaries, lapidaries, cosmic elements, or the stars; or else by a relational reality in extension or duration, such as the horizon, low, high, day, night, and the seasons.

For conceived reality, we can define the class of abstract, cultural (traditional), or a-cosmic symbolic components. Such terms are unsatisfying, since on the one hand, these symbolic signifiers have always a natural model, and on the other, their abstract character does not preclude their being sensible, either in the proper sense, or as an idea contemplated in its qualitative contents, its objective reality. If we take a geometrical figure as an example, such as the cross, the triangle, or the star, this symbolic signifier clearly does not exist *qua* figure in nature, for here form is always joined to some "matter." This is why they are qualified as "traditional," since they are given only by cultural tradition. As for their qualification as "abstract," this is in the sense of "drawn out," "considered independently," since such forms indeed find their model in corporeal structures (snowflakes, for example) but are considered specifically in themselves, apart from the natural beings realizing them. *Abstract* is here not opposed to *sensible*. This is seen more clearly in the case of color: color does not exist as such in nature, only colored objects. Yet it enters into the composition of a multitude of symbols. It is therefore an elementary abstract signifier which yet maintains its character as a sensible quality. The same is true for musical sound: it is a sensible or perceptible reality which does not exist as such in nature. It is a cultural product, which is why it is qualified as abstract.[18] And so while it is always possible to find a natural model for them, it is as cultural elements that they enter into the composition of symbolic signifiers. The difficulty comes in distinguishing entities from relations, since most elements in this order necessarily present a double aspect—entitative and relational—due to their belonging to a cultural *system*. This is the case for numbers, letters, ideograms, alchemical and astrological signs, music and vocal sounds, even colors. Finally, and especially, it is true of all *forms of language* (vocabulary and syntax), which represents the dominant class of

---

[18] These remarks find confirmation in the apparent antinomy in ordinary language between the words "abstract" and "concrete" with respect to art. We speak of concrete music and abstract painting, and are right to do so. If music using "natural" noises is called concrete, this is because normal music using "artificial" sounds is considered abstract, in the sense we have specified. In the same way, if a painting making use of forms and colors for their own sake, such that they form the very object of the artwork, is called abstract, this is because these elements are considered independently and in themselves, while ordinary (and so "concrete") painting always sees them as qualities of objects. In reality, the most abstract music always has moments of concreteness (and conversely, since the arrangement of noises is abstract). In the same way, the most concrete painting always plays with colors and forms for their own sake. Finally, it is interesting to observe that painting is directly concrete and music directly abstract, which indicates the externalizing function of vision and the internalizing function of the ear. We spontaneously believe that vision goes toward things, whereas sound enters the ear. Physically, this is inaccurate—rays of light also enter the eye. But the eye is mobile, while the ear is stationary in the head. We can moreover close our eyes: the eye is master of its own visionary capacity. We cannot close our ears.

traditional symbols, whether we think of Fr Jousse's "oral style" in mythic narratives (mythemes and structures), or the analyses of Lévi-Strauss. However, the *relational* element can also be considered in itself, as in the quasi-mathematical relations of sacred painting, ornamentation, statuary, or architecture. This element is typically called "proportion," and its fundamentally symbolic nature cannot be denied after even a brief study of metrology in religious monuments.[19] In music, in chant, in dance, the proportion of time is called rhythm, and its role here is as fundamental as that of proportion in architecture. In this class of symbols, relation appears as such, in its essence. Yet as we will observe, it is not at all reduced to a being of reason, but possesses rather the fundamental naturalness required by every element of the symbol.

According to the mode of lived reality, we can define the class of psycho-corporeal, human, or microcosmic symbolic components, terms as little satisfying as the preceding and used only for lack of something better. We also find here the entity-relation duality, but only under the form of psychic states, on the one hand, and that of gesture on the other. It will perhaps be surprising to discover psychic components of symbols, yet this is confirmed unmistakably. To stick to well-known data, we cite human love, which in the Song of Songs and in St Paul (Eph. 5:22–33) is taken as a symbol of the union of the Divine Principle with the human soul or the religious community; or tears, alchemical symbol of the heart's melting; or the state of infancy, taken as a symbol of spiritual innocence and faith; and so on. In fine, there is not a single human feeling, no human attitude which cannot become part of a signifier. These psychic states, sentiments, and attitudes are certainly not entities in the proper sense, but they enter into the composition of symbols based on their specific thematic unity, their "essence" or fundamental naturalness. Notwithstanding the general ambivalence of human feeling, which cultures have always known, the different psychic or psycho-corporeal qualities and states of individual man

---

[19] See the work of Matila C. Ghyka on this question: *Ethétique des Proportions dans la Nature et dans l'Art* (Paris: Gallimard, 1927) and *The Golden Number: Pythagorean Rites and Rhythms in the Development of Western Civilization*, trans. Jon Graham (Rochester, VT: Inner Traditions, 2016). We would like also to pay homage to a modest and little-known seeker, Colonel Ferraci, who to his last breath followed the field of metrology with the greatest interest. His publications are unfortunately few and dispersed in private publications.

generally present a homogeneity sufficient for playing the role of fundamental elements in symbolism. Many classifications forget elements of this kind, but we need only think of the semantic richness of the masculine/feminine couple as symbolic signifier to understand their importance.[20]

It remains finally to say something about gesture. It is proper to humanity, since the human body is its sole instrument. It could seem paradoxical to include it among the elementary materials of symbolic signifiers, since it is a corporeal act, a movement, and the idea of "material" evokes rather a sense of stability and immobility. But it is undeniably so, as evidenced in dance and most rites, from the Sign of the Cross or the Benediction to the Orthodox metania and Hindu *mudrā* or *āsana*. They are so fundamental that we could see them as the basic material of every symbol, that to which all else is reducible. This is the opinion particularly of René Guénon, who writes, "a symbol, understood as a 'graphic' figuration, as it is most commonly, is only as it were the fixation of a ritual gesture."[21] He alludes here to the important question of *ritual patterns*, which govern the realization of all traditional symbols, not only those of the *yantra* (esoteric diagrams) but also of sacred architecture: in the case of the Hindu temple, for example, the plan of the edifice is traced on the soil according to a precise and complicated ritual, which refers to the "sacrifice of *Purusha*" and fixes in consecrated space the rhythms of the celestial bodies.[22] One could find similar rules in the construction of medieval churches and,

---

[20] We would refer particularly to the Far Eastern symbol of the *yin-yang*, the signification of which is virtually universal. The error of Freudian psychoanalysis is not to have drawn attention to the sexual polarity, but rather to have considered sexuality as the primary and fundamental signified, the key and content (because unconscious) of every symbolic message of the human psyche, what every symbolic language *means*. But sexuality is itself a language and belongs to the order of signifiers, and what it *means* is not *essentially* sexual, or rather the essence of sexuality is not reducible to the accidents of its physiological manifestations.

[21] *Perspectives on Initiation*, 110–11.

[22] We are not able to elaborate on this point here, and refer to the study by Titus Burckhardt, "The Genesis of the Hindu Temple," in *Sacred Art in East and West: Its Principles and Methods*, trans. Lord Northbourne (London, Perennial Books, 1967), 17–43. This study relies especially on the works of Stella Kramrisch (*The Hindu Temple* [Calcutta: University of Calcutta, 1946]). Among the many works that could be read concerning sacred art, those of Burckhardt seem perhaps the most essential.

in any case, the Rite of Dedication.[23] Finally, Lanza del Vasto could maintain the existence of a sense of tracing "or a sense of movement and direction which is not reducible to any other or to their combination."[24]

We must also include within the category of gesture the vast domain of human action, which provides the fundamental content of mythic narratives and sacred acts. We are not dealing here with forms of language which are part of cultural elements, but rather directly human signifiers, linked to our psycho-corporeal nature. Actions are evidently relations, or sequences of dynamic relations, but they can nevertheless be analyzed into elementary units: "praxemes," corresponding to Lévi-Strauss's mythemes, yet viewed from the side of what the myth *is speaking about*, and no longer from the side of discourse itself. These praxemes, and their succession within a story, are incorporated into myth only due to their symbolic value. Their relation to speech remains essential, however, since as we have said, on the one hand, speech is a minimal gesture; and on the other, it is the most appropriate mode of expression for presentifying an action.

The Two Limiting Principles of the Symbolic Field

Such, in brief outline, is our classification of symbolic signifiers. One will doubtless object to its extreme generality: if anything can be a symbol, the symbolic field is coextensive with reality, and

---

[23] It can be confirmed that the procedure for establishing the plan and orientation of the edifice is rigorously identical between the Hindu temple and the medieval Christian church: see the indications given by Titus Burckhardt, as well as those given by Jean Hani (*The Symbolism of the Christian Temple* [Kettering, OH: Angelico Press, 2016], 18–25). See also the *Dictionnaire d'archéologie chrétienne et de liturgie*, under "Dédicace" (Eds. Fernand Cabrol and Henri Leclerq [Paris: Librarie Letouzey et Ané, 1920], t. 4, p. 1, 374–405).

[24] *La Trinité spirituelle* (Paris: Denoël, 1971), 41–42. In *Perspectives on Initiation*, Guénon argues that there are only two categories of symbols: audible and visual (*mantra* and *yantra*), with gestural symbols included in the visual category (excepting speech). Such a reduction is untenable. Certainly, a gesture is visible, as in the Sign of the Cross. But this visibility is not its specific property, its formative material: it is a secondary consequence of its corporeality, which may or may not be taken into consideration. A gestural symbol as important as the *samā* (spiritual concert and dance of the whirling dervishes) is often performed with eyes lowered or completely closed (cf. Eva de Vitray-Meyerovitch, *Rūmī et le soufisme* [Paris: Seuil, 1977], 124–25). On the other hand, we must account for abstract symbols: a number is neither visible nor audible, and yet it is a symbol, a "figure of thought," as Coomaraswamy would say.

to classify symbols amounts to classifying the different categories of reality. We would agree. However, there are two principles limiting or determining this field, which we initially posited in demonstrating the symbol's character as a mixed sign, and which we will conclude by recalling. The first is the principle of naturalness, the second that of institution or sacredness, with the second functioning on the basis of the first. What *a priori* makes a signifier appropriate to its signification is primarily its naturalness: this is the essential and decisive criterion. Next comes the fact of its being selected for such use by sacred or traditional institution, no institution bringing into play all possible signifiers. In other words, the principle of naturalness defines the entire field of symbolic signifiers, thus performing an initial selection within the set of realities within our experience. The principle of sacredness performs a second selection, based on the nature and requirements of a given religious form. Sacred dance is nearly absent from the Christian perspective for just this reason,[25] while architecture is absent from some nomadic traditions, for example that of the Native Americans.

These two principles regulate the symbolic field. But if the latter, referring to the fact of institution, presents no difficulty in application (a symbolic signifier is anything used symbolically by a tradition), this is not the case for the former. For naturalness to determine the symbolic field, we must be able to distinguish what is natural from what is not—modern thought is quick to mock any naïve recourse to some undefinable nature. The solution to this difficulty is given by the idea of the "relatively absolute."[26] Claiming that there is nothing entirely natural (in the order of human experience), the idea of nature (essentially, the nonhuman) is abandoned. Yet as Frithjof Schuon says, "There cannot be an 'absolutely relative,' but there is a 'relatively absolute' by virtue of which essential determinations maintain all their rigour on the relative plane, at least in respect of their qualitative content."[27] In

---

[25] David danced before the Ark. They say St Teresa of Ávila had her sisters dance to the rhythm of the tambourine. But it is significant that an edited volume like *Les danses sacrées* (Paris: Seuil, 1963) does not contain a section on Christianity.
[26] This idea was developed and often reiterated by Frithjof Schuon. It is found for the first time in *Stations of Wisdom*, trans. G.E.H. Palmer (Bedfont: Perennial Books, 1981), 27–30, 33–36.
[27] Ibid., 27.

other words, while it is true that all forms are relative, it is not therefore the case that the difference between two forms is purely relative, else they would not exist. Due to its infinity, the Absolute cannot but be reflected, positively or negatively, in relative forms. The difference between a natural and an artificial form is relatively absolute: "absolute," because the natural form is what more directly reflects the nature or essence of the thing or type to which it belongs; "relatively," because it is a reflection, and so an approximation involving degrees. As with the problem of the sorites, there comes a point where the form, in becoming more complex, no longer reveals anything of the essence and manifests nothing other than human ingenuity. A sheet of linen is closer to the essence of canvas than a sheet of plastic—whoever cannot see this will understand nothing about the sacred symbol. This is also why the numbers 6 or 8 are symbolic, while many others are not, unless reduced to less quantitative and more natural numerical forms. The difference between them is relatively absolute. Analogously, not all gestures are symbolic—only those which conform to a norm, a prototypical governing scheme, and finally a divine model. Such is yoga, one of the most important forms of sacred gesture: "It is said that, in the beginning, Shiva by taking all the postures created the species." And there are 8,400,000 of these.[28] The relational nature of symbolic gesture is confirmed here. Hatha yoga employs the subtle body, which is described as a diagram of nodal centers united by invisible channels. The different postures alter the figures composed by these nodal points, ordering these points with respect to one another according to relations which are new in each case. The criterion of a signifier's naturalness therefore suffices to perform a first selection of possible components and to refute the earlier objection.

This concludes the outline of our theory of the classification of symbols. We note once again that it is a classification of components of the symbolic signifier and not of symbols *per se*. A symbol is always, or nearly always, formed from multiple signifiers belonging to different categories, such that the unity (or individuality) of the symbol is variable. When we speak of a symbol, we are typically speaking of a symbolic complex whose

---

[28] Alain Daniélou, *Yoga: The Method of Reintegration* (London: Christopher Johnson, 1949), 25.

unity is of an essentially traditional order: sacred institution constitutes it as a symbol, not the unity of the signifiers composing it. This was clearly seen in the example of the Rublev icon. This point shows the major cause for variation in the classification of symbols, which can be classified differently depending on the component seen as dominant, given that all classes of symbols are "interconnected." Without rejecting such classifications, we yet believe that analysis should be followed down to elementary components, as we have attempted to do.

In any case, it will certainly have been observed that this classification of symbolic components into three fundamental categories corresponds to the triple articulation of the metaphysics of the symbol, discovered as the conclusion of our eidetics: symbols of a concrete nature refer directly to an ontology of the symbol; those of abstract or mental form refer to a noetics; and those of the human (psychic and corporeal) form refer to a ritualics. Our analysis of the symbol thereby hearkens back to and confirms our eidetics.[29]

---

[29] Cf. *supra*, 73, n. 12.

THE SYMBOL IS A SEMANTIC OPERATOR

IF WE ATTEMPT NOW TO DEFINE THE SYMBOLIC apparatus as sketched in the foregoing, expressing the general idea emerging from such an extended analysis, we will say that it is essentially a semantic operator.

By this term, we mean that a symbol functions as a meaning-producing apparatus, or more precisely, as an apparatus capable of transforming ontology into semantics, because it first transforms semantics into ontology; or again because, similar to chlorophyll in plants, it is able to fix the light of the intelligible in its own matter, restoring it in the form of an unlimited significance.

This semantic operator no doubt functions only for the intellect. But the symbol, not the hermeneut, "produces" the meaning. It awakens human consciousness to the reality of invisible Transcendence, revealing at once its own spiritual interiority as well as the endless exteriority of the created world, definitively separating our existence from its contingency and absurdity and bringing us into the infinite universe of the Spirit. It is a true cosmic athanor, the alchemy of its presence transforming the dust of things into the gold of glory. It fecundates the attentive intellect to embrace its natural order, teaching it the song of supreme Beauty as the wonders of its semantic energy grow inexhaustibly under the symbol's light.

Such is the mystery of the symbolic sign—a dynamic structure, an active and transformational form, a star fallen from heaven, consuming the substance of the world and returning it to the Principle. Like glowing sparks burning in all directions, symbols kindle the cosmic fire which will illumine all of creation in the sudden clarity of the Logos.

www.ingramcontent.com/pod-product-compliance
Lightning Source LLC
Chambersburg PA
CBHW020328170426
43200CB00006B/309